Arabesque

Greg and Lucy Malouf

Arabesque

Modern Middle Eastern Food

In loving memory of my father, Kevin Malouf.

This edition published in 2002
First published in hardback in 1999
by Hardie Grant Books
12 Claremont Street
South Yarra, Victoria 3141, Australia

National Library of Australia Cataloguing-in-Publication Data:
Malouf, Greg
Arabesque: modern Middle Eastern food
ISBN 1 86498 078 8
1. Cookery, Middle eastern. I. Malouf, Lucy. II. Title.
641.5956

Cover and text design by Danie Pout
Cover photographs by Bobbi Fabian and Robert Ashton
Photographs by Bobbi Fabian
Food styling by Deborah McLean
Typeset by J&M Typesetting
Printed and bound in Hong Kong through Phoenix Offset

10 9 8 7 6 5 4 3 2 1

Contents

Acknowledgements

Arabesque is the result of a lifetime's journey in, through and around food. It has been fuelled by my travels and the people I've met along the way, by the books I have read, and the countless meals I have cooked and eaten.

My first thanks must go to my family: to my mother, May, and my grandmothers, Adele and Madeleine. This formidable female trio taught me that a love of cooking and feeding others was a gift, not a chore. They influenced my childhood years and were the first to fuel my first interest in the classic flavours of the Middle East. I also especially thank my sister-in-law Amal Malouf and her mother Victoria Baroud for their constant support, and advice. Their breadth of knowledge and expertise in the cooking of Syria and Lebanon is unrivalled.

On a personal note, my appreciation also goes to Pat McDonald, who was one of the first to support and encourage my decision to become a chef. I thank too, Michelle Garnaut, my partner in Hong Kong, who was the first person to believe in and encourage my passion for the flavours of the Middle East. I have, too, always respected and admired Abla Amad, the undisputed queen of Lebanese home-cooking here in Melbourne. Over the years she has been a constant source of inspiration and encouragement. Other chefs I wish to thank are Andrew Blake, Fred Chalupa and Stephanie Alexander.

Throughout my career at O'Connell's Hotel I have been especially fortunate to work with many talented and dedicated chefs. My special thanks go to Harry Hajisava for twenty years of personal support and friendship, and for his help in testing some of the recipes in this book. I thank the entire dedicated O'Connell's team, and particularly Kurt Sampson and Miranda Epstein, for their loyalty and friendship and for their unstinting efforts in developing and refining many of my ideas to make them the dishes I dreamed them to be.

Over the years countless other talented individuals have passed through the O'Connell's kitchens, each making an invaluable contribution. They include Michael Bannerman, Cath Claringbold, Ben Hunt, Michelle Hoppener, Natalie Paull, Perry Peters, Adrian Richardson, Robin Sutcliffe, Paul Tek and Mark Tschappeller.

Still at O'Connell's Hotel, I know that my life would have taken a very different turn had it not been for the owners. I am particularly grateful to David Blackley, Geoff Burrows, Kent Lovell and Bill Regan, for their faith in my original vision for the hotel's restaurant. I thank them for giving me the freedom to develop my ideas within a framework of constant and unwavering support.

Lucy and I gratefully acknowledge the creative talents of designer Danie Pout, photographer Bobbie Fabian and food stylist Deb McLean. Their efforts have transformed our work into a stylish and elegant book of which we are very proud.

Our final and heartfelt thanks go to our publisher Hardie Grant. We are indebted to Sandy Grant for having the belief in our idea for *Arabesque*, and to the entire dedicated publishing team. We thank our editor Jane Angus, and most particularly, Julie Pinkham and Tracy O'Shaughnessy for their boundless enthusiasm, patience and encouragement, and for making the whole editorial and publication process such a joy.

Introduction

This book is intended for anyone who is interested in discovering more about the culinary influence of the Middle East and how to use these foods and flavours in their own kitchens at home.

Many people have some understanding of cooking from the Arab world, but it is usually based on their experience of limp pita bread and greasy kebabs from a grubby Lebanese takeaway. In more recent years there has also been a fashion for Moroccan food, with every other trendy bistro serving couscous and chermoula. But any deeper interest in Arab-influenced foods seems to have stopped here, which scarcely does them justice. The cuisines of the region we call the Middle East are as refined and complex as many other great cuisines of the world.

My own interest in food and cooking began in the family home in suburban Melbourne. My culinary instincts are rooted in the flavours and traditions of Lebanon, as cooked by my grandmothers and mother. When my classmates were munching on their lunchtime sandwiches of Strasbourg and tomato sauce, I was tucking into a garlic-laden falafel. Using ingredients such as chickpeas, allspice, vine leaves and rosewater has always been as natural to me as breathing.

When I embarked on my cooking career I followed the traditional route for a young Australian apprentice cook. I studied at trade school here in Melbourne while working in the kitchens of several outstanding local restaurants. The formal part of my training over, I then spent a number of years overseas, cooking in France, Italy, Austria and Hong Kong, honing my skills, extending my repertoire, and scarcely giving a thought to childhood dishes like stuffed vine leaves and kibbeh nayeh.

Over the last 12 years or so, since heading up my own kitchen, I have been able to synthesise the various influences of my culinary life and to produce the sort of food that I have always wanted to cook: not traditional Lebanese dishes, but rather food which, for me, captures the essence of the Middle East and expresses it in the best western tradition.

I am all for progress and evolution, in the kitchen as in any other field. Never before has the spread of information and ideas been as easy. As a result, most people know a little about many different cuisines, and are happy to incorporate ideas from Thailand, Mexico, Italy or Morocco in their own cooking.

There are, of course, those purists and traditionalists who abhor this evolution – and when it comes to the arbitrary mish-mashing together of completely incongruous ingredients, I too have been known to shudder. Such a lack of discrimination is, I feel, all about the quest for novelty, with little understanding or respect for the traditions of the cuisines used. But, surely things are no different than they ever were? There have always been fads and fashions in food. Over the centuries, as new ingredients spread to different regions they were quickly adopted and used ad nauseam until they found their own place and level in local culinary traditions. Without this eternal quest for new and different ideas we would still be munching on lentils and cabbage.

While I believe that good cooking is about understanding how to balance flavours and textures and respecting an ingredient's heritage, I also believe that this understanding does not necessarily have to be instinctual. It comes through experience. With this book I hope to encourage people to learn about and use ingredients which are close to my heart . Some, like rice or apricots are well known; others, like sumac or cardamom, may be less familiar. Most are relatively easy to track down, although a few will require a visit to a specialist Middle Eastern food store or good delicatessen. I have certainly not provided a comprehensive or definitive list of ingredients, but rather a subjective list of my own favourites, used in recipes which I feel best reflect the spirit of Middle Eastern cooking.

This book is not intended for the superchef – Middle Eastern food, is after all, largely just good home cooking. Many traditional dishes, though, are labour-intensive and time-consuming to prepare. They have evolved over hundreds of years, developed by Middle Eastern women whose day and social life revolved around highly labour-intensive cooking techniques. But these days few people have the time or inclination to spend hours stuffing little exquisite morsels.

Indeed, it seems as if the task of providing food every day for family, partner or oneself has become something of a chore. I firmly believe that one's daily dinner should not be complicated, time-consuming and overworked. In the western world we are blessed with an abundant and staggering array of fresh produce, and this should drive our repertoire. A dish can be transformed by the simplest things – and it is this detail which the following recipes are about. Remember then, that while some of the dishes might sound exotic and mysterious, they are based on traditions which are, after all, everyday fare in another culture.

In the pages that follow then, you will find a range of different dishes. Some, like the pickled pork belly, require a certain amount of planning ahead, even if they are not in themselves difficult and complicated to prepare; others are simple ideas, such as soft-boiled eggs sprinkled with dukkah, or a roast chicken stuffed under the skin with preserved lemon butter. Often it is simply a matter of looking at things from a different angle to make them exciting.

A word about health: my own past has been littered with angioplasty, bypass operations and even a heart transplant. Today I simply have to be conscious of my cholesterol intake, but I am firmly against the sort of food fascism which dictates many people's eating habits these days. For a healthy constitution, there must be balance. Don't banish all fats from your diet, but make sure, instead, that you eat 'healthier' fats such as olive oil, rather than saturated animal fats. Dairy foods are critical for bone and teeth strength – but make sure you don't eat a full-fat triple-cream cheese every day. You might opt instead for yoghurt. The desserts, cakes and biscuits in this book are not intended to be eaten every day. In the Middle East, they are rarely eaten, except on special occasions, and for the most part a meal will finish with fresh fruit.

Finally, a word about the construction of this book, and its co-author, my wife Lucy. I am a professional cook, she is not. On the other hand, she can write, whereas I (in good chef-like tradition) can barely manage a shopping list! As in all good partnerships, marriage included, it seems wise to divide the responsibilites on the basis of talents and inclinations. The text of this book has then, for the most part, been written by Lucy, and it is she too, who has been largely responsible for the translation of ingredients from commercial quantities to domestic. The recipes are written by me, but are the results of 40 years of eating, talking and experimenting with families and friends. The influences of my grandmothers, mother, sister-in-law and sister-in-law's mother, as well as countless other colleagues and mentors over the years, are all visible in this book.

Greg Malouf
1999

SPECIAL EQUIPMENT

Very few of us have the perfect kitchen and a complete batterie de cuisine, and yet we manage to cook and feed ourselves and our families very satisfactorily most days of the week. The recipes in this book are intended for the average cook, not superchefs, and for the most part can be made with the normal range of pots, pans, mixing bowls, baking tins, knives and wooden spoons.

Having said this, there *are* a few items of equipment that make life much easier, especially when cooking Middle Eastern recipes. Top of our list of essential items are a mortar and pestle. These are inexpensive and widely available from kitchen stores and Chinese supermarkets. They are indispensible when it comes to pounding and grinding nuts, seeds and spices. We also have a small coffee grinder, used for whizzing up larger quantities.

Also inexpensive and in constant use is our set of measuring cups and spoons. These are useful for measuring liquids and for ingredients which are measured by volume rather than weight. We have as well a set of electronic scales which conveniently weigh in metric and imperial. We discuss measurement and conversion ratios more fully in the next section.

It is a rare kitchen these days which has neither an electric mixer (we have a Kenwood) nor a food processor, and our recipes make use of both of these machines. Several dishes are also made much easier with a deep-fryer. However, we do not possess one and improvise quite successfully using a small saucepan or a wok for deep and semi-deep frying.

Moving further up the expense scale, there are several recipes in this book for ice-cream, and we are of the firm view that an ice-cream machine is essential for making the desired, velvet-smooth, light and creamy product. The freeze-beat-freeze-beat method will make an acceptable ice-cream, but it tends to be hard and dense by comparison with ice-cream made in a machine. If you love ice-creams and sorbets then you should do your best to buy, beg, borrow or steal a machine!

MEASUREMENTS

The recipes in this book were devised, tested and written in metric and will, in our view, work best if cooked according to the given measurements. Translating back to imperial is tedious and, as the future way of the world is undoubtedly metric, we urge you to try and get used to working in metric measurements – it really is simple. For those who are still in the transitional stage we include conversion tables (pages xiii–xv). The quantities are approximate – that is to say either rounded up or down.

We weigh dry ingredients, like flour, sugar and butter by grams. Small quantities of spices, however, we measure in teaspoons and tablespoons. Our set of spoons ranges from ¼ teaspoon to a tablespoon and is in constant use. One irritating and baffling fact is that American and English tablespoons are 15 ml, while Australian tablespoons are 20 ml. For the record, we use the American/English system, but are of the firm opinion that, for our recipes, the difference of 5 ml here or there is negligable.

Some items fall through the cracks when it comes to measuring. How do you give a precise measurement for a quantity of fresh herbs, for instance? Although we believe that the use of flavourings such as herbs and spices should be adjusted to the taste of the eater, for the purposes of our recipes we measure them by volume. Every bunch is a different size, depending where it is purchased, and weighing a few sprigs of parsley is surely taking things too far. In this book, then, fresh herbs are called for by the tablespoon or cup.

CONVERSION TABLES

WEIGHTS

Imperial	Metric
½ oz	10 g
¾ oz	20 g
1 oz	25 g
1½ oz	40 g
2 oz	50 g
2½ oz	60 g
3 oz	75 g
4 oz	110 g
4½ oz	125 g
5 oz	150 g
6 oz	175 g
7 oz	200 g
8 oz	225 g
9 oz	250 g
10 oz	275 g
12 oz	350 g
1 lb	450 g
1 lb 8 oz	700 g
2 lb	900 g
3 lb	1.35 kg

VOLUME

Imperial	Metric
2 fl oz	55 ml
3 fl oz	75 ml
5 fl oz (¼ pint)	150 ml
10 fl oz (½ pint)	275 ml
1 pint	570 ml
1¼ pints	725 ml
1¾ pints	1 litre
2 pints	1.2 litres
2½ pints	1.5 litres
4 pints	2.25 litres

DIMENSIONS

Imperial	Metric
¼ in	5 mm
½ in	1 cm
¾ in	2 cm
1 in	2.5 cm
1 ¾ in	4.5 cm
2 in	5 cm
3 in	7.5 cm
4 in	10 cm
5 in	13 cm
6 in	15 cm
8 in	20 cm
9 ¾ in	25 cm
12 in	30 cm

TEMPERATURES

°F	°C
275	140
300	150
325	170
350	180
375	190
400	200
425	220
450	230
475	240

TEASPOONS, TABLESPOONS AND CUPS

1 teaspoon	5 ml
1 tablespoon (3 teaspoons)	15 ml
¼ cup (4 tablespoons)	60 ml
⅓ cup	80 ml
½ cup	125 ml
1 cup	250 ml

You might also find it useful to know that in this book, unless otherwise stated:

- 1 egg = 61 g
- 1 medium onion = 130 g
- 1 large potato = 200 g
- 1 medium tomato = 100 g
- 1 large bunch herbs = 1 1/2 cups
- 1 lemon = 1/2 cup or 125 ml juice
- 1 cup dried beans or pulses = 160 g
- dried beans and pulses weigh about double once soaked.

It may appear that some recipes are very precise, particularly when it comes to baking and pastry making. Others, however, seem to be more flexible – a sprinkle or drizzle of this or that, a medium onion, a small zucchini or a large eggplant. This of course means that precision is not as important, and quantities are to be taken as guidelines, rather than hard-and-fast rules. Furthermore, unless stated otherwise:

- olive oil is listed either as extra-virgin olive oil, or olive oil (also known as 'pure olive oil')
- milk is full-fat
- thickened cream is 35 per cent fat
- pure cream is 45 per cent fat
- butter is unsalted
- eggs are free-range
- sugar is castor sugar
- chocolate is the best quality dark chocolate you can afford
- salt is sea salt, preferably from Maldon, not the iodised version available in supermarkets
- pepper is freshly ground white pepper, unless black is specified.

And finally, recipes serve four generously, unless otherwise stated.

Almonds

Many of our most popular foodstuffs are inedible and even poisonous in their wild state. And yet, as long ago as 3000 BC, in an extraordinary feat of primitive genetic engineering, our ancestors in the eastern Mediterranean learned how to select sweet, non-poisonous almonds from the bitter majority, and began the cultivation of one of the world's most important nuts.

The extreme bitterness of wild almonds comes from a chemical called 'amygdalin', which breaks down to form cyanide (also known as 'prussic acid'). A vestige of this remains today in bitter almonds, mainly grown for their volatile oil, which is used by confectioners to add flavour to marzipan. Their cousins, sweet almonds, are what we buy in the shops – usually in neat little plastic packages – either flaked, slivered or whole.

When the Arabs conquered Persia in the seventh century, the almond was just one of many new foods they discovered. From the Persians they learned to use whole almonds in a variety of sweet and savoury dishes. They also learned to grind them to a fine meal for use in cakes and biscuits, and to use them to thicken and enrich savoury dishes and sweet milk puddings.

As they expanded their empire westwards, the Arabs took with them many newly discovered foods, such as the almond tree, to cultivate in their new colonies and to trade with customers in Europe. As well as herbs and spices, vegetables and many varieties of fruit and nut trees, the Arabs also planted cuttings of the sugar cane they had found in Persia.

The sublime partnering of almonds with sugar remains a key element in European confectionary and patisserie today, especially in Spain and Sicily, where it is a legacy of their two hundred years under Arab rule. Callissons and dragées (sugared almonds), nougat, praline, macaroons and of course marzipan were all delicious outcomes of this marriage. When the Arabs retreated from Europe in the thirteenth century, the tradition of making sweetmeats, in both Spain and Sicily, was carried on by the skilled Arab servant women of Catholic convents, and became something of a closed industry.

The tradition and secrecy are still preserved today. On a recent trip to Andalusia we visited fancy sweet and pastry shops all around the region, and made a point of sampling as many convent sweets and cakes as we could manage! We can report that there are hundreds of different varieties – some flavoured with floral rosewater or orange-blossom water, some scented with spices such as cinnamon or cardamom. Others are enriched with egg yolks or chocolate, and many are mixed with candied citrus peel or chopped pistachio nuts for added texture.

Although almonds are probably best known in sweet dishes, they are also used extensively in the Middle East in a range of savoury dishes. Persians and Moroccans like to combine almonds with fruit in a range of tagines and braised dishes, in which they cook down to a buttery softness. In Syria and Lebanon they are fried and used as a crunchy garnish for all kinds of chicken and rice dishes.

SELECTING AND STORING ALMONDS

Almond trees have a lovely scented white blossom, making them an ornamental garden favourite. Soft, young green almonds are considered a real treat, and Greg recalls with great enthusiasm how he and his brothers would eagerly wait for spring, when the rush would be on to pick them straight from their backyard tree.

It is very hard to find green almonds in the shops, so, other than picking them straight from the tree, you will have to make do with the mature version. All supermarkets, whole-food stores and delicatessens stock almonds – mainly the blanched, prepackaged kind, which are certainly easier and more convenient to use, but you also run a greater risk of ending up with stale or occasionally rancid nuts. Around Christmas time there tends to be an abundance of the whole nuts, still in their shells. For cooking rather than nibbling, though, it is easier to buy shelled almonds, and they have a much sweeter, fresher flavour if you buy them in their papery brown skins and blanch them yourself as described below.

Probably the best place to buy nuts of any kind, if you want to ensure freshness, is from a Middle Eastern or nut specialist store, where you can be ensured a good brisk turnover.

Fresh nuts have a high oil content and will turn rancid if not stored correctly. For this reason it is preferable to buy all types of nuts in smallish quantities, and eat them within a month of purchase. Once you have opened a packet of nuts they should be stored in an airtight container in the fridge.

USING ALMONDS

It is not really practical to buy almonds whole in their shells – other than for the fun of cracking them around the Christmas dinner table. For cooking, the unpeeled nuts have a fresher flavour than the ready-blanched variety and it is very easy to blanch and skin them yourself. Soak the almonds in boiling water for around 3 minutes, then drain them well and pat dry. The skin will then slip off easily, although for more stubborn ones making a small slit with a sharp knife will help. Next, they should be thoroughly dried (either on the window sill in the sun, or in a low oven for 5–10 minutes) before use or before storage.

Blanched almonds can be ground to make a rich almond meal, which is infinitely superior to the ready-ground packaged stuff. One word of caution though: when grinding any nuts it is best to go slowly in short, quick bursts. Their high oil content means that they quickly mush down to an oily paste, rather than the light, fine crumbs you require.

Recipes for sweet biscuits and cakes often call for blanched whole almonds, or halved almonds. Savoury dishes are more likely to suggest dry-roasting or frying them to bring out a deeper, toastier flavour. Middle Easterners nearly always fry almonds, turning them an appetising golden-brown, and adding a heady savoury flavour and incomparable crunchiness to any dish. Surprisingly, less oil is absorbed in deep-frying than in shallow-frying. The nuts usually take only a few minutes to colour, so always watch them with an eagle eye, and drain them well on kitchen paper once you remove them from the heat.

ALMOND RECIPES

Fried almond risotto

Adding fried nuts and vermicelli threads to rice dishes is popular throughout the Middle East for the crunch and visual interest they add.

100 g flaked almonds

60 ml olive oil

50 g vermicelli nests, crumbled

60 ml olive oil, additional

I small onion, quartered

400 g Vialone Nano rice

I litre chicken stock, simmering

2 tablespoons celery leaves, roughly chopped

100 g butter, chilled and cut into small cubes

¼ teaspoon allspice

¼ teaspoon cinnamon

60 g parmesan cheese, grated

salt and pepper

• Fry the almonds in 60 ml olive oil until they are golden-brown. Remove them with a slotted spoon and drain them on absorbent paper. Return the oil to the heat and add the crumbled vermicelli. Fry until golden-brown, then tip into a sieve to drain. Dry the vermicelli on kitchen paper.

• Prepare the risotto using the four-stage method on page 230, adding the vermicelli to the onions and proceeding as described. Add the third quantity of stock and, when it is reduced by half, add the almonds, celery leaves, butter and spices, plus 80 ml of stock. Stir well until the butter is incorporated. Add the cheese and stir again. Cover the pan and take it off the heat for one minute, then check the consistency and adjust seasonings.

• Serve immediately as an accompaniment to barbecues, grills or roast meats.

Almond fritters

These golden puffs of airy choux pastry are rolled in toasted almond flakes before deep-frying and then drizzled with a floral honey syrup. A deep-fryer makes the task easy, but you can manage just as successfully with a small saucepan of oil. If you don't have a thermometer, the best way of testing whether the oil is hot enough is to throw in a small cube of bread. If it sizzles slowly to the top, turning golden-brown in about 30 seconds, you can proceed.

These fritters are delicious served with the rich and sophisticated Burnt Honey Ice-Cream (page 142), or perhaps a nutty Pine Nut Praline Ice-Cream (page 211).

50 g butter

3 teaspoons honey

100 ml milk

100 ml water

100 g plain flour

4 eggs

1 litre vegetable oil for deep-frying

150 g flaked almonds

icing sugar to dust

• Bring the butter, honey, milk and water to the boil. Add the flour and beat vigorously for 4–5 minutes until the dough comes cleanly away from the side of the pan and forms a ball. Place the dough in an electric mixer and beat in the eggs one at a time. Cover and refrigerate the mixture until ready to fry.

• Heat oil to 160°C (or test with a cube of bread). Shape fritter dough into smallish egg shapes using two dessertspoons. Roll each fritter in almond flakes and then deep-fry, four at a time, until the pastry is golden-brown and starting to split.

• Dust with icing sugar and serve immediately.

Basboussa

Versions of this semolina cake are found all over the Middle East. It is known as 'basboussa' in Egypt, while in Lebanese pastry shops it is served in little syrup-drenched lozenge shapes, and known as 'namoura', or 'harisa louz'. It is generally made with ground almonds, fried golden-brown in butter. Flaked almonds are used in this recipe to give added crunch.

100 g flaked almonds

225 g butter

200 ml yoghurt

125 g castor sugar

270 g fine semolina

50 ml Frangelico (optional)

½ teaspoon vanilla essence

1 ½ teaspoons baking powder

SYRUP

200 g castor sugar

150 ml water

juice of 1 lemon

- In a shallow pan, melt the butter and lightly fry the almonds until golden brown. Allow to cool.
- Beat the yoghurt with the sugar, then add the almond-butter mixture, semolina and Frangelico, vanilla and baking powder.
- To make the syrup, bring sugar, water and lemon juice to the boil and simmer for 5 minutes or until slightly reduced.
- Grease a baking tin and line with baking parchment. Pour the cake mixture into the tin and bake in a preheated 180°C oven for around 20 minutes, until the cake is just coloured. Then remove it from the oven and, with a sharp knife, mark out small diamond shapes on the surface of the cake. Spoon the syrup over the cake and return it to the oven for a further 5–10 minutes.
- Serve with a dollop of Lemon Curd Fool (page 158).

Other almond recipes

Apricots

Every summer we eagerly anticipate the arrival of the first stone fruits. Apricots, with their blushing rosy cheeks and syrupy perfume, are a visual delight. But sadly, in temperate climates – even the sunnier ones – they never quite live up to their promise and all too often are a furry, bland disappointment, requiring gentle poaching to bring them to life.

Originating in China, apricots spread along the ancient silk road to the Mediterranean, flourishing along the way in orchards throughout Persia and Syria, where they are still plentiful today. Some of the best apricots in the world are said to grow in Isfahan in modern Iran. Certainly they so delighted the ancient Romans when they invaded Persia in the first century AD that they took them back to Italy to plant, and within a few decades the cultivation of apricots had spread throughout western Europe.

The Arabs, who overran Persia in an explosion of religious fervour during the seventh century, were also seduced by the vast orchards of fruits growing in Persia – orchards of not just apricots, but also apples, plums, pears, pomegranates and quinces. It was in Persia that the Arabs learned to combine fruit with meat in fragrant, spicy stews and rice dishes. They took this new fashion, together with their new religion, back through the Mediterranean and the countries of North Africa, finally ending up in Spain. Of all their subjects, it was the Moroccans, at the extreme west of the Arab empire, who embraced this idea most enthusiastically, as can be seen from their national dish the tagine, which combines fruit, meat and spices in a very similar way to a Persian (Iranian) khoresht.

In the hot Middle East, it seems only natural that many fruits are also sun-dried and then stored to be enjoyed through the winter months. The best dried apricots are said to be the legendary Hunza apricots from

Kashmir, which need only a little plumping up in water and then gentle poaching to release their sublime tart–sweet intense flavour. They may look rather unprepossessing with their dull beige colour when compared with the bright-orange Australian and Californian apricots we see on our supermarket shelves, but looks aren't everything. The colour of the latter owes much to their treatment with sulphur dioxide, which is used to avoid spoilage and help preserve the colour of the fruit.

Sheets of dried fruit purée are also common throughout the Middle East. The only one we have found readily available here in Australia though, is apricot, known as 'amardine'. This is rather like an adult version of a fruit 'Roll-Up', and can be torn into strips and eaten as a chewy snack or cut into little shapes as a garnish for desserts, cakes or even rice dishes. Our sister-in-law, who grew up in Damascus, boils up Syrian amardine to make a thick, creamy summer pudding, studded with almonds and served with a big blob of whipped cream.

SELECTING AND STORING APRICOTS

Selecting apricots to eat fresh can be tricky. Always choose fruit which is unblemished and gives a little to the touch. Colour is not always a good guide, as fruit which is a beautiful pinky-orange and feels ripe to the touch may still taste unpleasantly furry and bland. The scent of the fruit is often a better guide to its flavour. If you plan to poach the fruit or use it in a cooked dish, though, the degree of ripeness is less critical.

Most dried apricots usually have a reliable flavour, and brightness of colour is not important, as the most expensive Hunza apricots prove. Dried apricots should be stored in an airtight container in a cool cupboard or pantry, where they will keep up to a year. In very humid climates they should be kept in the refrigerator.

USING APRICOTS

The intense syrupy sweetness of apricots is delicious in jams, preserves and jellies. It is also good in sweet tarts, crumbles and pies, or poached, puréed, and folded into cream for a bavarois or mousse. To prepare apricots for cooking, simply cut them in half lengthways, without peeling (the skin slips off easily once the cooked fruit has cooled a little). Don't discard the kernels, but add a few of them to the fruit for poaching – they contain minute quantities of prussic acid, which adds a slight bitter-almond flavour to the syrup. Dried apricots may be plumped up by soaking them overnight in water before poaching.

APRICOT RECIPES

Poached apricots

Poaching is the best and simplest way to bring out the intense sweet–sour apricot flavour. Cut the fruit in half and poach gently in a sugar syrup flavoured with lemon or orange zest, until soft. Be careful not to overcook them, and treat them carefully once they are poached as they will easily lose their shape. Poached apricots are delicious served warm with a big dollop of thick yoghurt and Cardamom-Orange Wafers (page 41). Or serve them, still warm, with Pine Nut Praline Ice-Cream (page 211) or spoon them over a sleek, trembling bavarois or custard.

1 kg ripe apricots

juice and zest of 1 lemon

1 cinnamon stick

250 g castor sugar

600 ml water

• Cut the apricots in half and remove their kernels. If you like, bash around 10 of the kernels to remove the nut inside, and add them to the syrup. Place all the ingredients in a pan and slowly bring to the boil.

• Then remove from the heat and allow the apricots to cool in their syrup.

Apricot-cardamom ice-cream

Apricots work equally well in an intense sorbet or creamy ice-cream. For this recipe you can use fresh apricots poached in a sherry-laced syrup, or, for a slightly different flavour, use intensely flavoured amardine sheets, as described on page 8. This ice-cream is also delicious if you omit the cardamom seeds and fold through Pine Nut Praline (page 210) toward the end of the churning process, for a toasty, nutty crunchiness.

250 ml sherry

250 ml water

16 cardamom pods, seeds only, crushed and sieved

1 packet amardine sheets (500g)

200 ml water

200 g castor sugar

50 g mild-flavoured honey

½ vanilla bean, split and scraped

8 egg yolks

600 ml thickened cream

1 teaspoon vanilla essence

• Combine water, sherry, and cardamom seeds in a heavy based pan and slowly bring to the boil. Lower the heat, add the amardine sheets and simmer gently until it all dissolves to a thickish smooth consistency. Remove from the heat and allow to cool.

• To make a syrup, bring the water to the boil with the sugar, honey and vanilla bean, then lower the heat and simmer gently for five minutes.

• Meanwhile, to make the ice-cream base, whisk the egg yolks until light and fluffy (about three minutes in an electric mixer), then pour on the hot syrup, whisking all the time. Add the cream and the vanilla essence, whisk briefly to incorporate then turn off the motor.

• Allow to cool completely, then fold the amardine fruit purée into the ice-cream base.

• Pour into an ice-cream maker and churn according to the manufacturer's instructions.

• Serves four to six.

Apricot and orange-blossom cream

Dessert wines such as Sauternes add another dimension to the flavour of poached apricots — fresh or dried. Of course if you don't wish to break the bank on a Sauternes, you could choose a Muscat or any one of many delicious Australian botrytis-affected 'stickies'. Other terrific combinations are Marsala, brandy or orange liqueurs or even orange-blossom water. This perfumed cream makes a delicious accompaniment to a rich chocolate cake.

300 g amardine sheets

150 ml water

70 g castor sugar

120 ml water

400 ml pure cream

60 ml Marsala wine

1 teaspoon orange-blossom water

• Gently cook the amardine in 150 ml water for about 10 minutes, until very soft. Remove from heat and whiz in food processor to a smooth purée. Chill.

• Next make a caramel with the sugar and 60 ml of the water. Once the sugar has caramelised add the remaining cold water to thin the syrup a little and prevent it from setting hard. Allow to cool completely.

• Combine the apricot purée with the cream, Marsala and orange-blossom water, and whip into soft peaks. Gently swirl in the caramel and serve straight away.

Artichokes

Maybe it has something to do with the fast pace of the world we live in, but many people consider artichokes to be much too much like hard work. It is true that they are not for those who like to eat on the run, as they require a certain level of commitment to prepare. Indeed, it must have been a brave and determined individual who first attacked the artichoke with a view to eating it. First you have to hack off the spiky outer leaves, and then do battle with the hairy, tickly central choke in order to arrive at the prized heart.

Artichokes are viewed much more favourably in the Middle East and Mediterranean countries, where they grow like the thistles they in fact are! They are particularly popular in Italy, not only for the antipasto platter, but also for a variety of Jewish–Italian dishes, such as the famous deep-fried artichokes (known as 'carciofi alla Giuda'), stuffed artichokes ('carciofi ripieni') or artichokes with rice ('riso con carciofi').

The Jews introduced artichokes to the northern cities of Italy in the sixteenth century, after their communities fled Sicily and the ferocious Spanish Inquisition. Sicilians often claim the artichoke as native to their island, but historians think it more likely that they were introduced by the Arabs during their occupation of the island in the nineth and tenth centuries. Whatever the truth, they were clearly greatly enjoyed by the Arabs, who named them al-kharsuf. This is the origin of 'carciofi' in Italian, 'alcachofa' in Spanish, and of course our English word, 'artichoke'.

Artichokes became popular in Renaissance Italy and then in France, thanks to Catherine de Medici, who moved there on her marriage to Henry II. Her fondness for them was considered most unseemly by the French court, given the artichoke's reputed aphrodisiac qualities – although this is no doubt the very reason that England's King Henry VIII took to them so eagerly!

Nowadays artichokes grow all around the Mediterranean and the Middle East, where they are cheap and plentiful. Fresh artichokes have a delicate, almost nutty flavour, which lends itself particularly well to Arabic styles of cooking. For instance, they are delicious crumbed or battered and deep fried, or braised in olive oil with other vegetables. Artichoke hearts with broad beans, in one of many common cross-cultural anomalies, are a popular Friday night dish in both Jewish and Arabic communities. They are also equally popular stuffed with a delicate meat and nut filling or a robust anchovy and crumbing mixture.

A good introduction to this refined vegetable is pickled artichokes, preserved in oil, which can be found in any good delicatessen. These are good scattered through salads, to which they add a lovely nutty flavour and a slight acidic bite. They also complement the richness of offal, and are particularly good with smoked tongue. Although the shop-bought versions can be good, they don't come close to those prepared at home. All that's required for their preparation, really, is a little courage.

SELECTING AND STORING ARTICHOKES

Artichokes come in all different sizes, but the ones most readily available in Australia tend to be quite small, when compared to the giant beauties on offer in Europe. However, the smaller size does not mean that they are inferior. Choose firm, crisp-looking vegetables which feel weighty. The stalk should still be attached and the leaves should be tightly packed together. Artichokes deteriorate quite soon after picking and as they age, the whole plant starts to droop. As they dry out they slowly turn brown and the leaves open up.

Quite a few of our recipes include pickled artichokes. The recipe for preparing them follows, but it may be more convenient for you to buy them. They are readily available, although quality is varied. The best are preserved in oil rather than brine, which gives an unpleasant 'tinny' flavour.

USING ARTICHOKES

Larger artichokes need first to be trimmed of their tough outer leaves, and the stalks sliced off so they will sit flat on a plate. Smaller artichokes may only need to be carefully washed and the stalks cut. Some people also like to trim neatly across the top leaves – this is best done with sharp kitchen scissors. Once cut, artichokes discolour quickly, so drop each trimmed vegetable into acidulated water straight away, where they will sit quite happily until you are ready to cook them.

The simplest way to cook artichokes is to boil them in plenty of boiling salted water and lemon juice. Cover them with a plate, to keep them under the surface, then cover the pan and cook them for 10–20 minutes, depending on their size. To check if they are cooked, carefully remove an artichoke from the pan and gently pull on a leaf. If it comes away easily, it is ready. The artichokes should then be drained and left upside down until you are ready to eat.

Artichokes cooked in this way are best eaten warm, rather than hot from the pan, and need lots of sauce to accompany them. At its simplest, this can be melted butter, with plenty of salt and pepper and a squeeze of lemon. Delicious variations might be a tangy vinaigrette, a rich hollandaise sauce or mayonnaise, or a light refreshing Avgolemono sauce (page 157).

Braising artichokes in a niçoise or à la grecque manner is merely a variation of the simple boiling method. The whole artichoke should be prepared as above, but cooked in a pan of water with plenty of olive oil and aromatics (see page 17 for recipe). They can be eaten straight away, or preserved in their poaching liquor for future use. We use artichokes cooked in this way in all sorts of dishes.

Other recipes require only the inner artichoke hearts, but these dishes are only worth preparing if you have large artichokes. Prepare them as above, with a pan of acidulated water close to hand. Trim the stalk and then start snapping off the leaves, rubbing the raw edges of the vegetable with half a lemon as you go. Keep going until you get to the pale, thin, tightly furled leaves inside the artichoke. At this point you can slice off the top part of the artichoke, scoop out the choke and discard these parts. Rub the heart all over with the cut lemon and then drop into your acidulated water.

ARTICHOKE RECIPES

Artichoke soup with Spanish sausage and roasted pistachio nuts

This is a version of a Renaissance soup which Greg learned in Mantova, Italy. The Italian version uses cock's combs instead of sausage, and the soup is garnished with jewel-like pomegranate seeds.

6 large artichokes

juice of 4 lemons mixed with 1 litre of water

2 medium onions

2 cloves garlic

2 medium leeks

100 ml olive oil

2 litres chicken stock

salt and pepper

3 semi-dried chorizo sausages, grilled and sliced into 1 cm diagonal pieces

2 egg yolks

150 ml thickened cream

juice of 2 lemons

GARNISH

½ teaspoon allspice
(freshly milled, if possible)

60 ml extra-virgin olive oil

100 g unsalted pistachio nuts, dry-roasted and coarsely crushed

• To prepare the artichokes, remove the outer hard leaves as well as the choke and immediately place the heart into lemon water.

• Slice the onions, garlic and leeks finely. Heat the olive oil in a heavy-based pot.

• Drain the artichokes and very quickly slice into thin (2 mm) slices. Sauté them in the hot oil with the onions, garlic and leeks, then cover and simmer for 5–8 minutes. Do not allow the artichokes to colour.

• Add the chicken stock. Bring to the boil and gently simmer for half an hour. Taste and season with salt and pepper.

• When ready to serve, bring the soup back to the boil and then add the grilled chorizo pieces. Mix the egg yolks with the cream and then add to the soup. Slowly return the soup to just below boiling, stirring constantly. Remove from the heat and adjust seasoning with salt, pepper and lemon juice.

• As you serve, finish each bowl with a sprinkling of crushed nuts and freshly milled allspice, and a drizzle of extra-virgin olive oil.

• Serves eight.

ABOVE:
Artichoke salad with bacon
and eggs (recipe page 18)
BELOW:
Pigeon stuffed with a cracked-
wheat pilaf (recipe page 33)

Salmon kibbeh nayeh - with a soft herb salad (recipe page 32)

Artichokes cooked à la niçoise

Prepare these in the spring, when artichokes are plentiful. There are endless uses for these artichokes, from soups and salads to braised vegetable and meat dishes. Having a jar of them in the larder will enable you to add that distinctive artichoke flavour and texture for many months after their season ends.

20 small artichokes, outer leaves trimmed

a small bucket of cold water acidulated with the juice of 2 lemons

1 litre water

juice of 4 lemons

½ litre white wine

¼ litre olive oil

1 teaspoon coarsely ground black pepper

4 shallots, peeled and quartered

1 bay leaf

2 sprigs thyme

1 teaspoon fennel seeds

2 cloves garlic

1 teaspoon salt

- Trim the outer leaves from the artichokes and place them in acidulated water.
- Bring to the boil 1 litre of water with the juice of 4 lemons, white wine, olive oil, pepper, shallots, bay leaf, thyme sprigs, fennel seeds, garlic cloves and salt. Boil the marinade for 20 minutes. Drain the artichokes and place them in the marinade. The liquid should just cover the artichokes – top up with boiling water if necessary. Bring back to the boil and cook at a rolling boil for about 5–10 minutes, or until they are just tender.
- Remove from the heat and allow to cool in the marinade. Arrange the artichokes in a 4-litre jar and cover with the marinade. Seal tightly and sterilise by placing the whole jar in a pan of cold water, bringing to the boil and simmering for 10 minutes.
- These pickled artichokes will keep unopened for 5 months. Once opened, they will keep in the fridge for up to a month.

Artichoke salad with bacon and eggs

This makes a good starter for four people or a light lunch for two, served with plenty of fresh, crusty bread. It is well worth making the dukkah for the fragrant nutty flavour which blends beautifully with the creamy richness of the runny egg yolks.

200 g bacon rashers

60 ml corn oil

I teaspoon honey

250 g artichokes cooked à la Niçoise (page 17) or good quality purchased artichokes, preserved in oil

2 shallots, finely shredded

½ cup whole parsley leaves

I tablespoon Dijon mustard

1½ tablespoons white wine vinegar

100 ml extra-virgin olive oil

salt and pepper

4 eggs

I tablespoon dukkah (see page 250)

• Cut the bacon rashers into little batons and fry in the corn oil until crisp, then drizzle the honey over the bacon pieces to 'candy' them for a few more minutes. Remove from the heat and strain through a colander or sieve. Cut the artichokes into quarters and place them in a large mixing bowl with the bacon, shallots and parsley.
• To make a vinaigrette, put the mustard in bowl and add a splash of vinegar to loosen. Whisk oil in very slowly so it emulsifies, until half is incorporated. Add another splash of vinegar to loosen again. Continue to add oil, whisking until all is incorporated. Taste and adjust seasoning.
• Poach the eggs, or boil them for 3–4 minutes from when the water boils. Peel and halve boiled eggs.
• Dress the artichoke salad with the vinaigrette. Place it on a plate and serve it with the eggs on top. Sprinkle with dukkah.

Other artichoke recipes

Fresh Broad Beans, Artichokes and Peas, page 26
Salmon Kibbeh Nayeh – with a Soft Herb Salad, page 32
Natural Oysters with Parsley-Bastourma Salad, page 191
Spring Vegetable Paella, page 233

Basque-style chicken

20 g dried porcini mushrooms

4 small-to-medium tomatoes

8 artichokes cooked à la niçoise
(page 17) or good quality purchased
artichokes, preserved in oil

1.8 kg corn-fed chicken

salt and pepper

60 ml olive oil

1 tablespoon honey mixed with
1 tablespoon water

8 shallots, cut in half

6 small cloves garlic, peeled

50 ml porcini juice from soaking

1 teaspoon tomato paste

100 ml red wine

300 ml chicken stock

8 leaves fresh sage

TO SERVE

200 g egg noodles

generous knob of butter

juice of half a lemon

salt and freshly ground black pepper

• Rinse the porcini mushrooms briefly in cold water to remove any clinging grit or dirt, then soak them in a cup of fresh cold water for 10 minutes. Reserve the liquid to be added to the stock later. Cut the tomatoes into quarters and gently squeeze out the seeds. If you are using fresh artichokes, remove the outer leaves and choke and drop the hearts into acidulated water. When you are ready to use them, cut each heart into quarters. If you are using pickled artichokes, cut each artichoke into quarters.

• Break the chicken down into 8 pieces, or ask your butcher to do it for you. Remove the skin and season with salt and pepper. In a large oven-proof pan, seal the chicken pieces in very hot olive oil, until they turn golden-brown. Towards the end of the frying time add the honey and then cook for a further few minutes to caramelise, but be careful not to burn. Remove the chicken from pan.

• Lower the heat and add the shallots and garlic to the pan, and sauté them briefly until they are just softened. Then add the artichokes, tomatoes and porcini mushrooms and sauté for two minutes. Mix the porcini juice, tomato paste and red wine with the chicken stock and pour into the pan. Place the chicken pieces back in the pan on top of the vegetables, sprinkle the sage leaves on top of the chicken and bake in a preheated 220°C oven for 20 minutes. Remove the pan from the oven and move the chicken pieces to a warm plate. On a high heat reduce the stock by about a third, and then return the chicken pieces to the pan.

• Cook and drain the egg noodles then sauté them briefly in butter. Add a squeeze of lemon, salt and freshly ground pepper.

• To serve, put sauce and vegetables on plate, then the chicken, and top with egg noodles twirled into a little mound on top.

Beans

In the beginning there were beans – broad beans, that is. These ancient, edible seeds grew abundantly all around Central Asia, the Middle East and the Mediterranean from the earliest times. In the days before humans learned how to cultivate plants, and had to scrabble around in the dirt for sustenance, broad beans were a godsend. They were easily gathered, were packed with stomach-filling starch, protein and other nutrients, and, most importantly, could be dried and stored for long periods of time.

Broad beans were also very easy to propagate, and became one of the first vegetable crops to be cultivated. Like other ancient crops such as lentils and peas, they belong to the leguminous plant group known as 'pulses', which have large nutritious seeds contained in an outer pod. Pulses were frequently combined with grains such as wheat, barley or millet to provide the main sustenance for early civilisations. As well as eating them, the ancient Greeks were said to have used broad beans as election ballot-counters. The Romans made them into cakes or porridge, while the Egyptians' passion for them endures today in little rissoles known as 'tamia' (elsewhere known as 'falafel') and ful medames, a humble peasant stew which has been adopted as the national dish.

Numerous other types of beans have been grown around the world since antiquity – soya beans in China and Japan; haricot, butter, lima, kidney and endless others in the Americas – but broad beans are the only variety native to the Middle East and Europe. Other beans didn't reach Europe until the fifteenth century, as part of the exciting new range of foodstuffs brought by explorer ships from the New World. As is so often the case, these new beans, which came in a dazzling range of colours, shapes and sizes, quickly overtook dull old broad beans in popularity. And so, tender little pale-green flageolets were taken up by the French, and the Tuscans' fondness for mild-flavoured borlotti beans led to their reputation as Italy's 'bean eaters'. The English preferred yet another sort of New World bean, the fresh 'green' bean.

Green beans are simply a variety of bean which have been cultivated for eating whole, rather than for their seeds alone. They also originated in the Americas, many thousands of years ago, and are grown today by home gardeners the world over. They come in a range of shapes and sizes – from the thin, elegant French beans to wider, flatter runner beans, or the long Asian snake beans. Green beans often used to be called 'string' beans because of the fibrous string growing down the seam, which had to be pulled off before cooking. Today, though, most beans have been bred to be 'stringless'.

SELECTING AND STORING BEANS

Fresh beans including broad beans and all varieties of green beans are seasonal and at their firm, snappy best during the summer.

When choosing any sort of green beans ensure that they are dry and unblemished, not wet and wrinkled, and, above all, crisp and firm, not limp and bendy. The freshness and age of fresh broad beans is a little harder to determine as they come hidden within their own fleshy pod. This pod is often misshapen and mottled, and it can be hard to tell the condition of the beans within – but certainly avoid soft and floppy pods. Later in the season, both the pods and the beans are likely to be larger. New-season broad beans, though, are small and tender, and can even be eaten in the pod.

Dried beans, of course, are readily available throughout the year, though it is impossible to know how long your particular choice has been sitting on the shelves. As with all pulses, we recommend you buy from a shop with a swift turnover and a knowledgeable clientele. Middle Eastern stores and health food shops are usually a good bet.

There are numerous different varieties of dried beans available, but for the most part, Middle Easterners tend to use dried broad beans (which can be large, dark and unpeeled, or smaller, split and peeled) and white beans such as haricots, cannellini and butter beans. Dried beans last well, but should be stored in an airtight container in a cool, dark cupboard.

USING BEANS

Green beans these days rarely need stringing, but usually require rinsing and a quick top-and-tail. Cook them in plenty of boiling salted water for 2 minutes or until they are just tender (personal preference should dictate whether you like them meltingly soft, or still with a slight squeak!). If you are eating them straight away, drain them thoroughly and then dress them immediately in a little butter or olive oil. If they are to be used later, they may be refreshed in cold water.

Fresh broad beans need to be removed from their furry pods before cooking. Unless they are baby-small they will also need to be peeled, which is easily achieved if you boil them rapidly for 2–3 minutes, then drain them and rinse them under cold water. When they are cool enough to be handled the tender beans can be easily squeezed out of their leathery skins. They need little further cooking, but just a gentle reheating, perhaps in a little butter or olive oil. From this stage they can also be added to pilafs and risottos, or dressed while warm for salads.

Dried beans and other pulses these days are pretty clean and it is unusual to find little stones and grit lurking among them, especially those in the plastic packages in supermarkets. If you buy them loose though, it is probably a good idea to wash them well, as they can be dusty, and to pick them over for alien matter.

Some people are put off cooking pulses because of the need to rehydrate them before cooking. But although it requires a little forethought, the soaking process really requires zero effort on the cook's part. Long soaking overnight in two to three times their volume of cold water is ideal, as it allows for a slow and thorough rehydration. The long soak is also helpful in leaching out some of the indigestible oligosaccharides which create gas in the gut – for this reason you should always throw away the soaking water. A pinch of bicarbonate of soda added to the soaking water is said to help loosen the skins. Some large beans with very tough skins (like giant dried broad beans) require even longer soaking (one to two days) in order to squeeze them out of their skins.

The quick soak method can be handy if you need to soak beans in a hurry (it is all relative, of course, as even the quick soak requires several hours). Rinse and pick over the beans as usual and then place them in a pan and cover them with twice their volume of cold water. Bring the water to the boil, and cook rapidly for 2–3 minutes. Then remove the pan from the heat and allow the beans to soak for at least 4 hours. Drain off the water and then proceed to cook.

After soaking, beans should be covered in plenty of fresh cold water, which is brought to the boil and then lowered to a simmer. The beans will take from 45 minutes to 2 hours to cook, depending on their size and age. As for all other pulses, do not salt the water until the very end of the cooking time, as it toughens the skins and slows down the cooking process.

BEAN RECIPES

White bean soup with spicy merguez sausages

Dried beans and pulses form the basis of all sorts of delicious soups, puréed into a delicious earthy smoothness. This version is spiced with sweet cinnamon and spicy merguez sausages, and has an underlying nuttiness from the hazelnut oil and the crunchy roasted nut garnish. Serve it with harissa toast – mix a spoonful of harissa paste into the Lebanese bread dough (page 267) and bake as usual.

125 g white haricot beans, soaked overnight in twice their volume of cold water

1 litre chicken stock

1 cinnamon stick

40 ml olive oil

75 g kaiser fleisch, diced

1 medium brown onion, finely chopped

1 clove garlic, finely chopped

1 stick celery, finely chopped

3 ripe tomatoes, skinned, de-seeded and finely chopped

1 teaspoon honey

1 teaspoon thyme leaves

zest of ½ lemon

1 tablespoon hazelnut oil

salt and pepper

1 cup spinach leaves, shredded

6 merguez sausages, grilled and sliced

80 g roasted hazelnuts, peeled and crushed

• Drain the haricot beans and place them in a pan with the chicken stock and cinnamon stick. Bring to the boil, then lower the heat and simmer for 1–2 hours until beans are tender, which will depend on their age and freshness.

• In a frying pan, heat the olive oil and sauté the kaiser fleisch, onion, garlic and celery for about 4 minutes until they are lightly coloured and softened. Add the mix to the beans and stock with the tomatoes, honey, thyme, lemon zest and hazelnut oil.

• To serve, bring the soup to the boil and season generously with salt and pepper, to taste. Throw in the shredded spinach leaves then garnish with slices of merguez sausage and crushed hazelnuts.

• Serves six.

Niçoise-style green bean salad

One of the best green bean salads around. Use fresh tuna, either seared medium–rare and sliced as described here, or cooked through and flaked into the salad. The dukkah adds a wonderfully nutty fragrance, and works beautifully with the creamy eggs and rich tuna.

DRESSING

1 tablespoon Dijon mustard

3 anchovies

1 teaspoon salted capers, rinsed well

juice of 1 lemon

1 tablespoon champagne or white wine vinegar

1 clove garlic crushed with ½ teaspoon salt

100 ml olive oil

6 eggs

2 medium waxy potatoes

1 large Spanish onion, thinly sliced

2 medium tomatoes cut into 8 wedges

150 g green beans

½ cup parsley leaves

60 g Ligurian olives

6 anchovies, cut in half

600 g fresh tuna

30 ml oil for grilling tuna

pepper

GARNISH

1 tablespoon dukkah (page 250)

- To make the dressing, put mustard, anchovies, capers, lemon, vinegar and garlic paste into a liquidiser and blitz to a paste. Gradually add the oil drop by drop until the mixture emulsifies. If the mayonnaise is very thick, thin it with a little water – the consistency should be like thin pouring cream.
- Place the eggs in pot of warm water. Bring to the boil and cook for 4 minutes. Drain and refresh in cold water, then peel and reserve.
- Steam the whole, unskinned potatoes for about 15–20 minutes, or until tender but still firm. While they're still hot, carefully peel and cut them into 3 mm slices. While the potatoes are steaming, prepare the onion and tomatoes and place them together in large bowl. Top and tail the beans, bring to them to the boil in salted water and cook for them for 2–3 minutes, or until they are tender. Drain and refresh them under cold water.
- Cut the tuna into three even steaks. Season well with salt and pepper. Heat the oil in a heavy-based pan until it is almost smoking. Sear the tuna pieces on each side (40 seconds per side for medium–rare) and then remove them from the pan and put them to one side.
- Cut each steak into six even slices.
- To assemble: While the potatoes and beans are still warm, place them in the mixing bowl with the tomatoes and onion, parsley leaves, olives and anchovy pieces. Gently mix with half the dressing. Choose a large shallow dish for serving. Cut the eggs in half, sprinkle them with dukkah and arrange them on the salad with tuna slices.
- Serves six.

Fresh broad beans, artichokes and peas

Use your own home-pickled artichokes, or good quality shop-bought artichokes in oil. This is a vibrant summery vegetable braise. Flood the plate with a big spoonful of the vegetables and then top with slices of grilled, barbecued or roasted meat, so the juices and flavours all mingle.

100 g fresh peas, shelled

150 g fresh broad beans, shelled

150 g shallots

artichokes cooked à la niçoise (page 17) or good quality purchased artichokes, preserved in oil

100 g bacon rashers

1 teaspoon honey

1 teaspoon butter

60 ml extra-virgin olive oil

1 small clove garlic, finely chopped

½ cup whole mint leaves

½ teaspoon sherry vinegar

salt and pepper for seasoning

• Blanch the peas in boiling water for 2 minutes, then drain them and refresh them in cold water. Blanch the broad beans for 2 minutes, then drain and refresh under cold water. When cool, peel off the skins. Peel the shallots and place them in a pan of cold, lightly salted water. Bring to the boil, then lower the heat and simmer until the shallots are just tender, which will take around 6 minutes. Cut the artichoke hearts in quarters.

• Cut bacon rashers into neat batons and fry until they are golden. Add the teaspoon of honey, cook a further minute, then remove the bacon pieces from the heat and strain them through a sieve or colander.

• In a clean pan melt the butter and oil together and lightly sauté the garlic. Add the whole shallots and mix well in the oil mixture. Add the broad beans and heat for a further minute or so, moving gently around in oil. Finally, add the peas, artichokes and mint leaves, and a splash of sherry vinegar.

• Season with salt and pepper and serve.

Other bean recipes

Whipped bean purée with Taleggio cheese

You can use any white beans, such as cannellini, haricot or even large butter beans. The idea is that the smooth creamy blandness of the starchy purée makes a terrific base for the strongly flavoured rind-washed Taleggio cheese. You could try all sorts of variations on the Taleggio cheese theme, such as crumbled fetta or freshly grated parmesan. A tablespoon of mustard, freshly grated horseradish or salty tapenade work well too, or, if you feel really extravagant, a liberal splash of truffle oil. Serve a dollop of this purée with grilled poultry or rabbit, or some good meaty sausages.

150 g white beans, soaked overnight in 2–3 times their volume of cold water

30 ml olive oil

1 medium onion, finely sliced

1 large clove garlic, roughly chopped

15 ml sherry

700 ml water

1 very small clove garlic crushed to a paste with ½ teaspoon salt

30 ml extra-virgin olive oil

juice of ½ lemon

60 g Taleggio cheese, cut into 1 cm dice

salt and pepper

- Strain the beans and rinse them well. In a heavy-based pot heat the olive oil and then add the onion. Sauté for a few minutes, add the chopped garlic and stir on a gentle heat for a minute. Add the beans, stirring well to coat them with oil, and then add the sherry. Add water and bring to the boil, then lower the heat and simmer uncovered for 30–40 minutes, or until the beans are tender and most of the liquid has evaporated.
- Towards the end of the cooking time raise the heat to boil off any remaining liquid, but watch carefully to avoid burning.
- Pour the beans into a sieve and strain any residual liquid, then tip them into a blender and add the garlic paste, extra-virgin olive oil and lemon juice.
- Blitz the mixture on high until it is reduced to a smooth purée. To serve, heat the purée through and gently fold in the Taleggio cheese.
- Taste and season with salt and pepper.

Rabbit hotpot with white beans and Spanish sausage

This rabbit hotpot is rich and smoky, similar to a French cassoulet. It needs only a big green salad and maybe a bowl of Goat's Cheese Mashed Potatoes (page 49) to make the perfect meal on a cold winter's evening.

100 g white beans, soaked overnight in 2–3 times their volume of cold water

1 kg rabbit hind legs cut in half, or rabbit pieces

salt and pepper

60 ml olive oil

1 tablespoon honey diluted with 1 tablespoon hot water

10 shallots

120 g small button mushrooms, stalks trimmed flush

6 cloves garlic

200 g semi-dried chorizo sausage, cut into 1 cm discs

100 ml white wine

2 large ripe tomatoes (or 1 × 400 g can), skinned, seeded and chopped

12 fresh sage leaves

½ teaspoon juniper berries, lightly cracked

peel of ½ orange

500 ml chicken stock

freshly ground black pepper

½ cup home-made Crumbing Mix (page 263)

6 kalamata olives, stoned and finely chopped

• Cook the beans in fresh water until they are just tender then drain and reserve. Pat the rabbit legs dry and lightly season them with salt and pepper. In a large oven-proof casserole dish, sauté the rabbit pieces in olive oil until they colour. Towards the end of cooking time turn up the heat and pour in the honey glaze. Sauté for a further 30 seconds until the mixture gently caramelises, turning the rabbit pieces so that they are coated with the glaze. Now add the whole shallots, mushrooms, garlic and chorizo sausage pieces and sauté for 2 minutes, turning everything in the glaze. Add the white wine and stir to lift all the golden bits stuck to the bottom of the pan. Then add the beans, chopped tomatoes, sage leaves, juniper berries, orange peel and chicken stock.

• Season with fresh black pepper.

• Bring to the boil, then cover the surface of the casserole with a circle of greaseproof paper and cover the dish with a lid. Cook on the middle shelf of a preheated 180°C oven for 30 minutes. Remove from the oven and check that the rabbit is tender and the meat is beginning to fall from the bones. Return to the oven and cook for a further 20 minutes. Preheat the grill to its highest temperature. Make sure you have removed the baking paper and sprinkle the surface with a mixture of the Crumbing Mix and the olives.

• Grill until golden-brown and serve immediately.

Burghul

Before tabbouleh took the world by storm, it is doubtful that there were many people outside the Middle East who even knew what burghul was. Even today, while recognising it as the little sand-coloured flecks in tabbouleh, not many of us have the first idea what else to do with it.

Burghul (or bulgar) is actually cracked wheat. To make it, grains are first boiled and then dried and roughly ground to produce the semi-processed wheat known as 'burghul'. This can then be steamed or boiled, moistened with a little butter or oil, and served as an accompaniment to all kinds of stews and braises. Its texture is a little like brown rice, and it has a nutty, earthy flavour.

As Middle Easterners know, burghul can be almost as versatile as rice. It is a prominent staple, traditionally considered peasant food (city sophisticates would mainly eat rice) and it features in everything from pilafs, stuffings and salads, as well as being a key ingredient in the Lebanese national dish, kibbeh.

Devotees of Lebanese restaurants know all about kibbeh. These are the little torpedo-shaped patties of meat stuffed into a crispy shell of burghul. The art of kibbeh making is the stuff of legend, and much is made of those special women favoured with 'kibbeh fingers'. Less well known outside Lebanon is kibbeh nayeh, which is a sort of Middle Eastern version of steak tartare. This uses the best quality lamb, pounded or minced to a fine paste with onion, burghul and spices, and served with a drizzle of fruity olive oil, salad onions, fresh mint and plenty of Arabic bread.

There are numerous versions of tabbouleh found all around the Mediterranean. In Turkey, for instance, they make a version called 'kisir', which includes green peppers and cucumber and is sometimes sharpened with pomegranate juice or verjuice (unripened grape juice) instead of lemon juice.

SELECTING, STORING AND USING BURGHUL

Burghul comes in several different grades and colours. The coarsest grade is usually cooked like rice, and used to make pilafs and stuffings. The finest grade is used in salads such as tabbouleh, where it is moistened and allowed to swell in a lemony dressing. In Middle Eastern stores you may also find that burghul is available bleached or unbleached. However, the colour of the burghul doesn't affect the flavour of the dish, so choose whichever you prefer the look of.

Fine burghul, which is what you use in tabbouleh, needs only minimal pre-soaking. The grains should be thoroughly rinsed in cold water and then allowed to soak for about 10 minutes to soften slightly. You then need to drain them well – tip them into a tea-towel and twist it tightly to extract as much excess water as you can.

For stuffings and pilafs, coarser burghul is cooked in the same way as rice. Like rice, it is better to measure both water and grain by volume rather than by weight – the ratio being 1.5 water to 1 burghul.

BURGHUL RECIPES

Watercress tabbouleh

Tabbouleh suffers much abuse at the heavy hands of deli and bistro cooks the world over. At its best, tabbouleh is a simple salad made at home, using whatever vegetables are best from the garden, and lavish amounts of fresh parsley and mint. In the West people often overdo the burghul, but tabbouleh is lighter and much more refreshing if less burghul is used. The individual vegetables and herbs may be prepared a little ahead of time, but should not be assembled with the lemon juice and oil until the very last moment.

100 g burghul, white, fine grade

2 bunches watercress, washed well
  and leaves picked (should yield
  1½ cups of leaves)

1 cup mint leaves, finely shredded

1 large purple onion, finely chopped

3 medium tomatoes, diced very small

juice of 2 lemons

½ teaspoon allspice

⅓ teaspoon cinnamon

½ teaspoon each salt and pepper

100–120 ml olive oil

- Soak the burghul in 1 cup of water for 10 minutes.
- Place the watercress leaves, shredded mint leaves, onion and tomatoes in a large mixing bowl. Squeeze the cracked wheat dry of as much water as you can (place in a tea-towel and twist). Add it to the mixing bowl and then pour on the lemon juice, allspice, cinnamon and salt and pepper. Add the olive oil and mix well using clean hands. Taste and adjust seasoning if necessary.

Salmon kibbeh nayeh – with a soft herb salad

Some people baulk at the thought of eating raw meat, which is what kibbeh nayeh is – a kind of Middle Eastern steak tartare, using lamb, burghul, onion and spices. However, most of us are familiar with sushi and sashimi, and are happy to eat raw fish – so this version of kibbeh nayeh uses fresh salmon or tuna, both of which work very well. The fish requires less mincing and pounding than the traditional lamb and results in a lighter dish which is delicious eaten with Arabic bread, white salad onions and a big blob of Yoghurt Cheese (page 289), or as below, with a fresh herb salad.

300 g Atlantic salmon, finely minced
    and chilled

2 purple shallots, finely chopped

150 g burghul, white, fine grade,
    soaked for 8 minutes in
    ¾ cup water, then squeezed dry

⅓ teaspoon allspice

1 very small bullet chilli, de-seeded,
    scraped and finely chopped

1 teaspoon salt

pepper

1 tablespoon extra-virgin olive oil

250 g natural yoghurt, hung in a cloth
    for 24–36 hours (page 289)

½ clove garlic crushed with
    ⅓ teaspoon salt

SOFT HERB SALAD

⅓ cup coriander leaves

⅓ cup mint leaves

⅓ cup flat parsley leaves

4 artichokes à la niçoise (page 17), or
    good quality purchased artichokes,
    preserved in oil

1 small purple onion, finely sliced

juice of ½ lemon

100 ml extra-virgin olive oil

salt and pepper

1 teaspoon sumac

• Chill a stainless steel (or glass) bowl, and in it mix the salmon, shallots, burghul, allspice, chilli, salt and pepper, with 1 tablespoon of extra-virgin olive oil. Form into 6 disc shapes and refrigerate.

• In another bowl, blend yoghurt cheese with crushed garlic.

• In another bowl mix coriander, mint, parsley and artichoke leaves with onion, lemon, 50 ml of the extra-virgin olive oil and salt and pepper to taste.

• To serve, place a disc of kibbeh in the centre of the plate. Place a small mound of salad on top and then a small dollop of the yoghurt cheese on top of the leaves. Drizzle the remaining extra-virgin olive oil around the salmon and sprinkle with sumac.

Cardamom honey-glazed roast duck (recipe page 40)

ABOVE:
Moroccan chickpea soup
(recipe page 55)
BELOW:
Grilled haloumy tart with a
white winter salad (recipe
page 46)

Pigeon stuffed with cracked-wheat pilaf

This pilaf makes a delightfully different accompaniment to all kind of meat dishes. Nutty, cinnamony and fruity, it also makes a delicious stuffing for farmed young pigeon. The poaching liquor will keep for a week in the refrigerator. Use it as a base to make soup, or for cooking savoury rice dishes.

PILAF

30 g currants

30 ml sherry

150 g burghul, coarse grade, soaked in 1½ times its volume of cold water for 5 minutes

salt and pepper

½ teaspoon allspice

zest of ½ orange

1 tablespoon butter

50 g toasted pine nuts

• Soak the currants in the sherry for 30 minutes.

• Rinse the burghul well in cold water and then put it in a heavy pot with 1½ times its volume of fresh cold water. Season lightly with salt and pepper. Bring the burghul to the boil and then simmer, covered, on low heat for 10 minutes. Drain the currants and add them to the burghul with the allspice and orange zest. Fork through and then cover again and allow to steam for a further 10 minutes. Add butter and season with salt and pepper. Allow to cool.

• Dry-roast the pine nuts over a high heat, shaking the pan continuously until all are even golden colour. Add to stuffing mix.

Recipe continued on next page.

PIGEON

4 size-3 squab pigeons (300 g)

pilaf (page 33)

2 large onions

2 cloves garlic

I stick cinnamon

½ teaspoon cinnamon

¼ teaspoon saffron (15 threads)

I bullet chilli, split

3 pods cardamom, cracked

enough water to cover

¾ teaspoon salt

I tablespoon honey

200 ml vegetable oil for frying

salt for dusting

• Stuff each bird with 2–3 tablespoons of the pilaf (not too full or they'll burst). Secure the skin at the opening with a toothpick.

• Cut the onions into quarters and smash the garlic roughly. Place them in a pan with the cinnamon stick and cinnamon powder, saffron, chilli and cardamom pods. Add the pigeons and pour on enough water to cover. Add salt and bring slowly to the boil. Cover the pan and lower the heat, then simmer gently for 40 minutes to an hour. When testing to see if the meat is tender, pierce the leg rather than the breast. At the 30 minute mark, add the honey to the poaching stock and stir well.

• When the pigeons are cooked, remove them from the poaching liquor and allow them to steam dry for 10 minutes. Dust the birds with salt and fry in moderately hot oil (a wok is perfect for this). Do two at a time, turning them around in the oil as they colour. Cook for about 4 minutes, by which time they should have turned a glossy, golden mahogany.

• Remove birds from the oil and sit them on kitchen paper for a couple of minutes to drain off excess oil.

• Serve with a little bowl of Cumin Salt (page 97) for dipping, and a Minted Cabbage Salad (page 170).

Cardamom

At our local Indian takeaway, there is always a pretty little brass dish of breath-freshening seeds and spices on the counter for customers to nibble on while waiting for their chicken vindaloo. In addition to the more familiar fennel seeds and whole cloves, tiny black cardamom seeds are almost always included in this mix. They are amazingly potent, and crunching them between the teeth releases a powerful citrussy flavour, with more than a hint of cleansing camphor. It is easy to see why they are chewed throughout India and in Arab countries as a digestive, and to sweeten the breath.

In western countries cardamom is still considered fairy exotic – a true spice of the Orient. They are, in fact, a member of the ginger family, and while they are native to India, they also grow in other tropical regions such as Asia, South America and even the South Pacific. We probably know them best for the refined and exotic flavour they add to Indian curries, dhals and rice dishes. But cardamoms also feature in Persian cuisine, and are an important ingredient in the bolder spice mixes of North Africa and Arabia. They add a curious, slightly camphorous undertone to the complex blend ras el hannout used throughout Morocco. In Yemen cardamoms are added to relishes such as the fiery zhoug and the musty, mysterious hilbeh.

Cardamoms also work deliciously well in sweet dishes and hot drinks. All around the Middle East they add a sweet perfume to Arabic coffee, while in some African countries they are added to both tea and coffee, usually combined with other spices such as cloves, cinnamon and ginger. Cardamoms add an exquisite flavour to creamy milk-based puddings, custards and even ice-cream. They work equally well in spicy biscuits and cakes, or with honey as a marinade for poultry and duck.

SELECTING AND STORING CARDAMOM

There are two main varieties of cardamom – green and a larger less common black one. The green cardamom is the one you are most likely to encounter. These are readily available from most decent supermarkets, although we tend to purchase them from Middle Eastern or Indian grocers, as there they tend to be plumper and fresher. Some suppliers prefer to bleach green cardamoms and sell them as 'white' cardamom, but they loose some of their fragrance and flavour in the process. As with all spices, it is really difficult to know when they were harvested and packed, or how long they have been sitting on the shelves. To ensure freshness it is best to buy them in small quantities and use them fairly quickly.

Cardamom seeds and ground cardamom powder are also available, which might seem more convenient, but the flavour is likely to be inferior to those you crack and grind yourself.

USING CARDAMOM

Cardamom's fragrant seeds are crowded into a pretty pale green pod, shaped like a miniature rugby ball. The pod may be used whole, or split to remove the seeds, which are usually ground into a fine aromatic powder.

To use whole cardamoms, crack them open (a heavy rolling pin does the trick nicely), and add them to rice pilafs, Moroccan tagines or sugar syrups with other flavourings such as cinnamon sticks and whole cloves. You will be doing your diners a favour if you fish these aromatics out before serving the dish – nobody wants to crack their teeth on a clove or end up with a mouthful of overpowering camphor.

Crushed to a fine powder, cardamom seeds are added to a range of spice mixes, particularly in North Africa and the Gulf States, where they are used to flavour savoury soups and stews. In the Middle East ground cardamom seeds are used more commonly to scent biscuits and cakes, custards and milky puddings, creams and ice-creams. Whack the pods with a rolling pin, or pierce them with the point of a sharp knife, and pry loose the tiny black seeds within. They can then be ground in a small coffee grinder or using a mortar and pestle. The essential oils in the seeds begin to dissipate very quickly once ground, so it is always better to grind them yourself at the last minute. The minute you start to pound away you will be rewarded by a waft of heady citrussy perfume, which will fill your kitchen with images of the Orient.

CARDAMOM RECIPES

Poussin roasted with cardamom and oregano

Cook the poussin slowly on a barbecue or grill, taking care not to burn or char, or you will overpower the fragrant spices. For four people you need four poussin, or you could use two smallish chickens (about 1 kg each).

18 pods cardamom

3 cloves garlic, roughly chopped

1 tablespoon salt

2 tablespoons fresh oregano or
  2 teaspoons dried oregano

80 ml olive oil

4 whole poussin (400 g each), cut
  down the back and splayed open

black pepper

• Using a mortar and pestle pound the cardamoms to loosen the husks. Remove these and continue to pound the seeds to bruise and release their flavour. Add the roughly chopped garlic, salt and chopped oregano leaves. Pound for a few minutes mixing all the ingredients together well. Then add 3 tablespoons of the olive oil and stir in well. Continue crushing until you have a thick, smooth paste.

• Rub three-quarters of the paste over the poussins, ensuring that you get in all the little cracks and crevices. Mix the remaining paste with the remaining olive oil and then pour over the poussins. Cover and marinate the poussins for 4–8 hours, turning occasionally. When ready to cook, preheat a barbecue or grill to high heat. Season the birds with plenty of freshly ground black pepper. Place them on the barbecue and cook them on high for a few minutes until the birds are golden all over. Then reduce the heat and cook slowly for a further 10–15 minutes, until they are cooked through. Towards end of cooking brush the birds all over with the remaining marinade.

• Serve with a robust salad, such as a traditional Greek salad, the Spanish Chickpea and Potato Salad (page 58) or even the Coarse Tapenade Salad (page 175).

Cardamom-crumbed lamb cutlets

2 racks lamb (best end – approx
  4 points per person)

5 pods cardamom – seeds only,
  lightly crushed

2 tablespoons Dijon mustard

I tablespoon mild honey

2 tablespoons sherry

black pepper

20 g freshly grated parmesan

60 g home-made Crumbing Mix
  (page 263)

2 tablespoons olive oil

salt and black pepper

• For better presentation, scrape the lamb rack bones back to the meat and then wipe them clean with kitchen paper.

• To make the glaze, put the cardamom seeds, mustard, honey and sherry in a saucepan with a grind of black pepper. Heat gently until the honey melts. Mix the ingredients together to make a thinnish glaze.

• Combine the crumbing mix with the olive oil. Add the parmesan to the breadcrumbs. Lightly season the lamb racks with salt and pepper. Spread the glaze generously onto the meat side of the lamb racks and then press the crumbing mix into the glaze, packing it on generously but neatly. Wrap tin foil around the bones to stop them charring.

• Drizzle the olive oil in a heavy oven tray, add the lamb racks and cook in preheated 210°C oven for 12 minutes for medium–rare or 15 minutes for medium. Allow to rest in a warm place for a further 10 minutes.

• Slice and serve with Goat's Cheese Mashed Potatoes (page 49).

Cardamom honey-glazed roast duck

Most new ovens these days have a rotisserie, which tend to be sadly under-utilised. This is a great shame, as they are easy to operate and result in superbly flavoured moist meats and poultry. If you are lucky enough to have a rotisserie, then immediately hunt down the instruction manual – it is the ideal way to cook duck, as it allows much of the fat to drip away. Of course, the best thing of all is to place a baking dish of vegetables under the rotating bird, which roast themselves in the delicious duck fat.

GLAZE

2 tablespoons honey

1 teaspoon sherry

3 tablespoons water

4 pods cardamom, seeds only, crushed
   (½ teaspoon of seeds)

½ teaspoon black peppercorns, crushed

1 teaspoon orange-blossom water

2 ducks (size 16)

salt and pepper

2 onions, quartered

2 lemons, quartered (or preserved lemon, optional)

1 bay leaf

1 cinnamon stick

few sprigs of rosemary or thyme

• Warm the honey gently with the sherry and water so that it dissolves. Then stir in the cardamom seeds and crushed pepper. As it cools down add the orange-blossom water.

• Wash and wipe the ducks and season with salt and pepper. Remove the wings and necks and stuff each cavity with an onion, a lemon, a bay leaf, half a cinnamon stick and a few sprigs of rosemary or thyme.

• Use small skewers or toothpicks to close the cavity. Pierce each duck with the rotisserie skewer and attach it securely using prongs and extra string. The ducks must be very securely attached to the skewer.

• Preheat the oven to 220°C. Fix the skewer to the rotisserie. If you want to roast some vegetables as well, place them in a tray underneath the rotisserie, where they will cook in the duck fat. After 30 minutes lower the heat to 200°C. After another 20 minutes increase the temperature to 220°C and brush the ducks liberally and evenly with the glaze while they are still turning. Close the oven and cook for a further 3–5 minutes until the birds are a glossy mahogany colour, but make sure you don't allow the glaze to burn.

• Remove them from the oven and allow them to rest for 15 minutes, covered with foil.

• Carve them and serve with roasted vegetables.

Cardamom-orange wafers

Cardamom's warm citrussy tones have a special affinity with orange. This combination features in all sorts of sweet dishes, ranging from ice-creams to crème caramels and brûlées. It works equally well in moist cakes and crisp, buttery wafers such as these. They will keep for around three days in a well sealed container.

60 g castor sugar

60 g plain flour

zest of 1 orange, finely grated

¼ teaspoon cardamom seeds, finely crushed

2 egg whites

75 g butter, melted

½ teaspoon orange-blossom water

small bowl of milk

• Mix together the sugar, flour, zest and cardamom seeds. Add the egg whites and mix to a smooth paste. Melt the butter and allow it to cool a little. Add the butter and the orange-blossom water to the mixture and stir to incorporate. The batter will be quite loose and sloppy.

• Preheat the oven to 160°C. Line a baking tray with baking paper and dot with small, well-spaced blobs of the batter. Wet your finger in the milk and carefully flatten and smear the batter out to circles about 1 mm thick. Refrigerate these for 10 minutes before baking in the centre of the oven for 5–7 minutes, or until golden-brown. Remove the tray from the oven and lift the wafers onto a wire rack with a spatula.

• When they are cool store them in an airtight container.

Other cardamom recipes

Cheese

When Greg was 19, and a young and foolish apprentice, he spent a magical time in France working in the dessert section of a Michelin-starred restaurant. He is fond of describing how he laboured from morning to night baking crisp buttery pastries, whipping up mounds of cream and lovingly stirring rich eggy custards. There is little doubt that he was eager to experience as many tastes and flavours as possible, and would have spent as much time licking the spoon as stirring it.

Naturally, the dessert section also included cheeses. This being France, there was an extraordinary variety of cheese on offer. The temptation to try every one was irresistible. Ah, but those were the days! The sad result of all this indulgence was that Greg ended up flat on his back on a hospital trolley awaiting bypass surgery. The next ten years saw more heart surgery, ballooning of the arteries and finally at the grand old age of 30, a heart transplant.

Not surprisingly, all this surgery has made him a more cautious, if not wiser man, and he has had no choice but to modify his eating habits. Cheese, with its very high fat content, is definitely off the menu, although, as a treat, we will sometimes make fresh yoghurt cheese – labna – at home. This is a Lebanese favourite, and dead easy to make. Being a dairy product, it is certainly not fat-free, but has about a third of the fat content of other soft cheeses such as brie or camembert, and a quarter that of hard cheeses such as cheddar.

Simple curd cheeses are still popular throughout Eastern Mediterranean and Middle Eastern countries today, where many households still make their own. The problem for those of us living in Australia (or North America, or any of the EC countries) is that all commercially available milk these days is pasteurised – and pasteurisation destroys the milk's natural bacteria. If you want to make fresh curd cheese at home, you have to add your own starter – something like cultured buttermilk works well. Another simple way to make your own fresh cheese is to use live natural yoghurt, which already contains its own cultures and in which the fermentation process has already taken place. The technique for making labna is described under Saffron-Yoghurt Cheese on page 289.

In Arabic countries there is nothing like the range of cheeses we have in the West. This is partly because few of them have a strong dairy tradition, and olive oil rather than butter is the main cooking medium. Such cheeses as there are tend to be made from goat's or sheep's milk rather than cow's milk.

However, cheese is widely consumed. Fresh curd cheeses are eaten at breakfast with bread, perhaps livened up with fresh herbs and a dish of olives. Other favourites are the very salty, crumbly fetta cheeses, which are also made from goat's or sheep's milk. These are popular throughout Greece and Turkey, and also Bulgaria.

Then there are the hard, almost rubbery cheeses, like haloumy, which are delicious dusted with flour and pan-fried, or baked in an Arabic-style calzone. Both Cyprus and Lebanon make excellent haloumy cheese – the Cypriot version is usually flavoured with dried mint, the Lebanese one with black cumin seeds.

Also used in cooking are milder flavoured hard cheeses such as kasseri and kashkaval, which are often mashed together as filling for savoury pies, omelettes and other egg dishes. Kephalotyri is closer to an Italian parmesan. It is strongly flavoured and usually small amounts are grated to add flavour to a dish.

A BRIEF HISTORY OF CHEESE-MAKING

The transformation of plain old milk into so many different products is quite extraordinary. It seems something of a quantum leap from that startling discovery in Neolithic times that the semi-solid curds produced from milk left to go 'off' in the sun could actually taste good, to the very sophisticated technology employed in cheese-making today. And yet the basic principles remain unchanged.

At its simplest, the curdling process occurs when the natural lactic-acid bacteria which are already present in milk are allowed to flourish – typically by heating. But there are still more things which can be done to speed up the curdling process. Food historians suggest that pastoral nomads in Central Asia used the stomach bags of animals as a sort of pre-historic Tupperware container. They would have discovered that rennet, an enzyme found in the stomachs of young calves, hastened the curdling of their milk, resulting in much firmer curds.

Once curdled, the next step in the cheese-making process is to drain off the whey. Today this is usually done in cloths, but in ancient times they used woven baskets. The French fromage, and Italian formaggio derive from the Greek word for basket, 'formos'. The Latin word for basket, 'caseus', became the German 'käse', the Spanish 'quesoa' and the English 'cheese'.

Variations in flavour and richness depend on the choice of cow's, goat's, sheep's or buffalo's milk. And on whether the animals have been fed on rich spring grass or winter hay. And in which part of the country the milk is from. The production of the whole range of cooked, smoked, aged, blue vein and surface-moulded cheese follows on from the initial curdling process.

SELECTING AND STORING CHEESE

Buying cheese is, of course, all about personal choice. Do you fancy a bitey piece of cloth-wrapped cheddar to munch on with an apple and a hunk of crusty bread? Perhaps you want to pop a slice of aged goat's cheese under the griller until it is all bubbly-brown, or to smear some perfectly ripe Brie onto an oat biscuit. Whatever your fancy, these days there is absolutely no reason why it should not be satisfied, unless of course, you buy plastic-wrapped slimy cheeses from the supermarket. Far better to visit a decent delicatessen or specialist cheese shop, where they understand that cheeses are living things which need nurturing.

So many of the cheeses which are unique to the Middle East and Mediterranean are simply not available here, although some local producers seem enthusiastic about experimenting with new varieties. All the recipes can be made with readily available cheeses – either imported or locally made equivalents, which are just as good.

Once home, cheese should be wrapped in a damp tea-towel, and stored in a cool, damp place – or failing that, the refrigerator. If you intend to eat it as is, then remove it from the fridge for at least an hour ahead of time, so it can slowly come up to room temperature.

Different cheeses have different life spans. As a rule, the very hard cheeses, with the lowest moisture content, will last the longest, and soft, fresh cheeses like curd, cottage and cream cheeses will spoil more quickly. As with so many foodstuffs, it really makes sense to buy in small quantities, and consume fairly quickly.

USING CHEESE

Preparing cheese for immediate eating involves first selecting a perfect, ripe specimen, storing it correctly and bringing it to room temperature before eating with crusty bread or hard biscuits, perhaps some fresh fruit, a wedge of quince paste or some dried muscatel grapes and, naturally, a glass of an appropriate wine.

CHEESE RECIPES

Grilled haloumy tart with a white winter salad

The simplest way of serving this rubbery-looking, slightly bland cheese is to grill or fry it. This transforms it to a golden, molten appetiser, which just needs a squeeze of lemon to bring it to life. Cypriot haloumy comes plastic-wrapped in brine and needs to be briefly rinsed and patted dry before use. Cut it widthways into slices about half a centimetre thick and dredge it in flour. Add cayenne or hot paprika to the flour for a spicier result. Fry the cheese slices in a little oil or butter and sprinkle them with thyme and a squeeze of lemon. Cook for a minute on each side and eat immediately. If they are allowed to cool down too much they go rubbery again. Eat them just like this, hot from the pan, as part of a mezze selection, or arrange them in this tart as a delicious starter or light lunch dish. The pastry may be made and even baked ahead of time and the tart easily assembled when ready to eat. This recipe makes enough pastry to line either four 8 cm tins or one 23 cm tin.

PASTRY

50 g plain flour

100 g self-raising flour

1 teaspoon salt

80 g butter, chilled

80 g crème fraîche, chilled

• Put the flours, salt and chopped butter into the food processor bowl. Then chill the whole bowl and blade in the freezer for 10–15 minutes. Remove from the freezer and pulse carefully until crumbs form. Add the crème fraîche and pulse until just incorporated (don't overwork). Work into a ball with your hands. Wrap in clingfilm and refrigerate for a minimum of 2 hours. Or, if you like, make the pastry a day ahead.

• When you are ready to make the tart, roll out the pastry, place it in a shallow 23 cm tart tin and allow it to rest a further 2 hours. Then line the pastry with foil, fill it with beans or rice and blind-bake it in an oven preheated to 180°C for 10–15 minutes until the pastry has set and is beginning to colour.

• Remove the beans and foil, lower the heat to 160°C and bake for a further 10 minutes until the pastry is golden-brown and crisp.

• Remove it from the oven and allow it to cool in its tin. Do not refrigerate it, but reserve it until needed in an airtight container (up to a day ahead)

• Snap the woody ends off the asparagus spears, and peel them up to the top. Drop them into boiling salted water for 10 mins or until tender. Refresh them in cold water and cut each spear into 3 pieces, on the diagonal.

FILLING

12 spears white asparagus
(approx. 2 bunches)

100 g portobello mushrooms, sliced
thinly

60 g frisée lettuce, torn into bite-size
pieces

½ cup watercress leaves

2 medium shallots, thinly sliced

1 block Cypriot haloumy cheese

plain flour for dusting

40 ml olive oil

1 teaspoon chopped thyme leaves

juice of ½ lemon

100 ml vinaigrette (see below)

salt and pepper

- When you are ready to serve, flash the tart in a preheated 200°C oven for 2 minutes. While it is heating, place the asparagus in a large mixing bowl with the mushrooms, frisée, watercress leaves and shallots.
- Remove the haloumy from its packet, rinse it briefly and pat it dry. Cut the haloumy widthways into 8 slices. Dust in a little plain flour. Heat the olive oil in a heavy pan. When the oil is almost smoking add the cheese slices and fry them for 30 seconds on each side, until they are a rich golden-brown. At end of frying, sprinkle them with thyme leaves and a squeeze of lemon.
- Remove the pan from the heat. Dress the salad with half the vinaigrette (see below), season with salt and pepper and pile the salad into warm tart shell, laying the haloumy slices on the top.
- Drizzle the remaining vinaigrette around the plate and serve while the haloumy is still hot.

VINAIGRETTE

5 dates

100 ml water

juice of 1 lemon

150 ml extra-virgin olive oil

salt and black pepper

- Bring water to boil, add dates and simmer until they are meltingly soft (around 15 minutes). Remove pan from heat and allow to cool. When cold, remove the seeds and skins. Chop the dates finely and whisk with the lemon juice and extra-virgin olive oil. Season with salt and black pepper.

Pease pudding with goat's cheese

1 medium brown onion, finely diced

30 ml olive oil

2 cloves garlic, finely chopped

200 g green split peas, soaked
  overnight

1 bacon or ham bone

300 ml water

1/3 whole nutmeg, grated

salt and pepper

80 g goat's cheese

• In a large saucepan, sauté the onion in the oil over medium heat until it is soft and translucent. Add the garlic and sauté for a few more minutes. Add the drained split peas, the bacon bone and the water (300 ml or enough to cover the peas by two finger-widths).

• Bring to the boil, then lower the heat and simmer gently for 30–40 minutes, until peas are mushy and water has nearly all evaporated. Remove the bone and season the mixture with nutmeg, salt and pepper. When you are ready to serve, heat the mixture and fold crumbled goat's cheese through it. Don't cook further – the heat from the peas is enough.

• This makes a delicious accompaniment to grilled lamb or roasts, pickled or boiled ham, or meaty sausages.

• Serves six.

Goat's cheese mashed potatoes

To make this with a really good consistency, mix ordinary brushed potatoes, which are light and fluffy, but rather tasteless, with flavoursome waxy Desirée potatoes. To get that lovely light texture, you should also push the mashed potatoes through a sieve, which is a bit tedious, but worth it for the result.

3 large brushed potatoes
  (about 600 g in total)

1 large Desirée potato (about 200 g)

60 ml extra-virgin olive oil

100 g butter

100 ml thickened cream

80 g mild-flavoured goat's cheese

salt and pepper

• Peel the potatoes and cut them into large equal-sized dice. Place them in a large pan and cover with cold salted water. Bring to the boil, then lower the heat and simmer gently for 15–20 minutes, or until the potatoes are cooked, but not mushy.

• As they are cooking, place the olive oil, butter and cream in another pot. Bring these to the boil and then simmer to reduce by a third. Keep warm. When the potatoes are cooked, drain and put them back into the pan and allow them to dry over the heat for a further 40–50 seconds. Then push them through a sieve and pour over the cream mixture. Beat with a wooden spoon. Adjust the seasoning.

• Roughly crumble the goat's cheese into the potato and mix it well with the mash.

• Serve immediately.

Bulgarian fetta fritters

These golden choux buns are bound to become a firm favourite. With their crunchy exterior and soft, melting centre they are good on their own, as an entrée with a small tabbouleh salad or as an accompaniment to barbecued meats. For a change, try drizzling them with maple syrup as you serve them. This recipe will make approximately 16 fritters.

1 medium leek, sliced

1 clove garlic, sliced

1 tablespoon butter

250 ml milk

250 ml water

125 g butter

250 g plain flour

6 whole eggs

150 g fetta

freshly ground nutmeg

salt and pepper

1 litre vegetable oil for deep frying

• Sauté the leek and garlic in the butter for 5 minutes or until soft, then purée.
• Place the milk, water and butter in a saucepan and slowly bring them to the boil so that the butter completely dissolves. As the liquid boils up, quickly add the flour, all at once, and mix well with a wooden spoon to incorporate it into the liquid. Continue cooking over a low heat for about 5 minutes until mixture is glossy and comes away from the sides of the pan in a smooth ball.
• Transfer the choux pastry to an electric mixer and beat for a few minutes on medium. Add the leek purée and then the eggs, one by one. When all is well mixed, quickly mix in the crumbled fetta and season with nutmeg, pepper and a little salt.
• Refrigerate the mixture for 2 hours before deep-frying in small balls, shaped with soup spoons if you like.
• Cook at 180°C for a couple of minutes, until the balls are golden-brown and starting to split.

Blue cheese and walnut terrine

For this rich terrine, use a sharp creamy blue cheese like Bleu d'Auvergnes, Roquefort or Foundation Blue. Serve it with walnut bread. Or for an unusual cheese course, serve it with a little Honey-Roasted Pear Walnut Salad (page 140)

250 g roquefort cheese

125 g butter

1 tablespoon cognac or brandy

30 g pure cream

pepper

125 g walnut halves, roasted and skins rubbed off

• Chill the bowl and blade of your food processor for about 15 minutes. Then add the cheese, butter and cognac and whiz to a paste. In a separate bowl, whisk the cream until it is thick, but not stiff. Mix a tablespoon of the cream into the cheese paste to loosen, then tip the mixture back into the cream and fold it in well.

• Season with pepper. Stir the walnuts through the mixture and set in a clingfilm-lined mould overnight.

• Serves eight.

Other cheese recipes

Chickpeas

What goes around, comes around. This is as true in food as it is in fashion – who would have thought that all those healthy, hippy dishes of the 1960s would return to favour so soon! In a delicious display of inverse snobbery, it appears that 'cucina povera' style – cuisine of the poor – is back in style in trendy restaurants the world over.

The fundamentals of this way of eating are reflected in the well-known 'food pyramid' philosophy, which recommends grains and pulses aplenty, an abundance of fruit and vegetables, fish as often as possible, poultry and lean meat in moderation, and cheese and other dairy produce for occasional treats.

Middle Easterners are great exponents of this style of eating, and are probably more inventive in their use of grains and pulses that anyone else in the world. Just look at what they do with the humble chickpea! A staple in Arabic cooking, chickpeas are used in countless soups, stews and stuffings. Roasted and salted, they are sold by street vendors as a snack all around the Middle East. Mashed, they form the basis for what are probably the most famous Middle Eastern dishes of all, hummus bi tahini and falafel. Dried chickpeas can even be ground into a flour for thickening stews and making all kinds of fritters, pancakes, dumplings and breads.

High in protein, easy to grow and handy to store through the long winter months, chickpeas are almost the perfect food. They are also one of the most ancient of foods, believed to be native to south-west Asia and having spread to the Middle East, India and southern Europe by Neolithic times. They were supposedly introduced to North Africa and Spain by the Phoenicians, and were later re-introduced by the Moors, who also established their popularity in Spain. They have remained a staple food in all these countries ever since.

SELECTING AND STORING CHICKPEAS

The variety of chickpea most readily available here in Australia is the creamy yellow garbanzo. It can be found in all supermarkets, dried and in tins. Tinned chickpeas are certainly more convenient, as they are ready to eat as they are. But they have a strong, almost metallic kind of smell and flavour, which can be quite off-putting. We would only recommend using them in an emergency.

Dried chickpeas vary enormously in age, size and quality. However, if you buy chickpeas (and indeed any pulses) from Middle Eastern or Indian grocers, where there is a swift turnover of stock, you are more likely to get a fresher, better quality product. In some specialist stores you may also be able to find a smaller, darker chickpea, which is believed to be closer to the ancient variety.

Chickpea flour, known as 'besan' and 'gram', can also be found in Middle Eastern and Indian stores. Both the flour and dried peas need to be stored in a well-sealed container and kept in a cool, dark cupboard.

USING CHICKPEAS

One of the most common complaints about dried chickpeas is that they take so long to prepare. Well, this is true up to a point, but bear in mind that most of the preparation involves soaking, which although time-consuming, requires absolutely no effort at all.

Always pick over chickpeas before use, discarding any which are dark and shrivelled, and rinse them well in several changes of water. Cover them with twice their volume of cold fresh water and leave them to soak, at least overnight, and preferably for 24 hours. Many Middle Eastern and Asian cooks add a teaspoon of bicarbonate of soda to the soaking water, especially in hard-water areas, which is believed to help loosen the skins.

If for some reason you forget to soak your chickpeas the night before, then a 'quick soak' will suffice. Rinse and drain the dried chickpeas and place them in a pan with twice their volume of cold fresh water. Bring to the boil and cook rapidly for several minutes. Remove them from the heat, and leave them to soak for 4 hours before draining and cooking.

When the chickpeas are ready to cook, drain the soaking liquid and rinse them well. Put them in a pan with fresh water and bring them to the boil. Do not add any salt at this stage as it toughens the skins and prolongs the cooking time. Turn the heat down low, cover the pan and allow the chickpeas to simmer. From here, the cooking time varies greatly depending on how fresh the chickpeas are. We have found that some take as little as 40 minutes, while others take up to 3 hours (yes really!). Towards the end of the cooking time you may salt the water.

If you are using tinned chickpeas, drain them and rinse them very well in several changes of cold fresh water.

CHICKPEA RECIPES

Moroccan chickpea soup with sautéed garlic prawns

Known as 'harira', this soup is a Moroccan favourite, particularly popular during Ramadan, when it is served after a day of fasting. Harira is traditionally eaten with dates and a wedge of lemon or lime. It is often made with lamb in a hearty meat stock. This is a lighter vegetarian version, all lemony and peppery. Garnish, if you like, with grilled seafood – delicate fillets of red mullet or garlicky prawns work well.

SOUP

60 ml olive oil

1 medium brown onion, diced

2 cloves garlic, crushed

100 g brown lentils

100 g chickpeas, soaked overnight

2½ litres chicken or vegetable stock

1 can crushed tomatoes (400 g)

¼ teaspoon ground cinnamon

¼ teaspoon ground ginger

1 pinch ground saffron, about 10 threads, lightly roasted and crushed

salt

½ teaspoon pepper

60 ml sherry

juice and zest of 1 lemon

1 tablespoon parsley, chopped

1 tablespoon coriander, chopped

1 tablespoon celery leaves, chopped

GARLIC PRAWNS

¼ teaspoon chilli flakes

2 cloves garlic crushed with ½ teaspoon salt

40 ml olive oil

12 king prawns, tails and heads removed

• Heat the olive oil in a large saucepan and gently sweat the onion and garlic until they soften. Add the lentils and soaked chickpeas and 2 litres of the stock. Simmer for an hour, or until the lentils and chickpeas are soft and beginning to break down. Use a hand-held electric beater on low speed to crush the pulses, but make sure not to turn them into a smooth purée. Add the tomatoes, cinnamon, ginger and saffron. Adjust the consistency with additional stock. Bring the liquid to the boil, season with salt and pepper and finish off with the sherry, lemon juice and zest, parsley, coriander and celery.
• Mix the chilli and garlic to a paste and rub it into the prawns. Allow them to sit for half an hour before cooking.
• Heat a grill, pan or wok, add the oil and, when it is smoking hot, add the prawns. Cook them on a high heat for 2 minutes.
• Serve on top of the soup.
• Serves six.

Hummus bi tahini

Creamy chickpea dips like hummus are popular around the Middle East. Some simple versions balance the sweet nuttiness of chickpeas with sharp lemon and garlic and a hint of savoury cumin. The best known version, though, is probably hummus bi tahini, which incorporates the earthiness of sesame paste (tahini).

200 g chickpeas, soaked overnight in
    2 times their volume of cold water
    with a pinch of bicarbonate of soda

juice of 2 lemons

2 cloves garlic crushed with
    1 teaspoon salt

100 ml tahini paste, well stirred
    (4 tablespoons)

salt and pepper

• Soak chickpeas overnight in water with bicarb. The next day rub the chickpeas well with your fingers in the soaking water to loosen the skins as much as possible. Remove the skins as they float to the surface. Place the chickpeas in fresh water and cook them for 40–60 minutes or until they are tender. Strain them, reserving the cooking liquid.

• Place chickpeas in processor with lemon juice, garlic paste and tahini and 2 tablespoons of the cooking liquid. Whiz until the mixture is very smooth. Add more liquid if the hummus is too thick. Taste and adjust seasoning if necessary.

• As the hummus cools down it thickens up, so adjust with more lemon or water, as needed.

Oysters in chickpea batter

Around India and the Mediterranean they grind chickpeas into a flour, known as 'besan' or 'gram', and use it to make all kinds of sweets and pastries. It also makes a lovely delicate batter, with a slight nutty flavour.

BATTER

500 ml beer

150 g besan flour (chickpea flour)

250 g self-raising flour

50 g cornflour

½ teaspoon cumin powder

1 pinch salt

1 pinch bicarbonate of soda

24 freshly shucked oysters, keep the shells for serving

flour for dusting

1 litre vegetable oil for deep-frying

• Pour the beer into a mixing bowl and whisk in the besan, the self-raising flour and cornflour. Add the cumin, salt and bicarbonate of soda and then allow to sit for half an hour before using.

• Heat the oil to 200°C. Test by throwing in a small cube of bread. If it sizzles slowly to the top, turning golden-brown in about 60 seconds, then the oil is hot enough.

• In batches of 6, dust the oysters lightly in plain flour, then dip into the batter and gently lower into oil. Fry for about 45–60 seconds, or until the batter is golden-brown.

• Serve immediately, back on their shells, with a lemon wedge and a little salad.

Spanish chickpea and potato salad

This Spanish-inspired salad combines waxy potatoes with sweet ripe tomatoes, savoury onions and fruity olives in a sweet–sour sherry vinaigrette. Serve it as a light lunch dish with plenty of crusty bread, as an accompaniment to Portuguese-Marinated Quail (page 68), or as part of a mezze luncheon.

2 large waxy potatoes

150 g cooked chickpeas

1 medium purple onion, finely sliced

2 medium tomatoes, de-seeded and
    diced very small

150 g whole green olives

½ cup parsley leaves

salt and pepper

80 ml extra-virgin olive oil

45 ml sherry vinegar

• Peel the potatoes and trim off the ends and sides. Cut into neat 1 cm dice – or roughly chickpea size. Steam for 10 minutes, or until they are tender.

• Combine the onion, tomatoes, olives and parsley in a large mixing bowl. When the potatoes are ready, season them with salt and pepper, pour the olive oil and sherry vinegar over them and stir gently.

• Tip the potatoes and dressing into the salad mixture. Toss gently and serve immediately after adjusting seasoning.

Other chickpea recipes

Falafel, page 84
North African Couscous Soup, page 89
Seven Vegetable Couscous with Onion Jam
and Green Harissa Broth, page 92
Battered Scallops with Cumin Salt, page 97
Battered Zucchini Flowers Stuffed with Goat's Cheese, page 295

Spicy prawn and mussel tagine

Chickpeas are a firm favourite in Moroccan cooking, featuring in all sorts of couscous dishes and tagines, such as this spicy seafood version. This recipe serves four as an entrée. Accompany with a dollop of Saffron-Yoghurt Cheese (page 289) or Basil Tzatziki (page 290).

½ kg mussels, bearded and well scrubbed

450 g king prawns (whole weight) approx 2 per person

60 ml olive oil

2 whole shallots, finely chopped

350 g waxy potatoes, cut into 1 cm dice

100 g chickpeas, soaked overnight and cooked

½ can crushed tomatoes (200 g)

2 tablespoons Tomato Chermoula (page 67)

250 ml stock or water

½ cup chopped parsley leaves

½ cup chopped fresh coriander (roots removed)

• De-beard and scrub the mussels thoroughly. Peel the body shells and legs from the prawns, leaving their heads and tails intact.

• Heat the oil in a large heavy-based pan. Add the shallots, chickpeas, potatoes, crushed tomatoes and tomato Chermoula. Then add the stock and stir well. Cover and cook for 8 minutes until the potatoes are just tender. Turn up the heat and add the mussels and the prawns. Cover the pan and cook until mussels open (1–2 minutes), then season with pepper and sprinkle with parsley and coriander leaves.

• Serve immediately with crusty bread and salad.

• Note: Do not add any salt as the mussel liquor is salty enough.

Chillies

When it comes to eating, we humans exhibit a sense of adventure in our willingness to try new and different foods and in our persistence with foods that are initially unpalatable. Think of chillies, black pepper, coffee, even alcohol – some of the most widely consumed foods in the world. On a first encounter, however, they are all either horribly bitter, or cruelly pungent, and can irritate or even burn the mouth's delicate lining.

We persist in consuming all these foodstuffs – in huge quantities too – because of their strange addictive power. With chillies, the thrill is all in the burn. They contain a chemical alkaloid known as 'capsaicin', which acts as both an irritant (the burn factor) and a stimulant. Capsaicin has no taste itself, but it does increase and intensify other flavours. This ability to enliven a limited range of bland ingredients is what makes chilli such an attractive food in impoverished countries around the world. More cunningly, capsaicin stimulates the brain to secrete endorphins, the body's natural opiates, which lift and exhilarate us. Chilli is said to be eaten daily by at least a quarter of the world's population.

This popularity has occurred only over the last 500 years, however. Chillies were unknown in Asia, Africa or indeed Europe until Christopher Columbus landed in the New World in 1492. Native to Central America, archaeological sites suggest that chillies were consumed in Mexico at least 9000 years ago and have long been cultivated there by native Incas, Mayas and Aztecs.

With the arrival of the spice-seeking Spanish and Portuguese, it was not long before chillies were being shipped back to Europe and thence to Spanish and Portuguese colonies in Africa, India and South-East Asia. In

Spain itself, chillies were eagerly received as a new kind of 'pepper'. Over time, they have been gradually cultivated to be larger and sweeter, although spiciness still remains in products such as chorizo sausages.

From Spain, chillies spread over the sea to Morocco, and the other countries of the Maghreb. People in these hot, desert-hugging regions loved the fiery heat of chilli and swiftly incorporated it into local spice mixes, such as the Tunisian tabil, and used it as a condiment in the form of chilli pastes and sauces. The best known of these is harissa, which is served all across North Africa, but is particularly popular in Tunisia and Algeria, where it is always served as an accompaniment to couscous. Moroccans tend to enjoy a gentler bite, and usually favour the sweeter heat of paprika. However, they are particularly fond of chermoula, a spicy marinade used for fish and seafood. Inhabitants of the Arabic Gulf States also enjoy the boldness of really hot chillies. The Yemeni relish zhoug, for instance, is hot enough to bring tears to the eyes.

In an interesting reversal of previous trends, the Spanish introduced chillies to the Arabs, who carried them eastwards again along well-established trade routes. Chillies tend to be too brash for Persian and Middle Eastern palates. They prefer other more complex and delicate spices which seduce the palate softly. However the use of chilli is spreading not only throughout western countries, but also through Middle Eastern countries such as Lebanon and Syria where it is being increasingly used, but often as a condiment. Dried chilli flakes, for example, are nearly always offered for sprinkling on minced lamb pizzas, or pickled chillies may be served as part of a mezze selection.

SELECTING AND STORING CHILLIES

All chillies and peppers (peppercorns apart) belong to the *Capsicum* family. There are many hundreds of varieties of chilli grown around the world, of all different shapes, sizes, colours and with varying degrees of heat. To the neophyte, chillies are merely hot, very hot or unbelievably hot, but to the true chilli aficionado each chilli has a particular aroma and flavour. Better known varieties include the jalapeño, commonly used in Mexican cooking;

the Jamaican Scotch bonnet, which is popular all around the Caribbean; the habañero, widely used in South America; and the bird's eye or bullet chilli, both red and green, which are common throughout South-East Asia.

Red chillies are merely riper than green chillies, and the colour is no real indication of heat. When buying chillies, select only those which are plump and firm, have no black spots on their skin and are not wrinkled or soft, especially close to the stem. Fresh chillies should be stored in the refrigerator, where they will last for several weeks. Remove any which seem to be getting soft, as they will quickly rot and spoil the rest.

Whole dried chillies have often been roasted to intensify their smoky, nutty quality. They tend to be very hot and are sometimes simply sizzled in hot oil to add chilli flavour without too much heat, and then removed before other ingredients are added.

Chilli powders also come in varying degrees of heat and intensity. The most commonly available are cayenne pepper (which is what most chilli powders are), and hot or sweet paprika. Cayenne is made from grinding several different types of chillies, and it is pretty hot. It should be added to dishes according to your personal taste. Paprikas will be labelled hot or sweet (mild). They vary in colour from bright orange to deep ox-blood red, and come from South America, Spain and Hungary. The Hungarian variety, widely used in Hungary as a mainstay ingredient, is generally considered to be the best.

As with other spices, dried chillies and chilli powders should be purchased in small quantities and stored in a cool, dark cupboard.

USING CHILLIES

When preparing chillies, it is best to err on the side of caution. Some people suggest rubbing the cut surface of a chilli on the back of your hand to give you an idea of its ferocity. It may cause your skin merely to tingle, or it could actually raise a blister – of course this won't tell you what it tastes like, but it will give you some idea of the likely effect on your mouth! You can also test the heat by cutting off a small piece from the centre of the chilli and cautiously licking it.

It is often recommended that you wear rubber gloves when preparing fresh chillies. At the very least, be careful not to touch the seeds or the whitish inner membranes. Wash your hands afterwards very thoroughly, and avoid touching your face, particularly your eyes.

Recipes often suggest removing the seeds and the inner white fibres, as these have the highest concentrations of capsaicin (this is rarely done in Asia or South America, of course, where they really believe in going for the burn). To do this, split the chilli lengthways and carefully scrape the seeds and fibres away with the point of a small kitchen knife. You should also use this method to remove the seeds from dried chillies.

CHILLI RECIPES

'Red Hot Chili Pepper' soup

This spicy soup was created when the American band was touring Australia in 1992. Use between one and three chillies – or more, of course – depending on your stamina. Squat, thick-skinned peppers are best for this soup, as they are easy to skin.

3 whole large red peppers

2 whole medium onions

2 cloves garlic

1–3 bullet chillies

60 ml olive oil

4 whole tomatoes, skinned and diced

40 ml sherry

600 ml vegetable or chicken stock

6 sprigs fresh thyme, tied with string

2 whole bay leaves

salt and pepper

1 teaspoon honey

• Roast the peppers over a gas flame, or under the grill, turning them constantly until they are blackened and blistered all over. This takes around 20 minutes. Put them into a bowl, cover with clingfilm and allow them to steam and soften for another 10 minutes.

• In the meantime, slice the onions finely and chop the garlic and chillies, seeds included. Sauté in the oil over a low–medium heat until they are soft and translucent. Then add the peeled, roughly diced tomatoes and sauté for a further 20 minutes. (To skin, pour boiling water over the tomatoes, pierce the skin and peel it off.)

• Once the peppers are cooled, peel off the skins, making sure you remove any blackened bits that will make the soup bitter and unattractive. Remove the seeds too, and then roughly chop them and add them to the tomato–onion mixture.

• Add the sherry and stock and cook a further 5 minutes. Season with pepper and salt. Add the bundle of thyme and the bay leaves and simmer for 15 minutes. Remove from the heat and stir in the honey. Taste and adjust seasoning if necessary. Liquidise the mixture until it is very smooth, which will take about 3 minutes on high speed.

• If you are fussy about presentation, tip the soup through a fine sieve which, will also remove any chilli seeds. Thin the soup down with a little extra stock or water if required.

• Serve it with a blob of goat's cheese and a drizzle of extra-virgin olive oil.

• Serves six.

Barbecued squid with zhoug (recipe page 81)

Whole roasted snapper with walnut-coriander dressing (recipe page 85)

Red harissa

In Morocco, harissa is simply rehydrated dried chillies mixed with tomato paste and salt. This version is closer to a Tunisian harissa, which is more complex with spices and garlic.

1 red pepper, roasted and peeled

10 small bullet chillies

2 cloves garlic

½ teaspoon salt

1 teaspoon cumin seeds

¾ teaspoon coriander seeds

60 ml olive oil

• Prepare the red pepper and chop roughly. De-seed the chillies, but leave the white inner fibres intact. Crush garlic with the salt. Roast and crush the cumin and coriander seeds. Place all ingredients in a blender and purée with the olive oil. Taste very cautiously for seasoning (it's hot!) and add more salt if necessary. This will make about 200 ml.
• Store in a sealed jar, under a thin layer of oil.
• Will keep a week in the refrigerator.

Other chilli recipes

Spicy Prawn and Mussel Tagine, page 59
Barbecued Squid with Zhoug, page 81
Green Harissa, page 82
Pickled Eggplants with Walnuts and Chillies, page 115
Devilled Lamb Loin, page 149
Chicken in Parchment with Moroccan Aromatics and Lentils, pages 164-165
Tunisian Briks with Brains, pages 196-197
Coriander and Prawn Briouats, page 198
Silverbeet Stewed with Tunisian Spices, page 256

Harissa-potato salad

A touch of harissa will liven up all sorts of soups and stews, or even a creamy potato salad such as this. If you are unable to make your own, then a good quality purchased paste will do.

6 medium waxy potatoes, steamed, peeled and cut into 2 cm dice

I tablespoon chopped capers

4 whole spring onions, finely chopped

MAYONNAISE

2 egg yolks

I clove garlic crushed with ½ teaspoon salt

75 ml extra-virgin olive oil

75 ml vegetable oil

juice of I lemon

I tablespoon Red Harissa (page 65)

salt and pepper

• Steam potatoes until tender, and while they are cooking, make the mayonnaise.
• Combine the olive and vegetable oils. Whisk the egg yolks well with the crushed garlic. Very gradually whisk in the oil, drop by drop, making sure each amount is thoroughly incorporated before adding the next drop. Once the mixture has thickened to a stiff paste, thin it with half the lemon juice. Continue to add the oil slowly, until all has been incorporated. Taste and adjust the seasonings and add the remaining lemon juice. Then stir in the harissa paste.
• Peel the potatoes while they are still warm and cut them into 2 cm dice. Mix them with the capers, spring onions and mayonnaise, thinned with a little cream if desired.
• Season with salt and pepper.

Chermoula

Since Moroccan food became all the rage, chermoula has featured widely on the menus of trendy restaurants around the world. In its homeland, chermoula is most often used with fish dishes. Its chilli-heat content may be varied to taste. This will keep for a month in the fridge – top up with a little oil each time you use it.

45 g cumin seeds, roasted and finely crushed

15 g coriander seeds, roasted and finely crushed

25 g sweet paprika

15 g ground ginger

2 cloves garlic, roughly chopped

2–4 whole bullet chillies, de-seeded, scraped and roughly chopped

juice of 2 lemons

100 ml olive oil

½ teaspoon pepper

½ teaspoon salt

- Put all ingredients into a food processor and blitz until garlic and chillies have been ground to a paste.
- For tomato chermoula, add 250 g crushed tomatoes.

Chermoula-roasted king prawns

12 king prawns (approx 1 kg)

1 ½ tablespoons Chermoula

salt and pepper

60 ml olive oil

1 medium onion, finely chopped

½ cup parsley leaves, roughly chopped

½ cup coriander, leaves, roughly chopped

juice of 1 lemon

- Peel the prawns, leaving the head and tail intact. With a sharp knife, split along the back and carefully pull away any intestines. Rub the prawns all over with the chermoula, season lightly and allow them to sit for an hour. Heat the oil in a wide, heavy-based pan. Sauté the onion for 2–3 minutes. When it is soft, raise the heat, add the prawns and sprinkle over the parsley, coriander and lemon juice. Turn the prawns in the hot oil for 2 minutes or until cooked. Serve immediately.
- Serves four as a starter.

Portuguese-marinated quail

This is a Portuguese-inspired twice-marinated and twice-cooked quail dish. The birds are rubbed with a spicy paste and then cooked in a tangy, hot–sour beer marinade. They are left in this marinade for up to three days and require only a quick grilling or frying to turn their skin a delightful golden-red.

4 whole quail

2 cloves garlic

I teaspoon salt

2 teaspoons sweet paprika

I teaspoon crushed cumin seeds

I tablespoon olive oil

200 ml beer

I tablespoon balsamic vinegar

I tablespoon white wine vinegar

I whole red bullet chilli, split in half

150 ml olive oil for frying

salt and pepper

• Trim the quail of necks and wing tips. Split down the backbone with a heavy knife and clean inside. Wash and pat dry.
• Pound the garlic with the salt to a smooth light paste, then pound in the paprika and cumin seeds for a few more minutes so you have a thick, stiff paste. Loosen the paste with 1 tablespoon of the oil and rub it all over the quail, thoroughly working it into all the cracks and crevices.
• In a bowl, mix together the beer, vinegars and chilli. Marinate the quail in this mixture overnight in the refrigerator.
• Place the quail and marinade into a heavy pot and bring to the boil. Lower the heat and cook gently for 12 minutes. Remove the quail and drain it on kitchen paper.
• Reduce the marinade by two-thirds until it is thick and syrupy, then pour it over the quail. Cover the quail and marinade with plastic wrap and allow to cool completely. Then refrigerate until you are ready to cook. You can do this up to 3 days ahead of time.
• To cook, you can grill the wet quails, straight from the marinade, on a griddle or barbecue or under the grill. They will need about 1½ to 2 minutes on each side. Or pat them completely dry, dust it in paprika flour (100 g flour to 1 teaspoon sweet paprika) and deep-fry until crispy. This will take about 1 minute in 200°C oil. To shallow-fry, heat about 2 cm of oil in a frying pan and fry, skin-side down for about a minute on each side, or until golden-brown.
• Season lightly and serve.
• Serves four as a starter.

Southern-fried chicken with eastern spices

This is a dauntingly long list of ingredients, but they are nearly all spices. Otherwise it is pretty simple to make. Serve this spicy fried chicken with wedges of lemon, a creamy Harissa-Potato Salad (page 66), or with crisp sautéed potatoes and a big green salad.

I corn-fed or free-range chicken
  (or 4 marylands)

6 pods cardamom, roasted and crushed

½ teaspoon black peppercorns,
  roasted and crushed

½ teaspoon fennel seeds, roasted
  and crushed

I teaspoon salt

½ teaspoon sugar

2 teaspoons sweet paprika

I teaspoon ground coriander

½ teaspoon turmeric

½ teaspoon cayenne pepper

½ teaspoon ground cumin

½ teaspoon ground cinnamon

¼ teaspoon ground allspice

100 g cornflour

50 g maize flour or very fine semolina

2 whole eggs

200 ml buttermilk

• Joint the chicken into eight pieces (or cut each of the marylands in half). Roast and crush the whole spices, salt and sugar, combine them with the other spices and then mix with the flours. Whisk the eggs into the buttermilk.
• Dip the chicken pieces in the flour, then into the egg mix and then back in the flour again. Shallow-fry them in vegetable oil until each piece is golden-brown all over.
• Place them on a baking tray and cook in a preheated 200°C oven for 20 minutes. Remove them from the oven and allow them to rest in a warm place for 5 minutes.
• Sprinkle with salt and serve.

Cinnamon

The smell of sweet cinnamon is as homely and comforting as your granny's kitchen, and conjures up happy memories of freshly baked apple pies, cinnamon buns and Christmassy mulled wine. We take it so much for granted that it is hard to imagine that the history of cinnamon, like that of so many other spices, is dark and violent.

The Spice Trade is almost as old as civilisation itself and the desire for spices such as cinnamon, pepper, cloves and nutmeg lured Phoenician, Egyptian, Greek and Roman ships out into unchartered seas. In the fifteenth and sixteenth centuries, enterprising buccaneers began the search for the Spice Islands in the East, which was the catalyst for great European voyages of adventure, the colonisation of new lands, the discovery, in fact, of a whole New World.

Cinnamon (and its rougher cousin, cassia) were two of the earliest spices to have been traded between ancient civilisations. Both were prized in early medicine and religious ceremony long before they were used in cooking. Cinnamon is mentioned in the Old Testament as an essential item in holy ritual, whilst the Egyptians used it for embalming their Pharaohs. The Queen of Sheba brought it with her as a precious gift for King Solomon; and the vicious Roman Emperor Nero, after murdering his pregnant wife Poppaea, reportedly burned her body upon the city's entire stock of cinnamon in a showy gesture of remorse.

Cinnamon is thought to have entered Europe's culinary repertoire in the last few centuries of Roman rule, but with the collapse of the Roman Empire, the supply of spices to the West dried up. Throughout the Dark Ages in Europe, however, Persia still had access to spices from the East via the overland route to China and across the Persian Gulf to India. The

Persians' imaginative and elaborate use of many spices and herbs in cooking is legendary. Indeed the lavish banquets enjoyed by Persian kings so dazzled the invading Arabs that they rapidly adopted many Persian dishes as their own.

During their Golden Age, the Arabs established a far-reaching empire and thriving trading networks from Persia in the east across North Africa and up to Spain in the west. Because of their strategic geographic position, Arab merchants had always played a key role in controlling the Spice Trade between East and West and, with the expansion of their empire between the eighth and twelfth centuries, they encouraged a renewed interest in spices all around Europe.

A lingering fondness for cinnamon in many Moroccan and Spanish dishes can be traced back to the Moorish occupation. In northern Europe, though, as cooking techniques evolved, the fondness for mixing sweet spices into one-pot savoury dishes declined. Cinnamon became, instead, the spice of choice for baking and sweet dishes, and to this day most English, Northern European, Scandinavian and American cooks limit its use to fancy baked goods, cakes and biscuits.

However, cinnamon remains an important spice in sweet and savoury Arabic cooking. It features heavily in Moroccan dishes – in the spice mix ras el hanout, or dusted onto soups, salads, couscous, tagines and, of course, bisteeya, the legendary pigeon pie. Lebanese, Syrian, Turkish and Egyptian cuisines use cinnamon in many dishes, and as a basic component of a range of different spice mixes.

SELECTING, STORING AND USING CINNAMON

Cinnamon is harvested from the inner bark of a tropical evergreen tree *Cinnamomum zeylancium*, grown mainly in Sri Lanka but also in Madagascar and the Seychelles. The bark is harvested during the rainy season, when it is pliable. As it dries it curls into long quills which are then cut into lengths and sold as the cinnamon sticks we use in casseroles and mulled wine, or ground into the powder we use for spice mixes or in apple strudel.

The quills of *Cinnamomum zeylancium* (or 'true' cinnamon) are a pale yellowish-brown with a mild sweet flavour. *Cinnamomum Cassia* (or cassia) is a darker reddish-brown and has a stronger, spicier flavour. Cassia is rarely seen in Australia or in Europe, but is apparently commonly sold and used interchangeably with 'true' cinnamon in the United States. Cinnamon quills may be added whole to soups and stews to infuse their flavour into the dish. They should always be removed before serving. The quills can also be ground into a powder, but in most instances it is far simpler to buy cinnamon already ground.

The aroma and taste of both cinnamon sticks and cinnamon powder fade with age. There is really no way of knowing how long the spices in the little plastic packets or glass bottles have been sitting on the supermarket shelves. It is really best to buy very small quantities at a time, rather than risk having a jar sit on your spice rack at home for years on end.

CINNAMON RECIPES

Ras el hanout

This is the legendary Moroccan spice mix, which loosely translates as 'house blend'. Cooks swear by their own particular combination of numerous spices and aromatics, which usually include cinnamon, nutmeg, dried rosebuds, ginger, cloves and chilli (as well as other more exotic ingredients such as Spanish Fly!). This is a humbler version which is quite spicy. Use it in soups or lamb tagines, or mix it with a little oil and rub it on poultry as a marinade.

6 pods cardamom, seeds only, roasted and crushed

½ teaspoon black peppercorns, roasted and crushed

½ teaspoon fennel seeds, roasted and crushed

I teaspoon cinnamon

I teaspoon ground coriander

I teaspoon turmeric

I teaspoon cayenne

2 teaspoons sweet paprika

I teaspoon ground cumin

I teaspoon salt

½ teaspoon sugar

½ teaspoon allspice

- Roast and crush whole seeds.
- Mix all ingredients together.
- Store in an airtight jar and use as needed.
- Makes 40 g.

Little pigeon bisteeya

This Moroccan specialty is baked for special occasions. However, nearly all Moroccan restaurants serve it, along with the ubiquitous tagines and couscous. It is traditionally made as one large pie, from pigeon spiced with saffron and cinnamon and enriched with eggs. A more prosaic alternative to pigeon is chicken, which is often substituted, but duck legs might be a better choice, with their dark, gamier meat. In Morocco, the whole pie is dusted with cinnamon and icing sugar and can be far too sweet for western palates. These little pies are only small, as the saffron and scrambled eggs make them extremely rich. Serve them on their own as a starter or maybe with some lemon-sautéed spinach as a main course.

3 pigeons (roughly 300 g each)

salt and pepper

100 ml olive oil

1 medium onion, finely chopped

2 cloves garlic, finely chopped

½ teaspoon ground ginger

8 threads saffron, lightly roasted and crushed

½ teaspoon cinnamon

½ teaspoon ground cumin

1 bullet chilli, seeded and finely chopped

60 ml sherry

600 ml chicken stock

3 eggs

⅔ cup parsley leaves, chopped

⅔ cup fresh coriander, roots and most of stalks removed, chopped

11 sheets filo pastry

150 g melted butter

100 g flaked almonds, fried in vegetable oil and drained

100 g icing sugar

20 g cinnamon powder

• Wash the pigeons and pat them dry with kitchen paper. Remove the legs and breasts, and season with salt and pepper.
• Heat half the oil in a heavy pan and sauté the pigeon pieces until they are golden-brown. Add the onion, garlic, ginger, saffron, cinnamon, cumin and chilli, adding more oil if necessary. Stir so the pigeon is well coated with spices.
• Add the sherry and stock, bring to the boil, then lower heat and simmer for 45–50 minutes, or until the pigeon is tender. When it is cool enough, remove the meat from the pigeon, discarding skin and bones, and shred it finely.
• Reduce the poaching liquid by half and then add the eggs and whisk until they are well combined. Pour this mixture into a small saucepan, season and scramble over a gentle heat until it is creamy and nearly set. Stir in the parsley and fresh coriander, and check the seasonings. Allow the mixture to cool completely. Stir the meat into the egg mixture, taste for seasoning and refrigerate until it is ready to use.
• To make the pies, work with one sheet of pastry at a time. Lay two sheets on the work surface and brush it with melted butter. Fold each one in half and

then cut into six equal squares. Put these to one side (you will need ten of them). Lay the remaining filo sheets on the work surface, one by one, and brush them with melted butter. Fold them in half and brush them with butter. Fold them in half again.

• Place a generous tablespoon of the meat–egg mixture in the centre of each filo square. Place one of the small pastry squares on top of the filling and scatter a teaspoon of fried almonds over the square. Brush around the filling with melted butter and then bring the surrounding pastry sides up and over the filling to form a ball. Turn the pie over and, with the palms of your hands, gently shape it into a raised circular pie. Flatten the top slightly and refrigerate the pie until you are ready to bake.

• Place the pies on a greased oven tray and bake in preheated 180°C oven for 10–15 minutes until they are golden-brown.

• Sift the icing sugar and cinnamon powder together.

• Remove the pies and sprinkle them with cinnamon dust to serve.

• Makes ten little pies.

Cinnamon-chocolate mousse

This is a heavenly chocolate mousse, made sweetly spicy with the addition of cinnamon. It is airy and fluffy and needs to set, so should be made a day in advance and allowed to firm in the refrigerator overnight.

300 ml pure cream

4 eggs

100 g mild honey

100 g castor sugar

400 g good quality dark chocolate

1 teaspoon vanilla essence

3 extra egg whites

1 tablespoon sugar

1 teaspoon cinnamon

TO DUST

1 teaspoon cinnamon

1½ teaspoons icing sugar

• Beat the cream to soft peaks and reserve in the refrigerator.
• Place the whole eggs, honey and sugar in a bowl over a pan of simmering water. Whisk for about 5 minutes until light and fluffy. Pour into an electric mixer and whisk on high for 5 further minutes. Meanwhile melt the chocolate over a pan of hot water and then allow it to cool slightly. Stop the mixer and fold the chocolate and vanilla extract into the egg mixture.
• In another bowl whisk the egg whites until they form very loose soft peaks. With beaters running, slowly sprinkle in the sugar and cinnamon. Continue beating for a little longer until they reach the shiny soft-peak stage.
• To assemble the mousse, fold the whipped cream into the chocolate base and then gently fold in the egg whites.
• Pour into a serving bowl and refrigerate overnight. When ready to serve, mix together the cinnamon and icing sugar and dust lightly over the mousse.
• Serve with fresh berries, caramel or a dollop of crème fraîche.

Cinnamon-dusted snow eggs

Serve these with a creamy Date Custard (page 108), or indeed any custard.

4 × 61 g egg whites

1 teaspoon lemon juice

100 g sugar

TO DUST

1 tablespoon cinnamon

1½ tablespoons icing sugar

- Three-quarters fill a deep baking tray with water. Place it on the heat and bring the water to a simmer.
- Put the egg whites into a mixer with the lemon juice and whisk at high speed until they start foaming up to form soft peaks. Then gradually add the sugar, still beating until the mixture is thick and glossy.
- Using two kitchen spoons dipped in hot water, scoop up a spoonful of meringue mixture and form it into an egg shape. Drop it carefully into the simmering water and poach it gently for about 5 minutes, basting continuously with the hot water. Do four meringues at a time. Turn them over and poach for a further 4 minutes. Remove the meringues with a slotted spoon and place them on a clean tea-towel draped over a cake rack.
- Refrigerate them until you are ready to serve.
- Dust the meringues with the cinnamon–sugar mix and float them on the date custard.

Other cinnamon recipes

Coriander

Coriander leads an exciting dual life as both a herb and a spice, and the need for one will not be satisfied by the other! When it comes to these harmless-looking lacy green leaves, passions start to run high – people either love them or loathe them. The scent and flavour of coriander are curiously hard to define. The name 'coriander' comes from the Greek word 'koris', meaning 'bug', and it is often said that the plant smells just like a bed bug. It is hard to imagine, though, that there are many people around these days who would recognise the smell of a bed bug if it jumped up and bit them on the nose. One of our very dear friends calls it 'stinkweed', which probably sums up the feelings of its detractors pretty succinctly!

Coriander – the herb – is a vitally important ingredient in cuisines as varied as Mexican, Thai, Vietnamese, Indian, Middle Eastern and North African. It is at its best very fresh – in salads or garnishes, or ground up, roots and all, into a paste. In cooked dishes it is best thrown in at the very last moment, otherwise it can add a soapy flavour to the entire dish.

In Middle Eastern food, fresh coriander is one of the most commonly used herbs. People buy it in great armfuls and use it with abandon. Its vivid green leaves are scattered into salads, and generous bunches are used to garnish grilled meat, seafood and poultry, numerous rice dishes and all kinds of mezze. Coriander is also responsible for the surprising bright-green colour you find in a falafel.

Used on its own, coriander adds a tantalising flavour to many dishes, but when combined with other ingredients such as garlic, lemon juice and chilli it really comes into its own, adding vibrant, zingy flavours which fairly dance across the taste buds. This can be best appreciated in the marinades and the numerous pastes and relishes which feature all around the Middle East. In Lebanon, for instance, roughly chopped coriander leaves and stalks are mixed with garlic and lemon juice to make a tangy marinade for grilled poultry and fish or to pour over rice pilafs. Some of the most popular relishes are zhoug – a fiery hot chilli–coriander salsa which originates in Yemen, but is now very popular in Israel as an accompaniment to just about everything – and tabil, a spicy coriander relish from Tunisia.

Even if you are not partial to fresh coriander, there is no reason why you should not enjoy the flavour of its dried seeds. These tiny golden balls are often found in pickling mixes where they create little citrussy explosions in your mouth. More often, they are toasted and ground to a fine powder to be used as a spice. Coriander is commonly combined with ground cumin and together they form the basis of numerous spice mixes throughout the Orient. Indian spice mixes, for instance, nearly all start with this classic combination, as do the North African mixes chermoula and ras el hannout, and the Egyptian dukkah. In many Arabic countries they use a spice blend known as 'baharat' (which literally means 'spices'). Every household will have its own particular blend of freshly ground spices, but all feature ground coriander and cumin, with the addition in varying quantities of peppercorns, cinnamon, cardamom, nutmeg, cloves and paprika.

SELECTING AND STORING CORIANDER

Sometimes all that you can find on the shelves are those flat vacuum-sealed plastic boxes of weedy little coriander sprigs. Buy these only as a last resort. It is best to buy big, healthy bunches with the roots still attached. The roots prolong the life of the herb and have a strong concentration of that spicy, citrussy flavour. Some recipes for pastes and relishes actually require the roots to be well pounded and incorporated into the mixture.

As with most fresh herbs, store coriander in the refrigerator. Place the plants, roots still attached, in a jug of water in the fridge, covered with a plastic bag to create their own little micro-climate. They should last 4–5 days – longer if you change the water regularly.

You can buy little bottles or plastic packets of ground coriander powder. Of course it is hard to know how long they have been sitting on the shelf and, once ground up, most spices quickly lose their aroma and flavour. It is far better to buy whole coriander seeds, which are also widely available, and to roast and then grind them yourself when needed. A coffee grinder (thoroughly cleaned first) will make easy work of the task, but it is really quite satisfying to grind them into a powder using a mortar and pestle.

USING CORIANDER

Before chopping, you always need to wash fresh coriander very carefully, as the leaves are often sandy and the roots harbour mud and dirt. If a recipe requires you to use the roots then you may even like to scrub them well to make sure you get rid of all the dirt.

When grinding coriander seeds to make a powder, first dry-roast them for a minute or so in a hot dry pan. This toasting really brings out the full flavour of the spice.

Seven vegetable couscous with onion jam and green harissa broth (recipe page 92)

ABOVE:
(from left) A la grecque dressing,
red harissa and green harissa
BELOW:
Barbecued salmon and eggplant
terrine (recipe page 116)

CORIANDER RECIPES

Barbecued squid with zhoug

Zhoug is a hot peppery relish that comes from Yemen. It is eaten with bread, and as a condiment to accompany grilled meats, poultry and fish. It is often blended with tomatoes to make a spicy sauce.

ZHOUG

4 pods cardamom, husks removed

1 teaspoon black peppercorns

1 teaspoon caraway seeds

4–6 bullet chillies, de-seeded and scraped

2 cups fresh coriander, roots removed

6 cloves garlic

¼ teaspoon salt

splash water

1 tablespoon olive oil

8 small squid tubes, tentacles still attached if possible (about 80 g each, whole weight)

80 ml olive oil

zest of 1 lemon

1 clove garlic, finely chopped

salt and pepper

• To make the zhoug, crush the cardamom pods, peppercorns and caraway seeds in a mortar and pestle. Sift to remove bits. Liquidise the chillies, coriander, garlic salt and water in a blender, then add the spices and mix in well. Cover with the tablespoon of olive oil.

• If you are not confident about cleaning and preparing the squid yourself, ask your friendly fishmonger to help you. You need the tentacles, head and beak to be removed, and the tube split and scraped clean. Keep the tentacles for cooking with the body of the squid.

• Score the outside of the squid in a criss-cross pattern. Marinate for a minimum of 6 hours in olive oil, lemon zest and garlic.

• When ready to cook, heat the barbecue (or very heavy pan). Season the tentacles and squid pieces and place on hottest part of the barbecue grill, scored side down. After 40 seconds, turn them over. In a moment, they will curl back up into a cylinder shape. Cook for a further minute then remove from the heat.

• To serve, stuff the tentacles back into the squid tubes and serve with lemon wedges and a small blob of zhoug on the side. (Beware, it is very hot!)

Green harissa

This is an adaptation of the traditional harissa, which is made with red peppers and fiery red chillies. To serve as a broth, bring stock or water to the boil, mix in the harissa, check for salt and pepper and serve as an accompaniment to tagines and couscous (see Seven Vegetable Couscous with Onion Jam and Green Harissa Broth on page 92).

125 g large green chillies, de-seeded, scraped and shredded

1 clove garlic

100 g fresh spinach leaves, stalks removed

2 cups fresh coriander, roots removed

1 teaspoon caraway seeds, roasted and crushed

1 teaspoon coriander seeds, roasted and crushed

1 teaspoon dried mint

400 ml vegetable stock or water

60 ml olive oil

salt and pepper

• Place all ingredients, except for the oil, salt and pepper, in a food processor. Whiz for a minute and then, with the machine still running, slowly add the oil until the mixture is the consistency of pouring cream. Season with salt and pepper.
• Transfer to a bowl, cover and chill.

Coriander and soft-boiled egg vinaigrette

Serve this vinaigrette straight away with Chicken Livers Pressed with Dukkah (page 251), poached brains, white fish or a cos lettuce-avocado salad.

2 whole eggs, cooked from the boil for 4 minutes

juice of 1 lemon

2 whole shallots, finely chopped

1 clove garlic, finely chopped

200 ml extra-virgin olive oil

1/3 cup coriander leaves and stalks, finely chopped

1 teaspoon coriander seeds, roasted and crushed

salt and pepper

• Separate the yolks from the whites. Blend yolks, lemon juice, shallots and garlic in a food processor and very slowly pour in the oil while the motor is running.
• Fold in the chopped egg whites and coriander, leaves, stalks and seeds.
• Season with salt and pepper.

May's marinated quail

These are a Malouf family favourite, as cooked by Greg's mother May. They are easy to prepare and bursting with tangy flavours. At home we eat them with a big bowl of risotto or Lebanese Nut Rice (page 150) and a simple mixed-leaf salad.

8 quail, or I large jointed chicken

2 cups coriander, roots removed and finely chopped

4 shallots, finely chopped

2 cloves garlic, finely chopped

zest and juice of I lemon

2 bullet chillies (optional), finely chopped

I teaspoon coriander seeds, roasted and crushed

200 ml olive oil

salt and pepper

• Trim the quail of necks and wing tips. Split down the backbone with a heavy knife and clean inside. Wash and pat dry.

• Combine the marinade ingredients and the olive oil in a very large mixing bowl. Place the quail in the marinade and rub it all over, thoroughly working into the cracks and crevices of the birds. Cover and allow to marinade for at least 6 hours, or overnight.

• To cook, season them first with salt and pepper. You can then grill the wet quails straight from the marinade on a griddle or barbecue or under the grill. Cook for 4 minutes, skin side down, then turn and cook for a further 4 minutes.

• Serves four (two quails each) as a main course.

Other coriander recipes
Spicy Prawn and Mussel Tagine, page 59
Chermoula, page 67
Chermoula-roasted King Prawns, page 67
Marinated Baby Lamb with Lebanese Nut Rice, pages 150-151
Chicken in Parchment with Moroccan Aromatics and Lentils, pages 164-165
Tunisian Briks with Brains, pages 196-197
Coriander and Prawn Briouats, page 198
Egyptian Eggs with Dukkah, page 250
Chicken Livers Pressed with Dukkah, page 251
Silverbeet Stewed with Tunisian Spices, page 256

Falafel

These spicy patties are a favourite snack all around the Middle East, and from Lebanese takeaway shops the world over. Different versions of falafel abound – in Egypt they are made using dried broad beans alone, whereas in Israel, Lebanon and Syria they are usually made with chickpeas. Others still, like the recipe which follows, use a combination of the two. These home-made falafel are far superior to any you can buy. They are spicy and fragrant and the fresh coriander adds a lovely bright-green colour. It is better to use skinless split broad beans rather than the whole, unskinned variety.

100 g split broad beans, soaked in
    I litre of cold water overnight

100 g chickpeas, soaked in I litre of
    cold water overnight

1½ cups fresh coriander,
    roots removed

I tablespoon ground coriander

I tablespoon ground cumin

I teaspoon bicarbonate of soda

I small chilli, finely chopped

½ medium onion, finely chopped

I clove garlic, finely chopped

½ teaspoon salt

750 ml olive oil for frying

• Drain the beans and chickpeas. Rinse well and dry.
• In a food processor, whiz the beans and chickpeas with a pinch of salt until they are the consistency of coarse, sticky breadcrumbs. Add all the other ingredients and whiz until they combine to form a bright-green paste which still has a fine crumb. Don't overwhiz – the paste should not be smooth and wet. Refrigerate for half an hour before frying.
• Heat the oil to 180°C. It is ready when a cube of bread sizzles slowly to the top and turns a pale golden-brown. Shape the falafel into little patties and fry for 6–7 minutes until they are a deep brown. Eat the falafel straight away, dipped into tahini sauce or stuffed into Arabic bread, with salad and a squeeze of lemon.

• Makes around thirty-six.
• Note: You can also use fresh yeast as a raising agent instead of the bicarbonate of soda. This will give you an even lighter crisper falafel. Use 15 g yeast blended with a tablespoon of warm water.

Whole roasted snapper with walnut-coriander dressing

DRESSING

100 g walnuts

1½ cups fresh coriander,
  roots removed

150 ml extra-virgin olive oil

juice of 1 lemon

1 pinch sumac

salt and pepper

1 clove garlic, finely chopped

1 whole shallot, finely chopped

4 whole baby snapper or black bream
  (approx 350 g each), scaled
  and gutted

salt and pepper

50 ml olive oil

• Roast the walnuts in a preheated 200°C oven for 5 minutes. Take them out and rub them briskly in a tea-towel to remove as much of the papery brown skins as possible. Wash the coriander, remove the roots and chop the leaves and stalks roughly. Whisk the oil and lemon lightly together with the salt, pepper and sumac. Add the shallots and garlic, and whisk lightly. Add the coriander and walnuts, and whisk gently.

• With scissors, trim the fins from the fish, and on both sides make three shallow slashes in the flesh. Lightly season the slashes with salt and pepper. Heat 20 ml oil in a heavy-based pan until it is close to smoking. Place two fish at a time in the pan and cook for about a minute on each side, until just coloured.

• Transfer the fish carefully into a large, deep baking tray, brushed with olive oil. Repeat the process with fresh oil for the remaining two fish. Place the baking tray on the top shelf of a preheated 200°C oven. Cook for 10 minutes, or until a pale milky fluid begins to ooze from the slits.

• Gently remove from the baking tray to serving plates and spoon the walnut dressing – which should be at room temperature – over the top.

• Serve with plenty of lemon wedges and a watercress salad.

Couscous

Until a few years ago, couscous was relatively unknown in western kitchens. Today it is marketed everywhere as the perfect convenience food, and even the big food manufacturers are hopping on the Moroccomania bandwagon, with a range of boil-in-the-bag and ready-to-cook versions. It all seems a far cry from Fez, and its legendary Seven Vegetable Couscous (see page 92).

Couscous is not a grain or cereal in its own right, but is made from semolina, which is itself a by-product of flour manufacture. Traditionally, the tiny pellets are laboriously rolled by hand to the correct size and consistency, and then steamed over a bubbling fragrant stew. The grains absorb all the flavours in the steam and slowly swell to a delectable light fluffiness.

Couscous is the name of the little granules, and also of the entire dish – including the savoury stew of meat or vegetables and an aromatic broth. Although we think of couscous as being particularly Moroccan, it is, with slight variations, the national dish of the entire Maghreb region (the North African countries of Morocco, Tunisia and Algeria). Algerian couscous dishes are fairly robust and spicy, while Tunisians like the fiery heat of lots of chilli, and often include fish and seafood. Moroccan versions tend to be subtler and more refined; they are often slightly sweeter and can include fresh dates or raisins, nuts and a touch of honey.

Couscous also appears in other Arabic countries, such as Lebanon, where it is known as maghrebia ('from the Maghreb'). Here the grains are much larger – almost the size of small peas – and are usually cooked in the broth, rather than steamed, with lamb shanks, or chicken and vegetables. Arab-influenced Sicily also has its own version, typically served with fish stews.

Today couscous is eaten as a daily staple throughout North Africa, but it originated as one of the traditional dishes of the indigenous Berbers. In its homelands it can be served in simple Berber style, with smen (the strongly flavoured preserved local butter) or it can be a lavish and complex medley of ingredients, eaten as part of an elaborate banquet or feast. Couscous can even be eaten for breakfast: a sweet version is prepared in milk with dried fruit and nuts, honey and a sprinkle of cinnamon. Traditionally, though, couscous is never served as a main course, but as a fill-up at the end of the meal, to ensure that no one goes home hungry.

Here in the West, we have taken couscous to our hearts and adapted it to our own eating habits. As well as being the perfect partner for exotically spicy tagines, it is the ideal accompaniment to all sorts of braises and stews, as it soaks up all the lovely juices. A handful of couscous thrown into a spicy soup thickens it in a most satisfying way. Couscous is even good just on its own, with a nob of butter, a grind of salt and pepper and maybe a dollop of thick yoghurt.

SELECTING AND STORING COUSCOUS

The packaged instant versions are anathema to food purists. However, it is virtually impossible to buy any other sort outside Morocco, and even in the Maghreb countries these days the lure of convenience food is irresistible. Very few Moroccans will make their own hand-rolled couscous, except for special occasions. Here in Australia most supermarkets stock several brands of the boxed instant varieties, which are all perfectly acceptable if cooked properly. In our view, the only ones to avoid are the boil-in-the bag, ready-flavoured versions which, in the way of one-minute noodles everywhere, end up tasting suspiciously similar and usually collapse into a soggy mess.

Some good delicatessens, specialist food stores and Middle Eastern grocers will also stock a fully dried, non-instant couscous. This is far more time-consuming to cook, requiring several cycles of steaming, separating and rubbing with well-oiled hands, but it results in a delicious mound of individually fluffy, light grains.

USING COUSCOUS

When cooked, couscous grains should be fluffy and separate, not gluggy and water-laden. Most of the instant versions come with poorly translated and completely inadequate instructions, or instructions in French and Arabic. For the traditional steaming method, see page 91.

For everyday speedy meals, the instant pour-on-boiling-water variety of couscous is really quite satisfactory, although obviously less tasty, as it doesn't allow the grain to absorb the flavours from the dish cooking below. However, it doesn't require any fancy cooking equipment, like a couscoussier, but only a bowl a fork and a kettle! The thing to remember, though, is that steaming couscous really does improve the flavour and texture of the end result – and is less likely to cause indigestion. Couscous has an amazing capacity to absorb liquid, and if inadequately cooked will continue to swell in your stomach! This problem is avoided in the traditional cooking method, which requires several sessions of steaming.

As a compromise, we suggest the following slightly-less-quick method. Pour on boiling water, following the instructions on the box. If these are unclear, the rule of thumb is to use twice the volume of water or stock as the volume of couscous. Leave it to stand for at least 10–15 minutes or until the liquid is completely absorbed. Then dot it with butter or drizzle it with olive oil, cover with clingfilm and microwave on medium for around 5 minutes. Alternatively, tip it into an oven-proof dish, add butter or oil, cover it with foil and leave it in a low oven for around 20 minutes. This second step allows the couscous to steam gently under cover and greatly improves its texture.

If you want to jazz it up a little, then add some aromatics (like a stick of cinnamon, a squeezed-out lemon half, a few sliced dried mushrooms, some raisins or even finely diced apricots) before the second heat-through. When you are ready to serve, fluff it up with a fork, season and serve. Or sprinkle on finely chopped parsley and mint, or some lightly toasted almonds.

COUSCOUS RECIPES

North African couscous soup

Similar to a traditional Moroccan harira, this soup is chock-full of nutty chickpeas and meaty lamb, and thick with couscous. Throw over handfuls of fresh mint and parsley and serve it with flat Arabic bread and a big dollop of creamy, soothing yoghurt for a filling winter lunch.

60 ml olive oil

250 g lamb, leg steak, cut into small chunks

1 medium onion, finely chopped

2 cloves garlic crushed with 1 teaspoon salt

1 tablespoon coriander seeds, roasted and ground

1 tablespoon cumin seeds, roasted and ground

1 teaspoon allspice

1 teaspoon chilli powder

1 teaspoon sweet paprika

1 can crushed tomatoes (400 g)

1 green chilli, de-seeded, scraped and finely shredded

1 teaspoon honey

100 g chickpeas, soaked overnight

800 ml chicken stock

500 ml water

salt and pepper

50 g couscous

1 tablespoon fresh parsley, finely chopped

1 tablespoon fresh mint, finely chopped

juice of 1 lemon

- Heat the olive oil and sauté the lamb pieces. Remove them with a slotted spoon and drain on kitchen paper. Add the onion and cook over a gentle heat until soft. Then add the garlic, coriander, cumin, allspice, chilli powder and paprika, and mix well with the onion. Cook for a further 2 minutes and then return the lamb to the pan. Next add the tomatoes, chilli and honey.
- Stir well before adding the chickpeas, water and stock. Cover and simmer on a low heat for 45–60 minutes, or until the chickpeas are tender.
- When you are ready to serve, taste and adjust seasoning. Add the couscous to the pot, cover and allow it to sit for 5 minutes.
- Serve garnished with the parsley, mint and lemon juice, a dollop of thick yoghurt (optional) and plenty of warm Arabic bread.
- Serves six.

Crab and couscous salad

60 ml extra-virgin olive oil

juice of 1 lemon

3 shallots, finely sliced

1 clove garlic, crushed with
  ½ teaspoon salt

200 g fresh crab meat

120 g cooked couscous (quick-cook
  method, see page 88)

½ large avocado (60 g), cut into
  1 cm dice

1 large tomato, seeded and finely diced

¾ cup coriander leaves, roughly chopped

½ cup watercress leaves

1 bullet chilli, de-seeded, scraped and
  finely shredded

1 teaspoon sumac

• Whisk together the extra-virgin olive oil and lemon juice with the shallots and garlic paste to make a dressing. Combine all the remaining ingredients, except for the sumac, in a bowl. Add two-thirds of the dressing to the salad and mix well.
• To serve, pile the salad into a high mound in the centre of the plate. Drizzle the remaining dressing around, sprinkle with sumac and serve with plenty of Arabic bread.

Buttered couscous – traditional method, per person

60 g couscous

cold water to moisten

few teaspoons olive oil

salt and pepper

aromatics

½ teaspoon butter

• Sprinkle the couscous in a shallow dish, add a quarter of a cup of cold water and let it sit for 10 minutes. This helps start the softening and swelling process. Then rake it through with your fingers. Add a teaspoon of olive oil, and lightly salt and pepper.

• Line a steamer or couscoussier with a damp cloth. Sit it on top of boiling water flavoured with aromatics if desired – such as a cinnamon stick, half an onion, lemon peel and a few twigs of thyme. Tip the couscous into the top section, steam for 15 minutes and then pour it onto tray. Fork it through lightly and allow it to cool for about 5 minutes. Sprinkle it with a tablespoon cold water and pour a teaspoon of oil onto your hands. Rub the couscous between the palms of your hands to break down clumps into individual grains. This will take about 5 minutes. Put the couscous back into the cloth and steam it again for about 20 minutes.

• Pour out and fork the butter through thoroughly.

Seven vegetable couscous with onion jam and green harissa broth

Serve with Green Harissa broth (page 82) in a separate jug, for each person to help themselves. A bowl of rosewater-flavoured Yoghurt Cheese (page 289) or basil tzatziki (page 290) on the side, although distinctly un-Moroccan, is also delicious.

ONION JAM

50 g butter

5 medium purple onions, finely sliced

250 ml dry sherry

250 ml tawny port

50 g currants, soaked in an additional 50 ml dry sherry

salt and pepper

240 g couscous

2 medium carrots, scraped and cut into wedges on the angle

1 small butternut pumpkin, peeled and cut into 2 cm dice

2 small turnips, peeled and cut into wedges

2 small parsnips, scraped and cut into batons

1 small eggplant, cut into wedges

1 medium zucchini, cut into wedges on the angle

100 g chickpeas, soaked overnight and cooked until just tender

4 small waxy potatoes, boiled until tender, peeled and halved

1 tablespoon sweet paprika

½ tablespoon powdered ginger

½ tablespoon dried chillies, crushed

½ tablespoon ground cumin

• Make the onion jam ahead of time. In a heavy-based pan, melt the butter and slowly sweat the onions until they are soft and translucent (about 5 minutes). Add the sherry and port and continue to cook for a further 45 minutes over a very low heat, stirring from time to time to ensure the jam doesn't stick to the bottom of the pan. Add the soaked currants and the soaking liquor and cook for a further 10 minutes, or until the onions have become very sticky and almost caramelised. Season with salt and pepper.

• If you have a couscoussier, stew the vegetables in the bottom section and steam the couscous on top. Otherwise proceed as follows.

• Prepare couscous with aromatics according to the base method (see page 91). During the second steaming, begin to prepare the vegetables. Preheat the oven to 200°C.

• In a mixing bowl, combine all the spices with the garlic, lemon juice and half the olive oil.

• Heat the remaining oil in a large ovenproof casserole and sauté the carrots, pumpkin, turnips, parsnips and eggplant for around 5 minutes, or until all are lightly coloured.

• Add the spice mixture and stir to coat the vegetables for a further 2 minutes. Add the stock and cook for 5 minutes.

½ tablespoon ground coriander

½ tablespoon pepper

4 cardamom pods, seeds only, crushed

I clove garlic crushed with ½ teaspoon salt

juice of I lemon

100 ml olive oil

500 ml vegetable stock

salt and pepper

2 teaspoons rosewater

• Add the zucchini, chickpeas and potatoes. Mix them in well then place the casserole in the oven and bake for 20–30 minutes or until the vegetables are tender. Remove from the oven, check for seasoning and sprinkle the rosewater over the top.

• To serve, pile the couscous high on a large serving platter and stack the vegetables on top. Serve immediately with a blob of onion jam, the harissa broth and Yoghurt Cheese.

Other couscous recipes

Perfumed Pumpkin Couscous, page 184

Cumin

Cumin seeds pack a powerful punch. Their earthy, savoury aroma reminds us immediately of Indian curries, but crunching them between the teeth releases a strong, spicy, almost aniseedy flavour, more reminiscent of caraway.

Cumin is indeed a member of the same family of umbillifers as caraway (and carrot and parsley), but whereas caraway is used in northern European cuisines as a flavouring for rye breads and smoked cheeses, cumin has its roots firmly in the East. The plant is believed to be native to Egypt, but has been cultivated around the eastern Mediterranean, Arabia and India for many thousands of years, and is one of the most ancient spices used in cooking.

Cumin was certainly grown in Egypt during the time of the Pharaohs, where it was used in the embalming process, as well as to flavour many savoury dishes, and it remains a favourite spice there today. The ancient Greeks and Romans probably imported cumin from Egypt, and also used it widely. While they enjoyed eating it, the ancient Greeks also considered cumin a symbol of meanness – a miserly person was said to be a 'cumin splitter'. In ancient Rome cumin was often used interchangeably with pepper.

The Romans were probably responsible for the eventual spread of cumin westwards, and by medieval times it was popular both in European kitchens and in early medicines as an antispasmodic and as a cure for flatulence! Interestingly, the faith in cumin's carminative qualities prevails in the Middle East today, where a pinch of ground cumin is often added to pulses while cooking.

Although cumin has rather fallen from favour in European cooking, it remains indispensable in the cuisines of North Africa, the Middle East and of course India. Its savoury, spicy flavour is added to all sorts of meat and poultry dishes, rice dishes, soups and stews. The seeds are typically dry-roasted before being ground to a fine powder, which further intensifies their pungency.

In Morocco cumin is an essential ingredient in chermoula, the hot and spicy seasoning paste used in many fish dishes. Cumin is also rubbed onto grilled lamb and used to season minced lamb for making kifta kebabs (brochettes). Throughout North Africa, a popular street food is hard-boiled eggs dunked in little dishes of cumin salt. The Egyptian spice mix dukkah, served with bread and olive oil, is also fragrant with roasted cumin. Middle Easterners use cumin and ground coriander seeds as the basis for many spice mixes. Cumin is often sprinkled onto onions and used to garnish rice and lentil dishes, or mixed with garlic and rubbed as a paste onto grilled meats.

SELECTING AND STORING CUMIN

There are three different kinds of cumin seeds – amber, white and black. The amber seed is the only one commonly available in supermarkets. This is also the variety most widely used in Middle Eastern and Asian cooking. White and black cumin seeds are usually only to be found in Asian or Middle Eastern stores. Black cumin is considered superior to the others as it is rarer and has a milder refined flavour, with smaller seeds. Naturally enough, it is also more expensive. Black cumin seeds are used on flat breads, especially in Turkey, Cyprus and Lebanon. In Lebanon they are also added to the brine in which haloumy cheese is stored.

Don't confuse black cumin seeds with nigella seeds, which are quite different. Nigella seeds are also tiny and black, and they have a strong peppery flavour. They are most commonly used in Indian cooking, especially in pickles and in spice mixes, and sprinkled over Indian flat breads.

Cumin seeds are available as whole seeds and as a ready-ground powder. Unlike many other spices, ready-ground cumin retains its potency pretty well – although as it ages you will have to increase the amount you use. For a full-on blast of flavour though, it is better to use whole seeds, roasted first and then ground with a mortar and pestle or in a clean grinder. As for all spices, buy cumin in small quantities and store it in a tightly sealed container in a dark, cool cupboard.

USING CUMIN

Cumin is potent, so it should be used sparingly. Recipes often suggest what looks like a ridiculously small amount of cumin, but a little really does go a long way. If you are unfamiliar with cumin, a good starting point is between one-eighth and one-quarter of a teaspoon of ground cumin, or half a teaspoon of the whole seeds for every four serves.

Dry-roasting cumin seeds reduces their faint bitterness and brings out their nutty, savoury taste. To dry-roast cumin seeds, put them in a heavy frying-pan on a medium heat and toss them around over the heat for few moments until they have darkened and begun to release their aroma. Tip them into a mortar and grind them up by hand, or pour larger amounts into a clean coffee grinder.

CUMIN RECIPES

Battered scallops with cumin salt

Savoury cumin salt is also good for dipping hard-boiled eggs into, or to accompany little grilled quail or pigeons. Serve these scallops with a wedge of lemon, or with a dollop of mayonnaise flavoured with preserved lemon and a small mixed leaf salad.

2 tablespoons cumin seeds

2 tablespoons salt

375 ml Chickpea Batter (page 57)

24 fresh scallops, cleaned, rinsed and dried

300 ml vegetable oil for deep-frying

plain flour for dusting

• To make the cumin salt, roast the cumin seeds until they are lightly coloured and then pound them to a fine powder using a mortar and pestle. Sieve to remove bits of husk. Crush the salt to a fine powder and combine with the cumin powder. Heat gently in a pan to release the flavour and then allow to cool and store in an airtight container.

• Make the Chickpea Batter and allow it to stand for half an hour. Meanwhile clean the scallops, wash them briefly and pat them dry. Heat the oil to 190°C (test with a blob of batter – it should sizzle to the top and turn golden-brown in about 30 seconds). Dust the scallops with plain flour, dip them into the batter and deep-fry, six at a time, for 45 seconds to 1 minute.

• Drain the scallops well on absorbent paper. Sprinkle them with cumin salt and serve straight away with wedges of lemon.

Cumin rouille

Use to accompany Prawns Wrapped in Almond Kataifi (page 199).

250 g potatoes

300 ml water or Crab Stock (page 247)

5 cloves garlic

10 saffron threads, briefly roasted
and ground

2 bullet chillies, de-seeded and
roughly chopped

2 red peppers, roasted, skinned
and diced

I tablespoon cumin seeds, roasted,
ground and sieved

juice of ½ lemon

250 ml olive oil

salt and pepper

• Cook the potatoes in water or stock with the garlic, saffron and chillies until the potatoes are soft and the water has nearly evaporated. Tip the mix into a blender with diced peppers, cumin powder and half the lemon juice and whiz to a purée. While the motor is running, slowly dribble in the oil, until all is incorporated, then add the remaining lemon juice.

• Season with salt and pepper. Taste and adjust seasoning, adding extra lemon juice if necessary. The consistency should be of a thin honey, not a stiff mayonnaise.

Other cumin recipes

Chermoula, page 67
Chermoula-Roasted King Prawns, page 67
Egyptian Eggs with Dukkah, page 250
Chicken Livers Pressed with Dukkah, page 251

Red mullet fried in cumin flour

Delicate little red mullet are adored around the Mediterranean and Middle East.
Deep-fried whole, as here, they make a spectacular but simple dish. You must use
whole, spanking-fresh fish. Ideally you should clean them yourself, as they are fragile,
and fishmongers tend to be heavy-handed, often crushing the flesh and impairing the
flavour. It is really not hard (see below) but if you are unsure, then ask your
fishmonger to be as gentle as possible. A deep-fryer with a basket is useful for this
dish, as you need the fish to maintain their shape for a spectacular presentation.

8 red mullet (120–140 g each)

salt

200 g plain flour

2 tablespoons cumin seeds,
   roasted, ground and sieved

1 teaspoon ground ginger

½ teaspoon pepper

700 ml vegetable oil for deep frying

• To clean the red mullet, leave the fins and tail attached for presentation, but scale using your thumb, running it against the scales from the tail to the head – they are delicate and come away very easily.

• Using a sharp knife, slice carefully along the underbelly. Hold the sides open and pull the insides away. Insert your finger into the reddish-coloured gills and pull them out too. Rinse the insides of the fish under running water, paying special attention to rubbing away the dark blood line against the back bone. Pat dry.

• Season the fish inside and out with salt. Heat the oil to 190°C. Season the flour with the cumin, ginger and pepper, and dust the fish all over with seasoned flour.

• If you are using a deep-fryer with a basket, then splay open the fish just under its chin/gills, so it sits up on its own. Place it like this in the basket – you should be able to do two or three at a time. Lower the basket gently into the oil and cook for 3–4 minutes, or until the fish are golden-brown and the flesh is firm to touch. They should 'set' into their new shape in the hot oil.

• Lift the basket out of the oil and place the fish on kitchen paper to drain.

• Serve them with lots of lemon wedges and preserved lemon mayonnaise.

Pickled pork belly roasted with cumin seeds

Pickled pork belly is used to make kaiser fleisch, and many good Continental butchers will have it in store. However, you will probably need to order it about a week ahead of time. Ask your butcher to remove the skin and ribs if you are unconfident about doing this yourself. Arrange to collect it at least two days before you want to eat it – it needs to be soaked in milk to tenderise it and remove some of the salt, and then marinated in a cumin-spiced oil before cooking. Cooked quickly over a high heat, pork belly strips resemble spare ribs. When cooked long and slowly they become meltingly tender and softly sticky. Either way, serve them with a hearty accompaniment, like creamy mashed potatoes or the spicy Harissa-Potato Salad (page 66). They are also good with a tangy braised cabbage dish or sauerkraut.

2 kg pickled pork belly, ribs and skin removed, soaked overnight in milk

2 cloves garlic crushed with ½ teaspoon salt

MARINADE

I tablespoon cumin seeds, roasted and lightly crushed

zest of I lemon

I teaspoon black peppercorns, lightly crushed

I teaspoon allspice berries, lightly crushed

I tablespoon fresh ginger, grated

150 ml olive oil

• Remove the pork belly from the milk, wash and pat dry. Cut the belly in half widthways, then cut each half into 2 cm strips. Rub the garlic paste all over the pork strips.

• Mix all the marinade ingredients together and add to the pork. Turn the pork so it is well coated. Cover and refrigerate for 6–24 hours, turning occasionally.

• The belly strips can either be seared in a hot pan to colour and then baked in a 200°C oven for 15 minutes, or placed on a rack and slow roasted in a 175°C oven for 1 hour until they are meltingly tender. They are also good barbecued on a hot flame for 15 minutes, until golden crispy brown.

• Serves eight to ten.

Dates

At first glance, dates are not immediately appealing. For many people, they are those hideously sweet, dried things that turn up in date slices, biscuits and steamed puddings. For some reason, dried dates are also a traditional Christmas gift, packed tightly into long oval boxes which are brightly decorated with palm trees, camels and mysterious foreign writing.

All it took for us to fall under the spell of these ancient fruit was a visit to the Middle East! Here were names and places familiar since primary school: Bethlehem, Jerusalem, Nazareth – and Jericho, the oldest continuously inhabited city in the world, described in the Old Testament as 'the city of palm trees'. Under the hot desert sun our guide pointed out a small oasis of date palms swaying gracefully in perfect, picture-postcard fashion. Clustered among the fronds were fresh dates, as big as amber-hued eggs. We could smell their sweetness in the air, and they were soft as warm toffee in our mouths.

It wasn't hard to imagine these most ancient of trees growing in the very same spot ten thousand years ago. As our guide explained, the date palm has been revered for its usefulness since Neolithic times. Although a tree takes up to six years to fruit, once mature it will yield up to 100 kilograms of fruit annually, for an average of sixty years! Furthermore, the tree itself provides shade and building materials, while its fronds are woven into mats and baskets.

Dates have been a staple food in desert lands for many thousands of years. Their high sugar content meant that they became the mainstay of the nomadic Bedouin's severe diet, and the prophet Mohammed was said to have survived entirely on dates and water during his self-imposed fast. Dates still have a special significance for Muslims during Ramadan – the day's fast is often broken with a bowl of dates and a glass of water, or they are served whole with a wedge of lime as a garnish for the traditional harira soup.

Today there are hundreds of varieties of date palm, which are grown in the Maghreb lands of North Africa through the Gulf States, Israel and Iraq to Pakistan, India and even California.

Australia's date-growing industry is still in its infancy, as date palms take a minimum of six years to reach full production. Most of the 'fresh' dates we enjoy have probably been imported from California or Israel. Although they can never match the buttery, brown sugar flavour of a sun–warmed fresh date eaten in its homeland, these are still quite delicious.

It is thought that dates first reached England in the thirteenth century. As with so many of the new foods brought across the seas by returning crusaders and merchants, they were very expensive and their use was mainly for sweet puddings and desserts. Even today English recipes for dates revolve around the bakery – recipes for date slices and loaves, scones, cakes and sticky puddings abound.

In the Middle East, however, they are not so restrained. Moroccan and Persian recipes frequently partner dates with lamb or pigeon. Rice and grain dishes are often garnished with chopped dates and a sprinkling of nuts. Dates are also used extensively in sweet dishes: they are preserved in syrup, cooked into a jam and chopped and stuffed into shortbread biscuits. Some of the most exquisite sweetmeats are made by stuffing dates with an almond, a pistachio nut, or a nob of rose-scented almond paste.

SELECTING AND STORING DATES

In North Africa and the Middle East, there is a seemingly infinite variety of dates to choose from, and their selection is a serious business. A purchase from the souks involves much sampling and deliberation together with long explanations of the differences between the numerous varieties on offer. In Australia we have to be thankful for what we can get, in most cases the deglet noor, which are a light golden colour. The other dates readily available in Australia are the luxurious medjool dates, which are darker, plumper and larger. When selecting dates, choose those which are unblemished and have a rich and fairly uniform colour. Although the wrinkliness of the skin varies, as a general rule, the drier and older the dates are, the more wrinkled the skin is. Because of their high sugar content, dates keep remarkably well. They do not need to be refrigerated and will keep for several weeks.

USING DATES

Really, the only think you have to remember when preparing dates is to remove the narrow pip inside. Simply slit them along one side and the pip will easily come away from the sticky flesh.

DATE RECIPES

Date-lemon chutney

This tangy spicy chutney is absolutely delicious with all kinds of grills, especially poultry. It also works well with rich creamy offal — serve it, for instance, with crumbed sweetbreads or golden brain fritters. Alternatively, use it as a last-minute glaze when barbecuing. Mix a spoonful with a little olive oil and simply brush it over the meat or chicken for the last turn on the flames. A spoonful of chutney added to a vinaigrette adds a lovely citrus-sweet dimension to a dressing for bitter-leaf salads (see Grilled Haloumy Tart with a White Winter Salad on page 46). If you can't wait the required time for the chutney to mature then make a simpler version by slowly cooking fresh dates until they collapse to a thick sludge. The reduction is then puréed and beaten with extra-virgin olive oil and lemon juice to make the vinaigrette.

6 medium lemons, zest and flesh
   finely chopped

2 tablespoons salt

4 cloves garlic, finely minced

100 ml extra lemon juice

100 ml cider vinegar

1 tablespoon fresh ginger, finely grated

1 teaspoon cardamom seeds,
   finely ground

1 teaspoon coriander seeds,
   finely ground

½ teaspoon chilli flakes

225 g brown sugar

200 g fresh dates, stoned and
   chopped small

• Mix the chopped lemon, lemon zest and juice with the salt and leave overnight. The next day place the lemon mixture in a heavy pan with all other ingredients except the sugar and dates. Bring slowly to the boil and simmer for 5 minutes. Then add the sugar and dates and simmer gently for 45 minutes to 1 hour, until thick and well reduced. Stir from time to time so it doesn't stick and burn. Pour into sterilised jars and store for at least 6 weeks before eating.

Pigeon tagine with dates and ginger

In the Middle East they get their pigeons live from the souks, and grill them over a hot barbecue. Here in Australia we have to make do with the less flavoursome farmed variety – usually sold as squab, which are tender baby birds weighing 250–400 g. Their rich, dark meat is delicious in this spicy sauce. The combination of pigeon and dates is a Persian and Moroccan favourite, although traditional recipes, which use large amounts of fruit, can be too sweet for western palates. In this version, the sauce is spiced with pungent saffron and ginger, which help cut the sweetness and richness of the dish. It needs only a simple pilaf or couscous accompaniment.

PIGEON STOCK

4 carcasses and trimmings

20 ml olive oil

I carrot, roughly chopped

I celery stick, roughly chopped

I onion, roughly chopped

I clove garlic, roughly bashed

I bay leaf

a few sprigs thyme

12 tablespoons sherry

1½ litres cold water

salt and pepper

• Prepare the pigeons by cutting off heads, necks and claws, trimming the wings and then neatly slicing away the breasts and marylands (thigh and drumstick) from each bird. Season each piece with salt. If you don't feel confident about preparing the pigeons yourself, ask your butcher to prepare them for you, and to keep the carcasses so you can make a stock.

• To make the stock, briefly sauté the carcasses to add colour, then add the vegetables, bay leaf and thyme and sauté a few more minutes. Add the sherry and scrape any bits from the bottom of the pan. Pour the water over the top and bring to the boil. Skim off any surface fat, then lower the heat and simmer for an hour, skimming off any additional fat from time to time.

Recipe continued on next page.

TAGINE

4 squab pigeons, breasts and
  marylands removed

1/2 teaspoon salt

500 ml water or pigeon stock

100 g butter

20 ml olive oil

2 medium onions, finely chopped

2 cloves garlic, finely chopped

1 tablespoon fresh black pepper

1/4 teaspoon powdered saffron (or
  10 strands, roasted and crushed to
  a powder)

2 teaspoons cinnamon

1 teaspoon ginger

200 g fresh dates, seeds removed,
  chopped

1/3 cup parsley leaves

• Melt the butter and oil and fry the onions and garlic over a medium heat until softened. Add the pepper, saffron, cinnamon and ginger and stir well. Season the pigeon pieces with salt and sauté in the spicy mixture for about 2 minutes, until they are well coated. Add the stock and bring to the boil. Lower the heat, cover and simmer for 15 minutes. Then add the chopped dates and stir in well. Cover again and simmer for a further 20–30 minutes, or until pigeon pieces are nice and tender.

• Sprinkle over the parsley leaves, taste and adjust the seasoning if necessary.

• Serve with plain buttered couscous or a simple rice pilaf.

Date brûlée with Kahlua

This is a thick, luxurious and totally seductive dessert, combining creamy coffee and buttery, toffee-ish dates. Cook the dates down to a soft jam-like consistency and use this as a base for petits pots, brûlées, soufflés and custards.

Serve the brûlée with Cardamom-Orange Wafers (page 41) or Sesame-Honey Wafers (page 252).

CUSTARD

1.25 litres pure cream

10 egg yolks

60 g castor sugar

1 vanilla bean, split and scraped

1 cinnamon stick

DATE CONFIT

125 g castor sugar

125 ml water

250 g fresh whole dates

½ cup Kahlua

100 g castor sugar for dusting

• To make the custard, bring the cream to a rolling boil and then pour it onto the egg yolks, sugar, split vanilla bean and cinnamon stick, whisking well to incorporate. Pour the mix back into the pan and cook gently for about 15–20 minutes, stirring constantly with a wooden spoon, until the custard thickens. It should be as thick as honey and just beginning to catch on the bottom of the pot.

• Pour the mixture into a stainless steel (or glass) bowl and sit the bowl on ice or in a sink of very cold water for 5–10 minutes. This is important, as it stops the custard from cooking further. Then remove from the ice and allow it to continue cooling down naturally.

• To make the date confit, heat the sugar with the water until it is completely dissolved. Add the whole dates and Kahlua and cover the surface with a circle of greaseproof paper to keep the dates submerged and stop a skin forming during cooking. Gently cook for 15–20 minutes. Remove from the heat and allow to cool. When cold, remove the seeds and skins from the dates and chop them finely. Place a heaped teaspoon of the confit at the bottom of each of ten small ramekin dishes or soufflé bowls (8 cm diameter), and then spoon in enough custard to fill the bowl to just below the rim. Chill until ready to serve.

• Set your griller to its highest possible level and heat for at least 5 minutes. Remove the custards from the fridge and lightly dust them with sugar. Place them under the grill for a few moments until they are brown and bubbling. Remove them and refrigerate for 5 more minutes. Dust them with a little more sugar and place them back under the griller for a second grill. Naturally, if you have a domestic blowtorch, this works even better.

• Serve straight away.

• Makes ten small brûlées.

Date custard

Custard might seem a little bit too much like nursery food, but this creamy caramel-like version is rather adult, and perfect served chilled with Cinnamon-Dusted Snow Eggs (page 77), as an accompaniment to Sticky Ginger Cake (page 135).

The date confit is made in a similar way as described in the previous recipe, but with orange and lemon juice for a lighter, tangier flavour. Either of these date confits can be folded through whipped cream to make a simple date romanoff, which would also be delicious served with the Sticky Ginger Cake, or with an orange cake.

CUSTARD

200 ml milk

100 ml thickened cream

4 egg yolks

50 g castor sugar

DATE CONFIT

125 ml water

100 g castor sugar

200 g fresh dates, stoned

150 ml fresh orange juice

juice of 1 lemon

• For the custard, bring the milk and cream to the boil. In a mixing bowl whisk the egg yolks with the sugar and then add the boiling milk and cream mix. Whisk well and tip back into the saucepan. Cook gently for about 10 minutes until the custard thickens. You should be able to draw a horizontal line through the custard on the back of a spoon, without it all running together. Allow the custard to cool a little.

• To make the confit, bring the water to the boil with the sugar until the sugar is completely dissolved. Add the dates, orange and lemon juice and cover the surface with a circle of greaseproof paper to keep the dates submerged and stop a skin forming during cooking. Bring back to the boil and then lower the heat and simmer for 15–20 minutes until the dates are meltingly soft. Remove the pan from the heat and allow to cool. When cold, remove the seeds and skins, chop the dates finely and return them to the syrup.

• To serve, mix the confit with the custard, pour into a large glass serving bowl and decorate with a few pieces of confit.

Eggplants

For many Anglo-Saxon cooks, the eggplant is something of a mystery. Its shiny, sensual curves are pleasing to the eye, and its deep purply-black hue hints of an opulence within, but many of us still don't really know what to do with it. Maybe make a moussaka? Or that famous Middle Eastern eggplant dip which seems to crop up everywhere these days? Possibly, if we feel a little more adventurous, we might even toy with the idea of stuffing it with a savoury rice filling.

This tentativeness is not surprising really, given that the eggplant has come into our kitchens, relatively recently. As with so many other good things which have come our way, eggplants were introduced to Europe by the Arabs. Eggplants were just one of many foodstuffs which they learned about on conquering Persia in the seventh century. From there, they spread the secrets of its cultivation and cooking to all the countries in their new empire, reaching through North Africa and up into Spain, and to the island of Sicily in the Mediterranean. However, it was not until the exodus of the Jews from Sicily in the fifteenth century that the eggplant reached northern Italy, and it didn't arrive in France until the eighteenth century.

The eggplant is surely the most adaptable vegetable on earth, as it lends itself to many diverse cooking styles and regional flavours. It can be fried, grilled, steamed, roasted and braised. Or mashed, stuffed, pickled or made into relish. It is equally delicious hot, warm or cold. The only way it cannot be eaten is raw.

When cooked, the eggplant has a unique subtle flavour and silky texture which allow it to showcase many other stronger flavours and ingredients without losing its own distinct identity. Blended with sesame paste it becomes a creamy, smoky purée; with tomatoes, onions and garlic, a robust braise. Add a touch of sugar, vinegar and a sprinkle of currants and it becomes a Sicilian–Arabic classic. With yoghurt and mint it turns Turkish; with minced meat, rice and pine nuts, Persian; and spiced with cayenne and saffron, a Moroccan tagine.

Some people are afraid of eggplants because of their reputation as oil-guzzlers. When they are fried, the spongy flesh does absorb extraordinary amounts of oil, but once they cool down, much of the oil seeps out again. Salting before cooking can help to reduce the amount of oil absorbed, as can dipping in seasoned flour before frying. The one thing which is critical, though, is to use really good quality olive oil as it becomes an integral part of the flavour of the dish. If you use cheap and nasty oil, it will only make the whole dish taste cheap and nasty.

SELECTING AND STORING EGGPLANTS

The variety of eggplant available these days is ever-increasing. We are probably most familiar with the large oval-shaped, purply-black variety. But this is just one member of the large eggplant family. These days we can also buy slim, trim little Japanese eggplants in most supermarkets, while better greengrocers will also offer plump little egg-shaped Lebanese eggplants or eggplants which are a delicate white-streaked mauve, the palest green or even a pure white.

Arabic folklore has it that when choosing an eggplant, you should look for an oval-shaped belly-button and leaves which reach down a quarter of the whole vegetable – these ones, so the theory goes, have fewer seeds and are less bitter.

Whichever variety or size you wish to use, always choose plump, firm eggplants with a taut, glossy skin. Any which are wrinkled, scarred or feel flabby should be rejected immediately. As with all vegetables and fruit with a high water content, choose eggplants which feel weighty for their size, as this indicates freshness. They should be stored in the fridge and used within a couple of days.

USING EGGPLANTS

If you are frying eggplants, remove the stalk and prickly leaves and slice the eggplant lengthways for an attractive presentation (about 0.75 cm thick). Eggplants do not need to be peeled – the skin not only adds an attractive colour, but also helps hold them together and maintain their shape.

You may wish to salt them to reduce the amount of oil they absorb on cooking. Place eggplant slices or cubes in a colander, sprinkling plenty of salt as you go. Put a plate over them to weight down, and leave them to drain for about an hour. Rinse them well and carefully pat them dry before frying. Bear in mind, though, that few eggplants we get these days warrant this degorging procedure just to rid them of bitterness.

Another good trick for limiting the amount of oil they absorb is to deep-fry slices of eggplant before further cooking. It sounds bizarre, but it does have the effect of sealing them and minimising further oil absorption. Another method is to dip slices in seasoned flour and shallow-fry them first. If you really want to be virtuous, you can, of course, always steam them or sprinkle them with a little water and microwave them instead of frying them. They do lose some of their rich, luxuriance, but if they are to be used in a highly flavoured dish, like a moussaka for instance, then it doesn't really matter.

Plump little Lebanese eggplants are ideal for stuffing and pickling whole. Medium-sized ones are perfect for stuffing and oven-baking. Large eggplants are best sliced and fried, layered for gratin dishes or cubed and used in braises or omelettes. To grill, brush slices with olive oil, and grill on a griddle plate, barbecue or under an overhead grill until soft. Depending on the thickness of your slices, this will take about 4 minutes on each side.

Larger eggplants are also good for making creamy dips. Soften the flesh by roasting the eggplant over a flame until the whole thing is blackened and collapses. The pulp can then be mixed with other flavourings, such as lemon juice, garlic or tahini paste.

EGGPLANT RECIPES

Smoky eggplant salad

The currants and pine nuts give this salad a distinctly Moorish feel.

I tablespoon currants

50 ml sherry

3 medium eggplants, charred and cut
    into 1.5 cm dice

40 ml olive oil

2 tablespoons pine nuts

I medium purple onion, diced

2 medium roma tomatoes, de-seeded
    and cut into 1.5 cm dice

I clove garlic crushed with
    ½ teaspoon salt

juice of I lemon

½ teaspoon sumac

I tablespoon whole oregano leaves

2 tablespoons whole parsley leaves

80 ml extra-virgin olive oil

salt and pepper

• Soak the currants in the sherry for 10 minutes. Char the eggplants as described in the next recipe. Once they are cool, carefully peel away all the blackened skin, cut them into rough 1.5 cm dice and place them in large mixing bowl.
• Heat the olive oil to medium heat and then fry the pine nuts for 3 minutes or so, moving them constantly to stop them burning. Remove and drain them on kitchen paper. Then sauté the onion until it is soft and translucent. Add it to the chopped eggplant. Mix the garlic paste and lemon juice and add to the eggplant. Sprinkle the sumac onto the eggplant, then add the extra-virgin olive oil and combine gently. Allow to rest for 5 minutes.
• Strain the currants and add them with the remaining ingredients to the salad. Mix gently, taking care not to break up the eggplant.
• Taste and adjust seasoning.

Baba ghanoush

This superb dip is found throughout the Middle East, Turkey and even Greece, and there are as many recipes as there are people making it! Local variations abound – with the addition of yoghurt, mint and cumin on top of the basic oil, lemon, garlic and tahini. It is really all about personal preference and a balance of flavours. The earthy tahini, sharp lemon or pungent garlic should not dominate, but all should meld into one rich, creamy, smoky whole, which is infinitely greater than the sum of its parts! One thing which we are adamant about, though, is that the eggplants simply must be roasted over a direct flame. It is the direct heat contact (which could also be got from roasting in the white hot ashes of a bonfire) which chars and blackens the skin, and results in that exciting, mysterious smokiness. If you have a gas stove, then cook them directly on the top burners. A similar effect can be obtained on the coals of a barbecue. If you have an electric stove, then you will have to roast them in the oven, but it just won't be the same! Serve as a dip with plenty of Arabic bread or as a deliciously different accompaniment to grilled or roast lamb.

4 medium eggplants

1 large clove garlic crushed with
  ½ teaspoon salt

juice of 3 lemons

3 tablespoons tahini

200 g natural yoghurt

salt and pepper

• Prick the eggplants all over with a fork and then sit them directly on the naked flame of your stove burners. Set the flame to low-medium heat and cook for at least 10 minutes, constantly turning until the whole eggplant is blackened and blistered and has collapsed in on itself. Remove them from the flame and place them on a small cake rack in a sealed container or plastic bag (so juices can drain off). Allow the eggplants to cool for about 10 minutes.

• If you prefer a milder smoky flavour then you can char the eggplants on the flame for 5 minutes and then finish off the roasting in a preheated 180°C oven for about 10 minutes.

• When the eggplants are cool, gently peel away the skin from the flesh with a small sharp knife. Allow the skin to peel away naturally, and do not scrape the flesh directly off the skin, as it will have a burnt flavour. For this reason too, be careful not to allow any pieces of the skin itself into the mix. Sit pulp in a colander and allow to sit for 5–10 minutes to drain further.

• When you are ready to assemble the dish, mix the garlic with the yoghurt then mix into the eggplant pulp with the lemon juice and tahini.

• Season with salt and pepper and mix to combine – the dip should be coarse, not smooth. Don't be afraid to taste and adjust seasonings as it should taste sharp. Serve with a big splash of extra-virgin olive oil.

Eggplant tonnato

These make a great accompaniment to fried or grilled fish, such as sardines, red mullet or whiting fillets. Serve as a light starter with a handful of dressed watercress leaves, or as a main course accompaniment to grilled or fried sardines.

3 medium eggplants

salt

50 g baby capers, finely chopped

I clove garlic, finely chopped

100 ml olive oil

TUNA MAYONNAISE

175 g canned tuna in oil

2 egg yolks

4 anchovies

I tablespoon mustard

juice of I lemon

150 ml olive oil mixed with 150 ml
    vegetable oil

I tablespoon white wine vinegar

salt and pepper

• Cut the eggplants widthways into 2 cm thick slices and lightly salt. Leave for about an hour and then rinse well and pat dry. Mix the capers with the garlic. Heat the olive oil in a heavy-based pan and fry the eggplants until they are lightly coloured on both sides. Sprinkle them with the capers mixture, pressing it well into the eggplants. Turn the eggplants and cook them for a few more minutes, and then remove and drain them on kitchen paper. Cover them with a tea-towel and place a heavy baking dish (500 g – 1 kg in weight) on top. Leave for about half an hour (this embeds the capers firmly into the eggplant, and squeezes out some of the oil).

• To make the mayonnaise, drain the tuna of its oil and place it in a food processor with the egg yolks, anchovies, mustard and lemon juice. Whiz to a smooth, fine purée. Dribble the oil in drop by drop until it is emulsified, then loosen it with half the vinegar. Slowly add the rest of the oil and, when it has all been incorporated, add the remaining vinegar. Taste and adjust seasonings.

• To serve, lay out eggplant slices in an overlapping ring and place a spoonful of mayonnaise and a lemon wedge on each slice.

• Serves six.

Pickled eggplants with walnuts and chillies

When we visited Lebanon a few years ago, we went to Zahle, the Malouf's home town. Zahle lies between Beirut and Damascus, in central Lebanon. It is surrounded by mountains, and is a popular summer resort. In winter though, the town is often snow-bound. People here are big on self-sufficiency and home-preserving – in the fruitful summer months they bottle, pickle and preserve in preparation for the cold, dark winters. It was here that we first tasted these eggplants pickled with walnuts and chillies. The recipe comes from our sister-in-law Amal Malouf.

1 kg baby Lebanese eggplants
(no more than 5 cm long)

100 g salt

150 g walnut halves

2 tablespoons oregano leaves

4 cloves garlic, thinly sliced

2–3 bullet chillies, split

1 litre olive oil

• Wash and dry the eggplants, and cook them in boiling water for 5 minutes. Refresh them under cold water and drain. Split the eggplant in half lengthways to within 1 cm of the stem. Open them up and rub salt into each side, then lay them in a colander, weight down and allow to drain for 24–48 hours.

• Chop the walnuts into quarters. Into each eggplant stuff a few oregano leaves, garlic slivers and walnuts. Pack the eggplants tightly in a sterilised jar and turn it upside down for an hour in a colander – this will allow more liquid to drain away.

• Invert, fill the jar with oil and drop in the chillies. Seal and leave for at least three weeks. Unopened they will keep up to a year.

• Once opened, keep refrigerated and eat within six weeks.

Barbecued salmon and eggplant terrine

This mosaic terrine is exquisitely pretty and a delicious light summery starter. When layering the ingredients, remember that the effect is meant to be a random mosaic, rather than neatly symmetric. If possible, try to get salmon from the head end of the fish, where it is thicker.

2 kg salmon fillet (approx. 30 cm long), skin removed

I clove garlic crushed with ½ teaspoon salt

pepper

40 ml olive oil

4 red peppers, roasted and peeled

200 g fetta cheese, crumbled

4 large leeks, steamed whole

12 Pickled Eggplants with Walnuts and Chillies (page 115)

2 teaspoons coriander seeds, toasted, ground and sieved

⅓ cup coriander leaves, roughly chopped

⅓ cup parsley, roughly chopped

• Generously line a 30 cm terrine mould (Le Creuset is ideal) with 4 layers of clingfilm (you need to enough to wrap up and over the terrine). Cut the salmon lengthways into 3 even-sized strips, rub them all over with the garlic paste and season them with pepper. Heat the oil in a large fying pan until it is smoking-hot. Sear the salmon pieces, one at a time, just colouring each side (no more than 20 seconds on each side). Remove them and place them on a wire rack to cool.

• Cut the skinned peppers in half, and trim to a neat shape. Lay half of them on the bottom of the terrine mould, skinned side down, trimming to fit if necessary. Sprinkle with a little crumbled fetta, then lay a piece of salmon down the centre, with a leek on one side and 4 pickled eggplants down the other. Sprinkle with half the ground coriander, fresh coriander and parsley leaves, and a little fetta cheese. For the next layer, place a leek down either side, and a strip of salmon and a line of 4 eggplants down the middle. Sprinkle with the remaining spices and herbs, and a little fetta, as before. For the top layer, lay a leek down the centre, the remaining piece of salmon down one side and the last 4 eggplants down the other side. Sprinkle with the last few bits of fetta and cover with the remaining red peppers. Bring the clingfilm over the top and seal.

• Cut out a piece of polystyrene, or a few thick pieces of cardboard just smaller than the mould, and place them so they fit inside the terrine, directly on top of the peppers. Weight the terrine down with a 2 kg weight and refrigerate it overnight. When you are ready to serve, unwrap the terrine and cut it into 2 cm slices. Serve it with a drizzle of olive oil, freshly made aïoli and hot, fresh crusty bread.

• Makes ten to twelve portions.

Quail baked in an eggplant

4 jumbo quail (180–200 g each)

4 small eggplants, about 12 cm long

salt

60 ml olive oil

salt and pepper

80 ml Cardamom Honey Glaze
  (page 39)

4 sprigs thyme

• Trim the quail by removing the neck flaps and wing tips.
• Cut the eggplants in half lengthways, leaving 1 cm intact close to the stalk (do not remove stalk). Sprinkle the insides generously with salt and leave in a colander for half an hour. Rinse them thoroughly and then sprinkle them with a little olive oil. Roast them in a preheated 180°C oven for 15 minutes. Remove them from the oven and allow them to cool, sealed in a plastic container.
• In a heavy pan, heat the olive oil and sauté the quail for a few minutes, until they are golden-brown. Season them with salt and pepper. Pour the Cardamom Honey Glaze into the pan and turn the quail around to ensure they are well coated. Remove them from the heat and allow them to cool.
• To assemble, place a sprig of thyme on one half of the opened-up eggplant and then insert the quail's bottom right into the centre of the eggplant and tie the drumstick legs together around the eggplant's stem. Cook in a preheated 200°C oven for 10 minutes. Remove and allow to rest for 2 minutes. Reheat the glaze and drizzle it over and around the quail.
• Serve with watercress leaves for a very attractive starter for four.

Other eggplant recipes

Soused Zucchini and Eggplant, page 296

Figs

There can be few greater pleasures in life than a fig. Not a dreary, brown, medicine-sweet disc of pressed dried fig, full of tiny little teeth-sticking seeds, but a perfectly ripe fresh fig, split to reveal its inner red secrets and glistening with a dew as sweet as honeysuckle.

The fig is regarded by many as a quintessentially Mediterranean fruit, but is believed to have originated in Asia Minor. Archeological remains suggest that fig trees were first found in Persia, Syria and Turkey, and then spread west along ancient trade routes to Greece and Italy and eastwards to India and China.

Figs – both fresh and dried – were an important part of the diet of the early peoples of the Middle East and eastern Mediterranean. The very high sugar content of dried figs has made them an ideal source of concentrated energy in lean times and a syrup of figs was used in many countries as an early sweetener.

Figs have long been celebrated for the simple and exquisite pleasure they provide. Baskets of figs have been found in Egyptian tombs, where they were left to accompany pharoes on their journey to the after-life. They were a favourite fruit of the ancient Greeks, who considered them a gift from the gods and fed them to their Olympic athletes. They were popular in the Roman empire, where they were grafted and cultivated with great success – figs are portrayed on the walls at Pompeii, and the Roman gourmet Apicius, writer of the first known recipe book, is said to have fed the best imported Syrian figs to his pigs to sweeten their flesh!

Figs and fig trees feature in the myths and legends of many civilisations from Ancient Egypt, Greece and Rome to India, East Asia and even North

Africa. The fig is also firmly entrenched in Christian symbolism. It is the first tree mentioned in the Bible, and its leaves were used by Adam and Eve to hide their nakedness. Fig leaves have been used as a symbolic device by artists ever since, to disguise nudity in their art.

SELECTING AND STORING FIGS

In Australia, many people are lucky enough to have a hardy old fig tree in the back yard and, come late summer, may gorge to their heart's content. In fact, the battle is on to get the fruit before the birds do and before the fruit becomes overripe. Most figs available commercially are black (or purple), green or white, but they are not sold by variety. The green ones are usually the first to reach our fruit stalls, followed by the larger deep-purple figs with their luscious deep-crimson flesh. Fig trees often crop twice, and true fig fanciers will often hold out for the smaller late-summer fruits with their intense honeyed perfume.

Whichever variety of figs are available, it is important to select fruit which are unbruised and unblemished. This is probably more important for figs than just about any other fruit. One of the reasons for their high cost is that they are delicate and highly perishable. Furthermore, they don't travel well, and once ripe they ferment rapidly. Figs need to be handled with a little tenderness, as they are so fragile. Reject any which are bruised or are sticky and weeping – they are almost certainly overripe and may even have started fermenting.

If possible, eat figs on the day of purchase, and certainly keep them refrigerated until you need them. Remove them from the fridge ahead of time, though, as chilling them dulls some of their flavour.

As in ancient times, the best dried figs are still imported from Turkey – the best being the legendary Smyrna figs. Turkish figs are large, plump white figs which are dried in the sun. Over time the sugar in them rises to the surface and gives them a characteristic white surface bloom. Dried figs may be bought loose or packed in little cardboard cartons (pressed figs), but the very best come strung on raffia loops like a chunky modern necklace.

USING FIGS

As with so many of the best things in life, a perfect fig really requires little tricking-up. Many are thin-skinned and don't require peeling, but if you like a fancy presentation you can cut a cross in the skin, intersecting over the top of the fruit, and peel the skin away from the flesh in petals.

Dried salty hams, such as prosciutto or pancetta, are natural allies of the fig, as are many cheeses. Soft, creamy cheeses, such as a fresh goat or soft blue cheese, are delicious with fresh figs; whereas hard sharp cheeses, like a good cheddar, are particularly good with the big dried Turkish figs.

Fresh figs make a perfect and easy dessert. Split them by cutting through the flesh to the base (but leave it intact) and eat exactly them as they are. If they are slightly less than perfect, then you might like to sprinkle them with a few drops of rosewater and a drizzle of honey. Or shake over Cinnamon Dust (page 76) and caramelise them under a very hot grill (or with a blow torch) and serve with thick yoghurt or mascarpone.

FIG RECIPES

Figs wrapped in prosciutto and kataifi

Partnering sweet fresh figs with creamy mascarpone and salty, piggy ham is a classic and delicious combination. Here they are briefly baked in a kataifi nest, which provides an extra crunch. The combination of hot juicy figs, salty ham, and cold melting mascarpone makes a stunning luscious starter.

12 small black figs

12 slices prosciutto

½ packet kataifi pastry

100 g butter, melted

150 g mascarpone

fresh black pepper

• Gently peel the figs and wrap the base of each one with a slice of prosciutto. With a small sharp knife, make a small cross over the top of each fig, and gently squeeze the base of the fig, so it opens out like a little flower.
• Carefully divide the kataifi into 12 long sections and brush liberally with the melted butter. Wrap it around the fig, leaving just the pointed top of the fig protruding. Bake the figs on the top shelf of a preheated 200°C oven for 8 minutes, or until the pastry is golden-brown.
• Remove from the oven.
• Serve with a blob of fresh mascarpone stuffed into the top of the fig and a grind of fresh black pepper.
• Serves six (two each) as a starter.

Fresh figs poached in ginger syrup

Fresh figs are barely poached with pieces of glacé ginger and sweet spices in a light syrup. When fresh figs are out of season, you could also use good quality dried fig, simmered in the syrup until soft and plump. Serve with thick Greek-style yoghurt and a drizzle of honey.

150 g castor sugar

400 ml water

peel of 1 lemon

4 cardamom pods, cracked

1 cinnamon stick

1 dried lime, cracked (optional)

60 g glacé ginger

12 fresh figs (or good quality
  Turkish figs, dried)

• Place the sugar in a pan with the water, lemon, 4 cardamom pods, cinnamon, lime and ginger. Bring to the boil, ensuring the sugar dissolves completely. Lower the heat and simmer for 5 minutes, then remove the pan from the heat.
• Peel the figs and place them in the syrup. Return the pan to a low heat and bring it slowly back to the boil. As soon as the syrup reaches the boil, remove the pan and allow the figs to cool down in the pan – no further poaching is required. (If you are using dried figs, simmer gently for 5 minutes, or until they are soft).
• Serve warm.

Other fig recipes

Dried Fig and Pistachio Chocolate Truffles, page 215

Toffeed fig tart

A simple filo-layered pasty base cooked crispy golden and drenched in syrup. Serve with a jug of delicate Ginger Cream (page 136), or if you prefer, a blob of crème fraîche.

10 sheets of filo pastry

200 g butter, melted

100 g castor sugar

100 ml water

a splash of rosewater (optional)

12 fresh figs

2 tablespoons castor sugar

1 extra tablespoon butter

100 g hazelnuts, toasted, peeled and
    roughly crushed

• Layer the sheets of filo pastry on the work surface, brushing each one with melted butter. Use a ramekin dish, or pastry cutter, about 8 cm diameter, and cut out 4 circles from the stack of pastry.

• Place the pastry circles on a baking tray lined with baking parchment and bake in a preheated 180°C oven for 10–12 minutes. Remove the tray from the oven and, while still hot, drizzle a little sugar syrup over each pastry circle.

• To make the syrup, place the sugar and water in a small pan and bring it to the boil, making sure the sugar is completely dissolved. Lower the heat and simmer for 5 minutes, then add a splash of rosewater if desired.

• Sprinkle the sugar into a frying pan and add the tablespoon of butter. Heat until the butter dissolves and the sugar caramelises. Cut each fig in half and place them cut side down in the caramel. Stir them gently in the caramel for a few moments, then remove them from the pan.

• To assemble, lay a circle of pastry on each plate and stack the figs, pointing outwards, in two layers of three halves. Sprinkle with hazelnuts, and serve immediately with Ginger Cream (page 136).

Garlic

Since the earliest days of civilisation garlic has been the culinary symbol par excellence of social snobbery and prejudice. Reviled by the aristocracy, garlic was always the poor person's food flavouring and medicine. The Egyptian pyramid builders and the Greek and Roman soldiers all ate garlic with their daily bread for strength and courage. It has traditionally been the common person's cold and flu remedy and an antiseptic for healing wounds and skin conditions; contemporary research suggests that it helps prevent blood clots and even some cancers. To this day in the Middle East, many people still string garlic over their front door to ward off evil spirits, and of course we all know it to be an essential weapon against vampires!

Even up until the last few decades, garlic has been firmly linked in the Anglo-Saxon mind with all that is 'foreign'. This prejudice centres around garlic's strong smell and the way it lingers on the breath. Generally, though, garlic has enjoyed a surprising reversal of fortune of late. Nowadays people tend to be considered miserably unsophisticated if they claim not to like it!

If you are not keen on garlic, you might think that Middle Eastern food is not for you, as garlic and its companion allium, the onion, are the fundamental savoury starting points for nearly every dish from Barcelona to Baghdad and Cannes to Cairo. The trick, though, is subtlety and a delicate hand. Everybody's garlic threshold is different; and besides, garlic shouldn't overpower every other flavour in a dish, but add an earthy depth and complexity.

Garlic is frequently combined with olive oil in a range of dressings, marinades, sauces and soups. At its most basic, this can be a simple emulsion, sharpened with a squeeze of lemon juice; at its most unctuous, the legendary aïoli, a rich garlicky mayonnaise much loved in the South of

France. In Lebanon and Syria they make toum – a sublime garlic sauce as light and fluffy as whipped cream. In Greece they pound garlic and oil with bread to make skordalia. In Spain they add tomatoes, peppers and onion to make the zesty summer soup gazpacho. The Moorish version uses almonds instead, and is at once creamy and refreshing. The Turks pound walnuts with garlic and oil to make the delicious sauce known as 'tarator'. While the Lebanese usually make their own version of tarator using pine nuts.

SELECTING AND STORING GARLIC

Garlic is available all year round, but is sweeter and more delicate in the spring. New season's garlic boasts plump, tightly packed heads of white juicy cloves, with soft, moist skins. By winter, the cloves are noticeably looser and harder, with dry, brittle papery skins that can even become woody. Older garlic can often begin to germinate and develop a green shoot in its centre. This has a bitter unpleasant flavour and should be pinched out and discarded.

Choose heads of garlic which are firm and weighty. Always check for bruising and blemishes, and avoid any heads that have shrunken withered cloves or are obviously mouldy on the outside. Store garlic in a cool, dry place rather than the refrigerator where it is more likely to go mouldy. It will start to sprout if kept too long, so use within a week or so of purchase.

USING GARLIC

To roast individual cloves or a whole head of garlic, they do not need to be peeled entirely. Simply tidy them up and remove any extra layers of papery skin. Individual cloves can be tucked in next to a roast, or you can oven-bake the whole head – some people like to wrap it in foil. When we roast a leg of lamb or a whole chicken at home, we always stuff a handful of garlic cloves alongside, or among the accompanying roast vegetables. The garlic cloves emerge from the oven all shrivelled, but when you pierce the skin you discover that the insides have transformed into a delicate, mellow, buttery paste, which is just divine mushed in with the gravy and smeared over a mouthful of meat or potato. One word of warning though: only add the garlic to the roasting pan once the initial blast of heat has been turned down. After the mellow creamy stage they quickly start to caramelise, becoming sticky and brown. Beyond that they turn to blackened cinders!

If a dish calls for whole cloves of garlic, the best way to peel them is to slice off the base of the clove and carefully peel the skin away with a small sharp knife. Otherwise, crush the clove firmly with the flat side of a broad heavy knife, as close the to handle as you can get, for maximum pressure. The skin should then peel away easily.

Many recipes call for finely chopped or minced garlic. The simplest way to achieve this is to crush the peeled garlic and a little coarse salt to a smooth paste using a mortar and pestle. It only takes a moment, as the gritty salt quickly breaks the garlic down to a silky smooth paste. An added benefit is that this paste dissolves away into the food, rather than hanging around as fierce little lumps. Chopping with a sharp kitchen knife is fine of course, but your fingers and chopping board always end up smelling of garlic!

The flavour and strength of garlic depends partly on its age, but also on whether it is eaten raw or cooked. It is at its most fiery when eaten raw, but both its flavour and texture soften and mellow on cooking. Dried-up old-season's garlic it can often be far too astringent to be enjoyable. One way of improving the flavour somewhat is to blanch it in boiling water for 30 seconds before use.

GARLIC RECIPES

Andalusian white soup

There are many garlic soups to be found all around the Mediterranean. Some are simple bread soups, other more sophisticated versions use a flavourful stock, instead of water, and others still enrich it with egg yolks. Some soups are served hot, others warm or even chilled. One hot day in Seville we ate a delicious version, thickened in true Moorish style with almond meal, sharpened with vinegar and served with a sprinkling of currants.

200 g day-old good quality white bread, crusts removed

150 ml milk

150 g blanched almonds

3–4 cloves garlic crushed with ½ teaspoon salt

120 ml olive oil

500–750 ml iced water

3 tablespoons sherry vinegar

salt and pepper

2 tablespoons currants, soaked in 2 tablespoons sherry

• Soak the bread in the milk for a few minutes, and then squeeze it dry. Place the almonds in a food processor and whiz to a coarse meal. Then add the bread and garlic paste and whiz to a smooth paste. With the motor running, slowly pour in the olive oil, drop by drop, as if making a mayonnaise. When all the oil is incorporated, add the iced water until the soup is the consistency of pouring cream. Add the vinegar and season with salt and pepper if needed.

• Keep the soup chilled until you are ready to serve. You can make it a day ahead if it suits.

• Serve at room termperature on a hot summer's day sprinkled with the sherry-plumped currants.

• Serves four to six.

Toum

This fiercely garlicky sauce is not for the faint-hearted, but if you enjoy garlic, you will love this Lebanese/Syrian sauce, which is traditionally served with chicken. Use it to brush on grilled chicken, seafood and meats at the end of barbecuing, or to accompany roasts or cold meats. Or thin it down with water to make a garlicky salad dressing. But be warned, don't plan any business meetings afterwards.

I whole head of garlic, cloves
  peeled (40 g)

I teaspoon salt

juice of I lemon

200 ml sunflower oil

30 ml water

• Peel and roughly chop the garlic cloves, then place them in a blender or liquidiser with the salt and lemon juice. Blend for about 2 minutes, until smooth, scraping down the sides occasionally. Next, very slowly start to add the oil, as if you are making a mayonnaise, and blend on high until it is emulsified. Continue to dribble in slowly, until all the oil is absorbed. Finally, add the water. The whole process will take about 5 minutes and you end up with a light fluffy garlicky sauce. This makes approximately 400 ml, which will keep in the refrigerator for about a week.

• If the sauce splits, you can save it by doing the following. Clean out the liquidiser. Put in 2 egg yolks and blend, then very slowly pour in half the split mixture. When it begins to emulsify and thicken add a teaspoon of cold water to loosen it. Then gradually add the rest of the mix. You end up with a mayonnaise rather than a sauce, but it is still delicious.

ABOVE:
Haloumy cheese
BELOW:
Quail baked in an eggplant
(recipe page 117)

Lamb kifta tagine with eggs (recipe page 148)

Garlic Yorkshire pudding

A touch of garlic makes a surprisingly different Yorkshire pudding batter. For an even bigger surprise drizzle the rest of the head of garlic with a drop of honey, wrap it in foil and bake it in the oven until it is soft (15 minutes at 180°C). Allow it to cool a little, then carefully peel each clove. Drop a soft, buttery clove into each pudding before baking them in the oven. These Yorkies are terrific with Devilled Lamb Loins (page 149) or any roasted joint of beef or lamb.

75 g plain flour

I egg

100 ml milk

2 cloves garlic crushed with
  ½ teaspoon salt

vegetable oil or dripping

- Sift the flour into a bowl, make a well in the centre and break in the egg. Beat the egg into the flour until it combines to a smooth, lump-free paste. Then add the garlic paste and mix in well. Gradually add the milk, incorporating each amount thoroughly before adding more. When all is mixed in, chill the batter for at least half an hour until you are ready to cook.

- Preheat the oven to 220°C. When it has come to temperature, pour a teaspoon of oil into each of six patty tins and heat them in the oven for 10 minutes or until the oil is sizzling. Pour in the chilled mixture and bake for 15 minutes.

- This quantity makes six small puddings or one large pudding.

Parsnip skordalia

Skordalia is a traditional Greek garlic sauce, often made with mashed potatoes, stale white bread, or even almonds. This version uses parsnip for a sweeter, mellower taste. Serve it as an accompaniment to any barbecue or grill.

1 kg parsnips

½ litre milk

2 cloves garlic crushed with
    ½ teaspoon salt

juice of 1 lemon

50 g fresh breadcrumbs

100 ml olive oil

salt and pepper

• Peel and core the parsnips and cut them into even-sized pieces. Cook them in the milk until they are very soft. Purée them in a food processor with the garlic paste, lemon juice and breadcrumbs. Add the oil, in a very slow dribble, until all is incorporated. Adjust the seasoning and allow to cool.

Other garlic recipes
Barbecued Squid with Zhoug, page 81
Honey-Garlic Aïoli, page 141
Marinated Baby Lamb with Lebanese Nut Rice, page 150–151
Saffron-Yoghurt Cheese, page 289
Basil Tzatziki, page 290

Ginger

Times and fashions change in the kitchen as surely as they do everywhere else. These days if you ask a shop assistant which aisle the ginger is in, they will almost certainly direct you to the fresh produce section, where fresh root ginger is to be found cuddling up next to the garlic. This gnarled, knobbly root certainly seems to have ousted the dried powdered spice in the popularity stakes in recent years. Those little bottles of sandy ginger powder, most commonly used in puddings, cakes and cookies, have been pushed firmly to the back of the kitchen cupboard.

It seems that speedy stir-fried dishes from China and South East Asia are better suited to our fast-paced lifestyles. Fresh root ginger combined with garlic and chilli forms the unmistakable fragrant and spicy basis for numerous dishes from this region. In traditional Chinese medicine ginger is also still used as a tonic, particularly for digestive disorders and for the female reproductive system. Ginger is eaten to boost the immune system and used for its general antibacterial properties – in fact ginger has always been widely used in many civilisations for its medicinal qualities as well as the clean, invigorating flavour it adds to food.

Botanically, ginger, like turmeric and galangal, is a rhizome – the tuberous root of an attractive flowering plant which probably originated in India or tropical Asia. It has been consumed in the Far East for many thousands of years, and was one of the first spices to be introduced to the Mediterranean, probably by the sea-loving Phoenicians. It was certainly known in the ancient civilisations of Egypt, Persia and Greece and was particularly loved in Rome, where it was used as lavishly as black pepper.

In medieval Europe powdered ginger was one of the most popular spices. It was used in baking, to make all kinds of biscuits, cakes and desserts, and was a popular flavouring in many savoury dishes too, often used very liberally to mask the smell and taste of bad meat. With the gradual evolution from one-pot cooking, the distinction between sweet and savoury dishes became more marked, and the use of ginger, like cinnamon, shifted to sweet dishes. This tradition remains in northern European and North American cooking today, in a wide repertoire of ginger biscuits, ginger cakes and puddings, gingerbreads and even ginger wines and cordials.

Dried ground ginger, rather than the fresh root, is used in Middle Eastern cookery and even more so in North African cookery. The Arabs transported ginger all around their empire from the eighth century onwards, introducing it to North Africa, where it became a key spice in savoury dishes, and where it remains one of the primary ingredients in spice mixes such as the Moroccan ras el hanout, which is used in all sorts of soups and tagines. As a result of the Arabic enthusiasm for spices, the Spanish too learned to love and value them. From the sixteenth century, both the Spanish and Portuguese introduced ginger to their colonies in the West Indies, West Africa and South America, where it is an important flavouring in local dishes.

The Arabs were also responsible for introducing Europeans to crystallised ginger. Once they invaded and conquered Persia they discovered sugar cane and, more importantly, the techniques for extracting and refining sugar. Preserved and candied ginger became a real delicacy – although perhaps its success was due less to its sweet flavour as to its reputation as an aphrodisiac!

SELECTING, STORING AND USING GINGER

When choosing ginger, try to buy the freshest, youngest looking rhizomes. As ginger ages it becomes woody and dry, and its flavour becomes hotter and more peppery. Certainly avoid ginger which is shrivelled and wizened. Store fresh ginger in the vegetable drawer of the refrigerator, where it will last for a couple of weeks.

To prepare fresh ginger, slice off a knob or section of the ginger and carefully peel it with a sharp paring knife. Cut it into thin slices across the grain. These can be used as they are, or sliced into batons and very finely diced. To grate ginger, use the shredding side of a grater, and then dice it more finely by hand. Large quantities of ginger can be whizzed to a paste in a food processor.

Ground ginger is available in little plastic packets or glass bottles from all supermarkets. Store it in a tightly sealed container in a dark, cool cupboard.

GINGER RECIPES

Rabbit terrine with ginger

750 g rabbit meat, minced

250 g pork belly, minced

250 g chicken livers, minced

1 egg

100 ml milk

1/2 tablespoon ginger powder

1/2 teaspoon cinnamon powder

1/2 teaspoon chilli powder

1/2 teaspoon ground coriander

4 shallots, finely chopped

1 clove garlic, finely chopped

50 g fresh ginger, grated

80 ml olive oil

1 tablespoon salt

1/2 teaspoon pepper

100 g unsalted, shelled pistachio nuts

300 g kaiser fleisch, thinly sliced

• Place the minced rabbit, pork belly and chicken livers into a large mixing bowl with the egg, milk and spices. Stir well.
• Sauté the shallots, garlic and ginger in the olive oil for 2 minutes, until they have softened. Allow to cool for a few minutes and add to the meat mixture and mix in well. To taste for seasonings, take a walnut-sized lump and fry on both sides until it is cooked. Taste and adjust with salt, pepper or spices if need be. Divide the mixture into three batches and pulse them in a food processor until they are smooth. Stir in the pistachio nuts.
• Line a 30 cm terrine mould with greaseproof paper and then line inside and up the sides with thin slices of kaiser fleisch, reserving enough to cover the top. Tip in the meat mixture and pack it in carefully. Cover with the remaining slices of kaiser fleisch, tucking any ends down the sides. Cover with foil, place in a deep baking tray half-filled with water and bake in the centre of a preheated 180°C oven for 1 1/2 hours. Remove the terrine from the oven and weight it down while it is still warm (a few heavy bottles or tins will do the job quite well).
• Leave it to cool overnight or for at least 8 hours. Turn it out, remove the greaseproof paper and slice thickly to serve.
• This terrine is good with crusty bread, pickled gherkins and plenty of hot mustard, or serve it with a lively salad such as Fattouche (page 261), Smoky Eggplant Salad (page 112) or Minted Cabbage Salad (page 170).
• Makes ten to twelve portions.

Sticky ginger cake

This cake uses both fresh grated ginger and dried ginger powder. It is deliciously moist, and mouth tinglingly hot and gingery. Serve warm at tea-time or turn it into a dessert with a generous dollop of crème fraîche, ginger cream or even Burnt Honey Ice-Cream (page 142).

220 g golden syrup

170 g sour cream

110 g soft brown sugar

2 eggs

4 teaspoons fresh grated ginger

1 teaspoon grated lemon zest

280 g butter

130 g plain flour

130 g self-raising flour

1 teaspoon baking powder

½ teaspoon salt

1 teaspoon ginger powder

• Whisk together the golden syrup, sour cream, brown sugar, eggs, grated ginger and lemon zest. Melt the butter and whisk it into mixture. Twice sift the flours, baking powder, salt and ginger powder. Fold into the warm batter, whisking gently if necessary to break down any residual lumps of flour. The batter will be fairly runny.

• Tip it into a well-greased 20 cm spring-form tin and bake in the centre of a preheated 180°C oven for 35–45 minutes, or until a skewer comes out clean.

Other ginger recipes

Pigeon Tagine with Dates and Ginger, pages 105–106
Fresh Figs Poached in Ginger Syrup, page 122

Ginger cream

Serve this alongside the Sticky Ginger Cake (page 135) or all kinds of steamed puddings. It is also good with Fresh Figs Poached in Ginger Syrup (page 122).

1 thumb fresh ginger

150 ml pure cream

½ teaspoon ginger powder

40 g palm sugar or soft brown sugar

2 egg yolks, whisked to combine

• Grate the fresh ginger on the shredder side of grater and chop more finely with a knife (don't use the fine side as it will just clog up the grater).

• Scald the cream with both the fresh and ground gingers and the palm sugar.

• Pour the cream onto the egg yolks and whisk well. Return the cream to the saucepan and heat it gently until the cream thickens slightly, which might take up to 10 minutes. Tip it into a bowl and allow it to cool.

• Whip the cream when you are ready to serve.

Ginger shortbreads

Rice flour gives a slightly sandy-shortbready texture. You could use cornflour instead for a softer, more melting biscuit.

150 g butter

75 g icing sugar

1 egg yolk

150 g plain flour

75 g rice flour

2 generous tablespoons of finely chopped crystallised ginger

• Chill the bowl and blade of your food processor for 10 minutes in the freezer. Then cream the butter and icing sugar. Add the egg yolk and mix in well. Sift in the two flours and then add the chopped ginger. Pulse carefully until the mixture just comes together. Tip the mixture onto a floured work surface and divide it into two. Roll each half into a log shape (approx 4 cm diameter), wrap in clingfilm and refrigerate them for at least 2 hours before baking in a preheated oven 150°C for 6–8 minutes. The biscuits should colour only very slightly. This dough will make 35–40 biscuits.

• Store them in an airtight container.

Honey

While the possession of a sweet tooth is far from being solely a twentieth-century phenomenon, it has never before been as easy to satisfy. These days confectionary is no longer confined to lolly-shops. In fact, it seems that wherever we go we are faced with sweet temptations – at petrol stations and video stores, supermarket checkouts and newsagents. It is easy to forget that these simple pleasures which we take so much for granted have only been readily available since the commercial cultivation of sugar cane and sugar beet during the last few hundred years.

The secret of extracting and concentrating the juice from sugar cane was known in India as early as 3000 BC, but didn't reach Europe until the Arabs took it to Spain in the eighth century. However, it was not until Spanish colonists took sugar cane to the West Indies in the fifteenth century that the sugar-refining industry really began in earnest.

Before refined sugar, people's taste for sweetness was satisfied by the concentrated natural sugars found in ripe and sun-dried fruits, and most of all by honey. Honey was one of the very first sweeteners known to our ancestors – prehistoric cave paintings in Spain depict a stone-age man carefully stealing honey from a nest of bees. By 2500 BC, the Egyptians had learned to avoid some of the danger involved in collecting honey from wild bees by taming them with smoke and forcing them to build their honeycombs in tall, cylindrical hives.

To ancient civilisations honey was a kind of miracle, a food given to us by the gods, rich in energy and delicious to taste. It was used for sweetening and flavouring foods, for making primitive fruit preserves and for coating all kinds of flowers, nuts and fruit to make sweetmeats. It must also be said that another of honey's key attractions was its propensity to ferment quickly when mixed with water — especially in hot climates — turning it into mead, one of the very first intoxicating drinks.

In the West, honey is no longer a key ingredient in most kitchens, as it is unable to compete with cheap white sugars in either cost or availability. For most of us, honey is merely a delicious spread to be enjoyed with lashings of butter on good hot toast. In the Middle East, however, honey is still an important basic ingredient in cooking and confectionary making. A spoonful of honey is often added to syrups for pouring over nut-stuffed pastries. Then there are all sorts of honey biscuits and puffs, like the Greek loukoumathes, honey pies and even honey-cheese cakes. Honey works well in nutty-earthy sweets, like nougat or halvah, and marries perfectly with several sweet spices, such as cinnamon, ginger and cloves. All around the Mediterranean gingerbreads and spice cakes are still made with honey. Honey's affinity with lemon is also well known, not just in throat-soothing winter drinks, but in syrups and marinades for roasts and grills. Honey even adds a warming, sweet base note to all kinds of savoury tagines and meat casseroles.

SELECTING AND STORING HONEY

One of the very best things about a weekend in the country is the opportunity it provides for visiting country markets. There always seems to be at least one stall boasting endless varieties of local honeys, and we find it almost impossible to go home without buying at least one jar. As a result we have a cupboard full of different honeys ranging from a mild-flavoured cheap supermarket variety, to several different intensely fragrant single-flower honeys.

Every honey is different. The flavour, strength and smell of each one is determined by the flowers visited by the bees, as their fragrance is retained in the honey. The cheap commercial brands always taste pretty much the same because they are blended from lots of different honeys. As a result they are consistent, reliable and a little dull, lacking the complexity and subtlety of the finest single-flower honeys. Honeys from small producers tend to be costlier. Like the finest boutique olive oils or wines, the flavour of these honeys is also dependent on the local climate, terrain, fauna and flora that the bees visit.

In Australia we are lucky enough to enjoy some of the best floral honeys in the world from a wide range of native plants. Some of the best include the distinctive and world-renowned Tasmanian leatherwood honey, as well as milder flavoured honeys from red gum, blue gum or yellow box. Some are strongly floral, like orange blossom and apple flower, or more aromatic, like lavender and clover. Some have strong herbal qualities, like rosemary, fennel and thyme.

Honey should not be kept in the fridge, and should always be stored in a cool cupboard, well away from light. All honeys start off fairly runny and clear, though some are darker and stronger smelling. Over time, and more quickly if exposed to light, they slowly crystallise, becoming thicker and cloudier, until they eventually set solid. (Don't confuse them with creamed honeys, though, which are whipped to a creamy opaque consistency). This is an inevitable process which affects neither the flavour or quality of the honey and is easy to reverse by submerging the entire the jar in a pan of very hot water. Leave it for half an hour or so, until the honey becomes runny again.

USING HONEY

Everyone knows that honey is delicious on hot, buttered crumpets or drizzled over a bowl of thick, creamy yoghurt with the lightest dusting of cinnamon. If you want to use it in cooked dishes though, use it with discretion – honey is not simply interchangeable with sugar, and some very strongly flavoured honeys are not suited for cooking at all. Furthermore, heat destroys the more complex and distinctive flavours of the most interesting single-flower honeys, so in many cooked dishes it is better to use a milder flavoured supermarket brand.

HONEY RECIPES

Honey-roasted pear and walnut salad

Top this salad with slices of grilled haloumy to make a delicious starter. It is a lovely light accompaniment to all sorts of earthy vegetable dishes and risottos.

3 ripe pears

2½ tablespoons mild-flavoured honey

3 cardamom pods, seeds only

1 tablespoon orange-blossom water

3 teaspoons sherry

25 g butter

120 ml extra-virgin olive oil

100 g walnuts

2 packets Cypriot Haloumy cheese
(250 g packets), sliced 3 mm thick

100 g plain flour for dusting

60 ml olive oil

juice of 2 lemons

1 teaspoon fresh thyme leaves,
chopped finely

1 purple onion, finely sliced

2 bunches watercress, leaves picked

100 g black olives

salt

½ teaspoon black pepper

• Peel the pears and cut them into halves (or quarters if they are quite thick), and cut out the core. In a small pot, warm the honey, cardamom seeds, orange-blossom water and sherry.

• In a heavy frying pan, melt together the butter and 2 tablespoons of the extra-virgin olive oil until bubbling, then sear the pears for 1 minute on each side. Add the honey mixture and sauté for a further 2 minutes until it is a warm caramel colour.

• To roast the walnuts, place them in a very hot oven for 5 minutes. Rub away some of the papery brown skin in a tea-towel and cut them into quarters.

• To grill the haloumy cheese, dust the slices in flour. Heat the 60 ml of olive oil in a frying pan over a high heat and cook the cheese slices until they are golden-brown. Turn them and colour the other side. Pour the lemon juice over the cheese and sprinkle with the thyme leaves.

• Slice the onion finely and rinse it under cold running water for 5 minutes to reduce its sharpness.

• In a large bowl gently mix together the pears and haloumy cheese with the watercress leaves, olives, onion and two-thirds of the walnuts.

• In a separate bowl, gently whisk together the remaining extra-virgin olive oil and the lemon juice and season with the salt and black pepper. Pour the dressing over the salad and gently combine them.

• To serve, place a mound of salad on each place and sprinkle the remaining walnuts over the top.

Honey-garlic aïoli

If you find that aïoli is often just too garlicky, then you might prefer this version, which tempers the pungency of garlic with a softer, sweeter flavour from a mild-flavoured honey.

3 whole heads of garlic

1 tablespoon honey

2 egg yolks

1 teaspoon Dijon mustard

60 ml champagne vinegar

150 olive oil combined with 100 ml vegetable oil

juice of 1 lemon

salt and pepper

• Cut the garlic heads in half crossways and drizzle them with honey. Wrap them in tin foil and roast them in a preheated 180°C oven for about 20 minutes or until they are very soft.
• Squeeze out the garlic into a blender and whiz with the egg yolks, mustard and half the vinegar before adding the oil, drop by drop, until the mixture emulsifies.
• Loosen with the remaining vinegar and lemon juice, then add the remaining oil and season with salt and pepper.

Burnt honey ice-cream

Caramelising honey just to the point of burning takes it from super-sweetness to the very edge of bitterness. It makes a very rich ice-cream and is delicious served with puffy Almond Fritters (page 5), Sweet Nut-Stuffed Quinces (page 225), or alongside a slice of Sticky Ginger Cake (page 135).

200 g sugar

6 tablespoons water

6 tablespoons honey

500 ml milk

1 litre cream

8 egg yolks

• Dissolve 100 g of sugar with the water and boil until it reaches the soft-boil stage – that is 240°C on a sugar thermometer. This takes approximately 8 minutes. Then add the honey and cook to a dark caramel, which will take an additional 8–10 minutes. Be careful it doesn't burn and remember that residual heat will continue to cook it once you remove it from the heat.

• Meanwhile, bring the milk and cream to the boil. In a mixing bowl whisk the egg yolks with the remaining sugar. Pour the hot cream onto the eggs, whisking vigorously, then return the mix to the saucepan. Mix in the caramel and stir over a very gentle heat until it thickens. You should be able to draw a clear line in the custard on the back of a spoon.

• Remove the pan from the heat and cool it in a sink of cold water or ice, stirring from time to time. When the custard is completely cold pour it into an ice-cream machine and churn according to the manufacturer's instructions.

• Serves four to six.

Honey mousse with pine nut praline

In this light-as-air dessert, sweet honey mousse is spiked with nutty, earthy Pine Nut Praline (page 210), which also adds a very pleasing crunch to the smooth creaminess.

3 leaves gelatine

4 tablespoons mild honey

400 ml cream

4 egg whites

I teaspoon Cointreau

100 g Pine Nut Praline (page 210)

• Soak the gelatine leaves in cold water for a few minutes to soften, then squeeze out the excess water. In a saucepan heat the honey, then add the gelatine and allow to cool down to room temperature (don't refrigerate).

• Whip the cream and egg whites in two separate bowls.

• Fold the honey, Cointreau and Pine Nut Praline into the cream. Then fold in the egg whites and chill until ready to serve.

Other honey recipes

Almond Fritters, page 5
Cardamom Honey-Glazed Roast Duck, page 40
Cinnamon-Chocolate Mousse, page 76
Preserved Lemons with Honey, page 155
Orange-Blossom Clotted Cream, page 185
Honey-Curd Pies with Rose-Scented Figs, page 204
Spiced Quinces, page 223
Sweet Nut-Stuffed Quinces, page 225

Lamb

When it comes to meat, there is little doubt that in the wealthy West we are well and truly spoilt for choice. Whether it is the ham in our lunchtime sandwich, the minced beef in our takeaway burger, or our Sunday roast, most of us are used to eating meat in one form or another, virtually every day. The vegetables, salads, grains and pulses which accompany it are often eaten only in a grudging nod to nutritional balance or as mere stomach filler-uppers. Consumption of meat, once upon a time an expensive treat and a symbol of wealth and extravagance, has now become the norm.

This is certainly not the case in most developing countries (and this means the majority of the world's population), where meat is still considered something of a luxury, eaten more as a condiment to flavour starchy staples, and often only on religious feast days and special family celebrations. Many countries around the Middle East and Mediterranean are in this category, even though times are changing and different types of meat are more freely available. What little meat is eaten, however, is almost certain to be lamb. In fact, older Arabic cookery books often vaguely refer to 'meat' without specifying from which animal it should come! This is because traditionally the term 'meat' was virtually synonymous with lamb or mutton (or sometimes kid and goat), as they were the only meats readily available.

Sheep were one of the very first animals to be domesticated, as early as 9000 BC, by the nomads of the Central Asian steppes who reared them as much for their woolly coats and milk and their tallow fat as for their meat. Sheep were easy to tame, having a strong herd instinct, being quick to breed and easy to graze on scrubby hillsides and grasslands. By the time cattle were domesticated, several thousand years later, they were generally

Devilled lamb loin (recipe page 149)

ABOVE:
Preserved lemon and lime
with honey (recipe page 155)
BELOW:
Preserved lemon guacamole
with smoked eel and pine nut
wafers (recipe page 156)

considered far too valuable as draught animals to be eaten and, to this day, much of the terrain around the eastern Mediterranean and Levant countries is too poor for cattle breeding and dairy farming.

In the hot Middle East, pig farming was not viable, as pigs are temperamental animals, generally resistant to herding, and greedy scavengers rather than grass-grazers. Although pork was widely eaten and enjoyed by most early civilisations, the annoying tendency of pigs to roam, coupled with their reputation for spreading disease and parasites, eventually led to taboos surrounding their consumption among two of the major religions of the Middle East, Judaism and Islam.

Lamb, on the other hand, has become strongly associated with many different cultural and religious festivities around the world and particularly in the Middle East. For Christians, a paschal lamb has a deep spiritual significance at Easter as the symbol of Christ. Lamb is also the meat of choice at Jewish and Muslim feast days. The Jewish celebrations of Passover and New Year would be unthinkable without lamb, and Muslim countries ritually slaughter and feast on whole roasted lambs on religious holidays and at wedding feasts or other family celebrations.

SELECTING AND STORING LAMB

Lamb is eaten at every age from a few weeks to several years old. The animal that we eat most of the year around is generally between 3 months and a year old. New season spring lamb is also available – usually at a higher price – and is tender and juicy, although its flavour is often milder.

Two other extremes are baby milk-fed lambs (2–4 weeks old), weighing 4–6 kilograms, which are available from some specialist butchers and are a special delicacy in the Arab world. Their meat is sweet, delicate and buttery-soft, as befits an animal which has not yet tasted a blade of grass. At the other end of the age spectrum is mutton, which is hard to find. At least two years old, it has a strong pungent flavour, which some people adore, and its mature meat requires really slow long cooking to tenderise.

Young lamb is a vivid rosy-pink, whereas the older animals and mutton turn a deeper, more purple red. Avoid meat which looks brown and tired. The fat should be white and dry, not yellow and wet.

USING LAMB

There are myriad different cuts available to consumers these days and you need to choose the appropriate cut for each particular dish.

In the Middle East, whole lambs roasted on a spit for festive occasions are often baby or milk-fed lambs, which are greatly enjoyed for their delicate and very tender meat. Cuts from older lambs also lend themselves very well to roasting. The European tradition is usually to roast the leg, shoulder or racks (from the best end of the neck), perhaps flavoured with garlic and rosemary, and eat with roasted vegetables and gravy. In the Middle East, lamb is more likely to be stuffed with rice, fruit and nuts.

Braised dishes are often simmered long and slowly, using cheaper cuts from the shoulder, neck or shank and eked out with lots of vegetables and pulses. Much of the thrill of these dishes comes from the elaborate and subtle combinations of many different spices and herbs, or from simmering with fruits such as apricots, dates or quinces.

And then there are minced meat dishes, which are a mainstay of Arabic, Jewish and Turkish cooking. These offer an economical way of using tougher cuts of meat, by pounding or grinding them into a fine paste, adding a generous pinch of carefully selected spices, and then rolling into tiny meatballs for frying or for cooking in a thick sauce or casserole. Spicy minced lamb is also shaped into long sausages around skewers for grilling over hot coals. It is also the main ingredient for the legendary Lebanese dish kibbeh, which can be fried or eaten raw.

All around the Middle East and eastern Mediterranean the air is filled with the savoury aroma of sizzling grilled lamb, known as 'meshwi', which is sold from humble street stalls and kiosks everywhere. The technique of packing tender tasty little morsels of meat onto skewers or spits, and then grilling them over flames or glowing charcoal was reputedly first used by Ottoman soldiers during their long battle campaigns. Being constantly on the move, camping out of doors and having only small amounts of fuel led to this practice of quickly grilling tiny pieces of meat over intense heat.

This style of quick grilling over fierce heat is perfectly suited to the most tender cuts of lamb. These days they are marketed as 'trim', with much of the fat removed to suit the anti-fat brigade. They are usually fillets, cut from the loin or leg. Because the meat is lean, it needs to be brushed with oil to keep it moist and to stop it from sticking.

LAMB RECIPES

Sticky lamb shank soup with fresh fenugreek and molten mozzarella

This amazingly fragrant soup is really more of a meal. Fresh fenugreek can be hard to find – try an Asian or Middle Eastern grocer.

50 ml olive oil

6 lamb shanks

salt and pepper

2 medium brown onions, coarsely chopped

3 celery sticks, coarsely chopped

2 medium carrots, scraped and halved lengthways

2 medium leeks, washed and halved lengthways

4 cloves garlic, peeled

100 ml sherry

2 litres chicken stock or water

1 tablespoon fenugreek seeds, rinsed and lightly cracked

1 teaspoon cumin seeds

2 sticks cinnamon

1 teaspoon allspice berries, lightly cracked

1 small butternut pumpkin, peeled, de-seeded and cut into 1 cm dice

2 medium turnips, peeled and cut into 1 cm dice

2 medium potatoes, peeled and cut into 1 cm dice

¾ cup fresh coriander, roughly chopped

1 bunch fenugreek leaves (or flat-leaf parsley), leaves picked

200 g mozzarella cheese, sliced

• Heat olive oil in a heavy-based casserole dish and season lamb shanks with salt and pepper. Brown all over. Remove from pan and drain on kitchen paper.

• To the casserole dish add onions, celery, carrot, leeks and garlic and sauté over a low heat for 5 minutes. Return the lamb to the pan, add the sherry and stock and bring to the boil. Skim, then lower the heat.

• To make the spice-bag, combine the fenugreek seeds, cumin seeds, cinnamon stick and allspice in a small muslin cloth and tie with string. Submerge the bag among the vegetables and shanks. Place the casserole on the middle shelf of a preheated 180°C oven for 1¾ hours, until the lamb is falling from the bones.

• Remove the casserole from the oven and strain the mixture through a sieve, pressing on the vegetables to extract maximum flavour. Discard the vegetables and spice-bag, remove the meat from the bones and shred it coarsely.

• Cook the pumpkin, turnip and potato in the strained stock until tender, then strain and reserve with the meat. Bring the stock to the boil and reduce it by one-third, skimming constantly.

• Return the meat and vegetables to the pan and heat through, then add the coriander leaves and adjust the seasoning. To serve, ladle the soup into serving bowls, top with mozzarella slices and sprinkle with fenugreek leaves.

• Serve with crusty bread. Serves ten.

Lamb kifta tagine with eggs

Meatballs with a difference! This makes a tasty supper dish and with its spicy tomato sauce and rich runny eggs is bound to become a firm favourite.

MEATBALLS

500 g lamb, finely minced

1 medium onion, finely chopped

3 tablespoons parsley, finely chopped

1/4 teaspoon cayenne pepper

salt and pepper

2 tablespoons olive oil for frying

SAUCE

2 tablespoons olive oil

2 medium onions, finely chopped

1 clove garlic, finely chopped

2 cans tomatoes (400 g), drained and chopped

1 teaspoon cumin powder

1 teaspoon cinnamon

1/2 teaspoon cayenne pepper

salt and pepper

500 ml water

1/3 cup parsley leaves, finely chopped

1/3 cup coriander leaves, finely chopped

6 eggs

- To make the meatballs, combine all the ingredients well and, with wet hands, form into walnut-sized balls. Heat the oil and brown the meatballs all over. Drain well on kitchen paper.
- For the sauce, heat the oil in a heavy-based casserole dish and lightly sauté the onions and garlic until they are translucent. Add the remaining ingredients (except the water, fresh herbs and eggs) and stir well. Then add the water, stir again and bring to the boil. Lower the heat and simmer the sauce, uncovered, for around 30 minutes, or until it has reduced to a very thick gravy.
- Add the meatballs to the sauce and continue cooking for a further 8 minutes. Carefully break the eggs into the sauce, cover it with a lid and cook until the eggs are just set, which will take around 5 minutes.
- Serve at once, straight from the pot, liberally garnished with the fresh herbs and with plenty of Arabic bread to mop up the runny egg yolks. Alternatively, accompany with a dish of plain buttered couscous and a dollop of thick natural yoghurt.
- Those who enjoy a more piquant dish may add one finely chopped bullet of chilli while sautéing the onion and garlic.

Devilled lamb loin

4 whole lamb loins (approx 200 g each)

fresh black pepper

3 teaspoons hot English mustard

3 teaspoons Chermoula (page 67)

• Carefully slice away any excess fat on the lamb loins then grind the fresh black pepper on both sides. On one side, spread a little mustard and then over that a little Chermoula. Turn over onto a piece of clingfilm and repeat on the other side.

• Grill or barbecue the lamb for 2 minutes on each side, for medium-rare, turning twice to stop it burning. Serve with creamy Harissa-Potato Salad (page 66) or Preserved Lemon Guacamole (page 156) and Garlic Yorkshire Pudding (page 129).

Marinated baby lamb with Lebanese nut rice

This is a traditional favourite at Easter time, when a whole baby lamb is stuffed with a rice-and-nut mixture and barbecued or spit-roasted for a real family feast. If you can procure a baby lamb, and your oven or barbecue can accommodate it, go for it. Otherwise try this adaptation, which is equally delicious if not quite as spectacular.

MARINADE

4 cloves garlic crushed with
    1 teaspoon salt

juice of 2 lemons

1 teaspoon pepper

1 teaspoon ground allspice

2 teaspoons fresh thyme, finely
    chopped

250 ml olive oil

1 small lamb shoulder (1.5 –2 kg)
    with shank, cut at ball joint

2 × 6-point lamb racks from the neck
    end (bones trimmed and scraped
    back to the meat)

salt and cracked pepper

RICE

50 ml olive oil

1 large onion, finely diced

150 g lamb mince

650 g short-grain rice

1 litre chicken stock

1 cinnamon stick

salt

1 teaspoon cracked pepper

• For the marinade, blend the garlic paste, lemon juice, pepper, allspice and thyme with the olive oil. Marinate lamb pieces overnight.

• Pre-heat the oven to 220°C. Remove the lamb from its marinade and brown it all over in a heavy-based baking tray (there will be enough oil in the marinade). Sprinkle it with salt and cracked pepper and place it in oven. Roast the shoulder for 50 minutes to 1 hour, and the racks for 30 minutes, then remove them from the oven and allow them to rest in a warm place, covered with foil.

• While the lamb is roasting, prepare the rice. Heat the olive oil in a large heavy-based pot and sauté the onion and minced lamb until the onion is soft and the meat has browned. After about 4 minutes, add the rice and boiling chicken stock. Turn the heat down to a simmer, and add the cinnamon stick, salt and pepper. Cover and cook for 16 minutes.

TO SERVE

80 g pine nuts

80 g pistachio nuts (shelled)

80 g blanched whole almonds

100 ml olive oil

2 cloves garlic crushed with
    ½ teaspoon salt

juice of 1 lemon

1½ cups fresh coriander, roots
    removed

• Fry the nuts separately in 100 ml olive oil until they are golden-brown.
• To serve, turn the rice out onto a large serving platter and sprinkle it with the nuts. Cut the lamb racks into three, and carve shoulder meat for each person, arranging the pieces around the rice. Pour the juices from roasting into a small pan, bring quickly to the boil and add the garlic paste and lemon juice. Pour over the lamb and garnish the whole platter with fresh coriander. Accompany with thick Greek-style yoghurt and a fresh green salad.
• Serves six.

Other lamb recipes

Lemons

The inner city suburb of Melbourne where we live sports the usual signs of a neighbourhood on the up-and-up. We are surrounded by skips full to the brim with cast-off furniture and the noise of builders' drills fills the air. In recent years a number of bright young things (like us!) have moved into the area, but the streets around us are peopled by the same Greek and Italian families who moved in during the 1950s. Many still live in the same old workers' cottages, some have renovated, or added grand extensions, but the one thing they have in common is a lemon tree in the garden!

For our Greek neighbours it is inconceivable that they could live without a lemon tree close at hand. It is easy to understand why. The lemon must surely be the most indispensable item for any cook. Lemon is one of the most popular flavours for desserts – both its juice and its zest add a refreshing zing to cakes, tarts, puddings, sorbets and refreshing summer drinks. Lemon juice adds a piquant tang to salad dressings and brings grilled meat and poultry to life, while fried fish and seafood are unthinkable without an accompanying lemon wedge. As well as bringing out the flavours of most foods, lemon juice is also useful as a tenderiser and colour preserver. Rubbing the cut surface of an avocado with lemon juice will stop it going brown, and similarly, fruits and vegetables such as apple and artichoke can be prevented from discolouring by keeping them in acidulated water.

We tend to think of lemons as being quintessentially Mediterranean, but it seems likely that the lemon and its forebear, the citron, originated in northern India, and from there spread to Mesopotamia and Persia. But lemons and other citrus fruits (apart from the thickly pithed bitter citron, which was widely cultivated by Jews for use in religious ceremonies) were not widely known in the Mediterranean until the spread of Islam in the seventh century.

The Arabs loved citrus trees, not just for their fruit, but for their fragrant blossoms and leaves. They treated their empire in Spain as a big citrus orchard – it was they who planted the courtyards of the Alhambra with orange and lemon trees, and who filled the *Patios de los naranjos* outside the Great Mosques in Cordoba and Seville.

The Arab and Persian penchant for sour flavourings is evident in their use of ingredients such as verjuice, tamarind, pomegranate and, of course, lemon in many dishes. A lemony tang is the unifying characteristic of most Middle Eastern dips – baba ghanoush, hummus, skordalia and taramasalata all have a distinctive lemon flavour. This preference also underpins many of their fruit and meat combinations. The strong, fatty mutton which is the basis of most meat dishes benefits enormously from sharpening with fruits like apricots, pomegranates and lemons. One of the characteristics of Moroccan cuisine – learned from the Arabs – is the use of whole preserved lemons in meat stews known as 'tagines'.

SELECTING AND STORING LEMONS

If you have had the foresight to plant a lemon tree in your backyard you are very fortunate. The rest of us have to make do with lemons from the local market, greengrocer or supermarket and there are a couple of things to bear in mind. Firstly, choose organically grown fruit if you can. Most commercially grown lemons are picked green, when they are most acid – this is also what makes them keep so well. Once picked, though, lemons do not ripen any more, so to make them that bright sunshiny yellow we all love, lemons are treated with ethylene gas. This destroys the chlorophyll and leaves behind only the yellow pigment.

Thin-skinned lemons tend to be juicier and are ideal for preserving. Thick-skinned lemons are good for zesting. However, any lemon you buy should feel weighty, an indication of its juiciness. Lemons should be wiped dry, as they have a tendency to go mouldy if damp. They can sit happily in a bowl on the kitchen table, where they will cheer up the room with their sunny hue. In a humid climate, though, they will last better if refrigerated.

Lemons, and indeed other citrus fruits, are often waxed to a shiny gloss before they are stored. So if you are planning to use the zest, make sure you wash and dry the skins very well before zesting.

USING LEMONS

To improve the yield of juice from lemons, soak them in warm water for 20 minutes of so before squeezing. Lemon juice will keep for 4–5 days in the refrigerator and can also be frozen. To maximise the lemony flavour, add lemon zest to a dish, as it is the skin of the lemon that contains the intense essential lemon oil. To zest a lemon, carefully remove the yellow skin (avoid the pith, which is bitter) with a zester. This will peel away long, thin threads of lemon skin, which usually need to be chopped more finely with a sharp knife. If you don't possess a lemon zester, then a vegetable peeler will also do for removing thin slices of peel, which, again, will need to be chopped finely. A grater will also work, but tends get clogged up with a wet, sticky mess.

LEMON RECIPES

Preserved lemons with honey

Preserving lemons in salt, Moroccan-style, adds complex spicy undertones to the sourness of the lemons. The addition of honey, cinnamon and coriander seeds gives further depth and a more rounded sweetness. This version uses a trick learned from Claudia Roden, which involves freezing the lemons first to speed up the whole maturing process. For a delightful change you can try the same recipe using limes.

Use only the rind of preserved lemons and discard the flesh. Add the finely chopped skin of ½ a preserved lemon to 80 g of butter and use it to stuff a chicken under the skin before roasting, or rub over skewers of tiger prawns before barbecuing. Thinly sliced, it adds a piquancy to tagines and other braises and fricassees. Use it to make a sensational Preserved Lemon Oil (page 181) for vinaigrettes and salad dressings. Or finely chop it and add to mayonnaise, hollandaise sauce or even guacamole.

1.5 kg thin-skinned lemons

350 g salt

1 tablespoon coriander seeds, lightly crushed

2 cinnamon sticks

2 lemon leaves or bay leaves

¼ cup honey

1 cup lemon juice

3 cups warm water

• Wash and dry the lemons. Cut them lengthways into quarters from the point of the lemon to three-quarters of the way down, but leaving them joined together at base. Place them in a plastic bag in the freezer for 24 hours.
• Remove the lemons from the freezer and allow them to defrost. Stuff the centre of each lemon with a heaped teaspoon of salt. Arrange them neatly in a 2 litre jar, sprinkling each layer of lemons with salt and crushed coriander seeds.
• Place the sticks of cinnamon down the sides of the jar along with the lemon leaves or bay leaves. Mix together the honey and lemon juice with the warm water until the honey dissolves. Pour into the jar, covering the lemons entirely, and screw the lid on tightly. Place a piece of cardboard on the bottom of a large pot and sit the jar on top. This stops it vibrating. Add warm water to cover the jar completely and slowly bring it to the boil. Boil for 6 minutes then remove from heat. Gently lift the jar from the pot.
• Store in a dry cool place a month before opening. Once opened, keep refrigerated. If the lemons are not frozen first, then the maturation process will take at least 3 months.

Preserved lemon guacamole with smoked eel and pine nut wafers

GUACAMOLE

1 large ripe-but-firm avocado, cut into ½ cm dice

1 small tomato, skinned, de-seeded and cut into ½ cm dice

⅓ cup coriander leaves, chopped

1 fresh green chilli, seeded, scraped and finely chopped

juice of 1 lime

1 clove garlic crushed with ½ teaspoon salt

½ preserved lemon, skin only, finely chopped

½ medium purple onion, finely chopped

1 small smoked eel, skinned and filleted

8 Pine Nut Wafers (page 209)

30 ml extra-virgin olive oil for sprinkling

1 teaspoon sumac (optional)

salt and pepper

• Gently combine all guacamole ingredients in a large mixing bowl.
• Carefully divide the eel into two long fillets. Depending on the size of the eel, you will probably only need to use one of these. Cut it into strips about 5 cm long, and cut each piece in half lengthways to give a total of 12 strips.
• To serve, lay a wafer on the plate and place 3 strips of eel on top. Place a heaped spoonful of guacamole on top of the eel, and finish with another wafer.
• Drizzle a little extra-virgin olive oil around the plate and sprinkle with sumac and salt and pepper, if desired.

Preserved lemon butter

Use this tangy-salty butter to stuff under the skin of a chicken before roasting.

175 g softened butter

1 Preserved Lemon with Honey (page 155) skin only, finely chopped

2 shallots, finely chopped

½ clove garlic, finely chopped

1 tablespoon parsley, finely chopped

1 teaspoon thyme leaves, finely chopped

½ teaspoon sumac

• Add all the ingredients to the softened butter and mix thoroughly.
• Shape into a rough sausage shape and place onto a square of greaseproof paper. Roll to a smooth log and then wrap in cling film and refrigerate until needed.
• It will keep in the freezer for 3-4 weeks.
• Cut off discs and use as required.

Avgolemono

This egg-and-lemon combination is a Greek favourite sauce and soup. But the combination is also considered a cornerstone of Sephardic cooking. Claudia Roden's fascinating book of Jewish food has several recipes for this as a sauce, and she suggests that it was probably Portuguese or Spanish in origin. Made like a custard, it is similar in flavour to a hollandaise, but much lighter and fresher in the absence of large amounts of butter.

2 whole eggs

1 egg yolk

juice of 1 lemon

100 ml chicken stock

pinch sumac

• In a small pan, whisk together the whole eggs and egg yolk with the lemon juice. In a separate pot bring the stock to the boil and add one tablespoon of it to the egg mixture. Mix in well, then pour the whole thing back into the hot stock, stirring well.

• Cook gently over a very low heat, stirring constantly with a wooden spoon. It will gradually start to thicken. Continue cooking and stirring until the sauce is thick enough to hold a line drawn across the back of a wooden spoon.

• Remove from the heat and straight away pour the sauce into a clean bowl.

• It can be served hot or cold and is a light tangy accompaniment to most seafood and fish, oysters, brains or even simply steamed vegetables.

Lemon curd fool

Serve this lemony fool with Sesame-Honey Wafers (page 252), or to accompany Sticky Lemon-Yoghurt Cake (page 291), or any other nutty, citrussy syrup cake. The curd can also be folded into an ice-cream base for a stunning lemon ice-cream.

juice and zest of 2 lemons

90 g butter

175 g castor sugar

3 eggs, beaten

½ litre pure cream

60 ml caramel

• To make the lemon curd, finely chop the lemon zest and place it with the juice, butter and sugar on the top of a double boiler. Heat and stir until the sugar is completely dissolved, then pour in the eggs. Continue to heat gently, stirring all the time, until the mixture thickens. Do not allow it to boil.

• Strain and chill. When you are ready to serve, whip the cream to soft peaks and swirl in the lemon curd and caramel. Serve in a glass bowl, or individual glass dishes for the full effect.

Other lemon recipes

Date-Lemon Chutney, page 104
Marinated Baby Lamb with Lebanese Nut Rice, pages 150–151
Preserved Lemon Oil, page 181
Preserved Lemon Gremolata, page 190
Risotto with Zucchini, Prawns and Preserved Lemon, page 231
Sticky Lemon-Yoghurt Cake, page 291

Lentils

As with so many of the world's subsistence foods, lentils have received bad press through the ages! Sneered at by the wealthy, and moaned about by the poor, who have so often depended upon them as their staple diet, they are also considered dull and bland and worse still, suffer a disturbing reputation for causing flatulence.

And yet, despite all this, people have been stolidly munching away on lentils for many thousands of years. Their place of origin is believed to be somewhere in the Middle East, and archaeologists have found evidence of their cultivation as early as the seventh century BC, in sites ranging from Iraq, Turkey and Egypt to China.

The reason for the lentil's unpopularity really has little to do with its taste, but rather its relentless availability. Through long dark winters when other fresh vegetables were lacking, families could always rely upon their store of lentils for the cooking pot. Similarly, when meat is scarce – as indeed it has been for most of the world's population since the beginning of time – lentils and other pulses have always been cheap and easy to grow.

Furthermore, in the world of pulses, lentils are second only to soya beans for their high protein content and when combined with other grains, cereals or nuts they provide us with nearly all our necessary daily proteins. Lentils are also high in fibre and a variety of minerals, low in fat – and very politically correct!

The combining of various plant foods to boost the protein value of a dish is a common practice throughout the Middle East. Lentil and rice dishes feature everywhere: the Lebanese have their mjaddarah (lentils and rice), while the Egyptians call a similar dish megadarra. In Iran they enjoy addas polow, a creamy lentil-rice dish enlivened with chopped dates and raisins. In India they pour dhal on rice and scoop it up with flat breads. Lentil soups around the Arab world also usually include cracked wheat, noodles or rice.

Although many people think lentils are dull and flavourless, it is this same soothing blandness which makes them the perfect vehicle for herbs, spices and other aromatics. Think of spicy Indian dhal and Moroccan harira soup, or lentil and spinach soup, all tangy with lemon, and a favourite all around the Middle East. Gently braised with a piece of smoked bacon, in the northern European tradition, lentils are deliciously earthy and comforting and act as the perfect foil to rich smoked meats and sausages.

SELECTING AND STORING LENTILS

Most lentils are readily available from supermarkets, health food stores and Middle Eastern and Indian specialist stores. They can be divided into three broad colour groups: brown/green, red and the grey Puy lentils from France. These latter lentils are available from smart delicatessens and specialist food stores.

There are several different varieties of brown and green lentils (often also called 'Continental lentils') which taste very similar and can be used more or less interchangeably. They are large, whole and unskinned, so keep their shape and texture when cooked.

Red lentils are also sold as Egyptian lentils. They are small, skinned and split, so cook down rapidly to a soft purée and are best used for soups and dips.

Puy lentils are currently the darlings of the foodie world. These tiny blue-grey lentils have become ultra-fashionable, as they have an excellent flavour and, though small, maintain their shape and texture well. They are ideal for salads or as a simple lentil braise to accompany meaty sausages or smoked pork dishes.

As with all pulses, store lentils in an airtight container in a cool, dark cupboard. They will keep well for about a year, but will begin to age and deteriorate from then, losing their shape and texture on cooking.

USING LENTILS

Most of the pre-packaged varieties of lentil have been thoroughly washed and checked over for grit and gravel. If you buy them loose, though, you should certainly give them a good wash in several changes of water and check them carefully.

Unlike many other pulses, lentils don't need to be soaked. After washing and draining they should be cooked in plenty of stock or plain water. The cooking time for lentils will vary depending on their type and on the dish – for example, in salads they need to be tender but still retain their shape, whereas for soups and purées they can be cooked down to a creamy mush.

LENTIL RECIPES

Green lentil soup with saffron-scrambled eggs

This is one of the best soups we can think of for a cold winter's night. It is deliciously warming and subtly spiced, and the creamy scramble of eggs makes it comforting and filling.

1 medium onion, finely chopped

80 ml olive oil

1 clove garlic, finely chopped

2 green chillies, de-seeded, scraped and finely chopped

350 g green lentils

1 teaspoon allspice

1 teaspoon honey

juice and zest of 1 lemon

1½ litres vegetable stock or water

salt and pepper

1½ cups fresh coriander leaves

5 eggs

10 saffron strands, lightly roasted and crushed

80 ml thickened cream

salt and pepper

50 g butter

extra-virgin olive oil

extra fresh coriander leaves to garnish

• Heat the oil in a heavy pan and sweat the onion for 2 minutes until it is softened. Add the garlic and green chillies, and cook a further minute. Add the lentils, allspice, honey, lemon juice and zest, and then the vegetable stock or water. Season with salt and pepper and bring to the boil. Skim, lower heat and simmer for 45 minutes until the lentils are very tender. Add the coriander and remove from the heat. Allow to rest uncovered for 10 minutes before blending to a purée in liquidiser or food processor.

• Taste and adjust seasoning and thin with a little more stock if necessary.

• Lightly combine the eggs with the saffron, cream and a little salt and pepper. Melt the butter and cook the eggs over a very gentle heat until they are very softly scrambled.

• To serve, bring the lentil soup to the boil, skim and pour into serving bowls. Top with a spoonful of the scrambled eggs, drizzle with a little extra-virgin olive oil and garnish with fresh coriander leaves.

• Serves six.

Mjaddarah

Just about every country and region of the Middle East has its own lentil and rice dish. The Turks have their lentil pilafs, the Persians their addas polow and everywhere there are versions of mjaddarah (Lebanon and Syria), moudjendar (Cyprus) or megadarra (Egypt). It must be said that this homely dish doesn't look very special – just a brown sort of mush. But it is fantastic comfort food – sweet and earthy, and topped with heaps of caramelised onions. It is a great home-cooked favourite in Lebanese and Syrian families, and is often eaten during Lent, or on Fridays and other meat-free days with a sharp lemony salad such as Fattouche (page 261).

80 ml olive oil

1 medium brown onion, diced small

185 g brown lentils

4½ cups water

80 g long-grain rice, washed well
    and drained

½ teaspoon cumin

2 medium onions, sliced

- Heat half the oil and sauté the diced onion until soft. Add the lentils and half the water, cover and cook for 15 minutes (or until lentils are just cooked). Add the rice, mix well and continue cooking for a further 15 minutes, stirring every now and then and gradually adding more of the water as it is absorbed.
- The dish is ready when lentils have broken down almost to a purée and the rice grains have swelled and almost burst – in fact, it looks rather like an unappetising khaki brown porridge! Add the cumin and stir well. Heat the remaining oil and cook the sliced onions over a low to medium heat for 5–8 minutes until they have caramelised.
- Serve the mjaddarah at room temperature garnished with the onions.
- Serves four to six.

Chicken in parchment with Moroccan aromatics and lentils

This is an ideal dinner party dish. Everything can be prepared ahead of time, and needs simply to be reheated for serving. Served in individual parchment parcels, it also brings a touch of drama to the dinner table.

100 g French Puy lentils

½ medium onion

1 cinnamon stick

4 stalks thyme

1½ kg chicken pieces on the bone

1 cup plain flour

1 teaspoon sweet paprika

1 teaspoon salt

60 ml olive oil

1 large brown onion, finely chopped

400 g potatoes, peeled and cut into 2 cm dice

200 g carrots, scraped and cut into 2 cm dice

2 tablespoons Chermoula (page 67)

1 can crushed tomatoes (400 g)

½ preserved lemon, skin only, finely chopped

1 litre chicken stock

300 g pumpkin, peeled and cut into 2 cm dice

salt and pepper

¼ cup parsley leaves, finely chopped

¼ cup coriander leaves, finely chopped

- Place the lentils in three times their volume of cold water with the onion half, cinnamon stick and thyme. Bring to the boil, then lower the heat and simmer uncovered for 20 minutes, or until they are just tender. Strain.
- Mix the flour and paprika. Dust the chicken pieces in the spiced flour. Heat the olive oil in a large heavy-based pan, add the chicken pieces and sauté until they are golden all over. Add the onion, potatoes and carrots and mix well. Add the Chermoula, coating all the ingredients, then add the crushed tomatoes, the chopped preserved lemon and the chicken stock. Bring to the boil, then lower the heat, cover and simmer for 8 minutes. Add the lentils and pumpkin, and cook without the lid for a further 5 minutes, by which time the vegetables should all be just tender and the chicken just cooked. Remove the pan from the heat. Allow to cool and then refrigerate overnight.
- To serve, preheat the oven to 180°C. Using non-stick baking parchment, cut four 40 cm lengths to make four squares. Fold each square into sixteenths, trim around the ends then open up to form the rough circle. Place the circle into a fairly deep bowl and heap in a quarter of the mixture, ensuring even amounts of chicken, vegetables and sauce. Sprinkle with the chopped parsley and coriander. Gather the edges of the paper together above the mixture and tie with kitchen string so you have a little

bag. Place the parcels in a baking tray and cover with tin foil (this stops the tops from getting crispy and the string from burning).

• Cook for half an hour and serve individual parcels for each person to break into it to release the delicious aromatic braise within.

• Serve with Buttered Couscous (page 91), Cracked-Wheat Pilaf (page 33) or even Fried Pine Nut Gnocchi (page 208).

Other lentil recipes

Moroccan Chickpea Soup with Sautéed Garlic Prawns, page 55
Green Olive and Lentil Dip, page 176

Mint

Minty things are all around us, from breath-freshening toothpastes and chewing gums to palate-cleansing after-dinner sweets. Yet in western kitchens not nearly enough is made of the humble mint. The most exciting thing that many of us do with it is to chop and scatter a handful on new season's potatoes and garden peas, or drown it in vinegar to serve with roast lamb.

Why this reluctance to use one of the most readily available herbs? Mint must surely be the easiest herb in the whole world to grow! Unless vigorously pruned, it runs rampant in most backyards. It is ideally suited to a window box, which contains its aggressive root system better. Even if you have no patch of earth in which to plant a few mint cuttings, these days, neat little bunches of the fresh herb are available from supermarkets pretty much all year round.

In the Levant countries and all around the Mediterranean people buy great armfuls of all kinds of fresh herbs and use them lavishly. Mint is certainly one of the most popular, loved for its cleansing fresh flavour during the long hot summer months. In Lebanon, Syria, Iraq and Iran freshly picked mint leaves are tossed into mixed-leaf salads. Mint is also a key ingredient in the Lebanese favourites tabbouleh and fattouche. Fresh mint is often eaten with soft white cheeses and fresh bread, perhaps with a dish of olives or a drizzle of olive oil. Small bunches of mint are a classic garnish for all kinds of mezze dishes, in particular the Lebanese national dish, kibbeh nayee. Often fresh mint and other herbs are set on the table in a small jug to be nibbled at during the meal.

In Morocco, fresh mint is essential for the sweet green tea served endlessly throughout the day and night. Although it is traditionally served very sweet, its mintiness makes it surprisingly refreshing. Mint, with its sharp clean taste, is an ideal palate-cleanser, and is frequently partnered with cucumber or yoghurt to make dressings, chilled soups and cooling relishes, which make a terrific foil for hot and spicy dishes. This combination is used throughout the Middle East and eastern Mediterranean (and also in India, where raitas are a popular accompaniment to spicy curries). Fresh mint is also used to add a characteristic sweet flavour to a number of hot savoury dishes – either mixed into rice and meat stuffings, or packed on top of braised dishes such as vine leaves or koussa while they are cooking.

Mint is one of the few herbs which retain their flavour when dried. All around the Middle East and in countries like Turkey and Greece, many households dry their own mint and use it even more than the fresh herb. Dried mint works particularly well with fresh white cheeses such as fetta or curds, and is often added to flavour little cheese pies. In Cyprus dried mint is used to flavour haloumy, and you can see little flecks in the surrounding brine. Egg dishes are commonly flavoured with a sprinkle of dried mint. A great Lebanese favourite is eggah – a classic flat omelette, coloured bright-green from its addition. The Lebanese version of tzatziki, khiyar bi laban, also uses dried mint rather than fresh.

SELECTING AND STORING MINT

If you grow your own mint you will need to pick it constantly to keep it at bay. But this shouldn't be too burdensome – even if you can't face eating it at every meal, its fragrance fills the kitchen delightfully. Growing it at home also means you have the luxury of choosing different varieties – not just common old spearmint (or garden mint) but also peppermint (cultivated commercially for pharmaceutical and food flavourings), applemint, lemon mint, pineapple mint and old-fashioned pennyroyal.

If you buy mint in the shops it is likely you will get spearmint, which is the most common variety grown commercially. This is available all year from supermarkets and greengrocers, but it is most abundant in summer. When purchasing, try to avoid bunches with wilted drooping leaves, especially if they appear to be turning black. Don't wash mint until you are ready to use it, as water makes the leaves blacken and rot more quickly.

Store it in the refrigerator and use it within a few days. A sprig of mint in a glass on the window sill won't last very long, but will make the kitchen smell fresh, sweet and clean for a day or so.

As for dried mint, you can find little packets at the supermarket, which are fine, but drying it yourself is even better. Strip the leaves from the stalks and lay them on greaseproof paper to dry over several days – or place them outside in the sun until completely dry.

USING MINT

Wash and dry fresh mint well before using. If you need it chopped, do so at the last minute with a sharp knife – using a blunt knife only bruises it. If you must use mint as a garnish, don't use timid, little individual leaves, but big, generous bunches.

Other mint recipes

MINT RECIPES

Minted split pea soup

This is a fabulously minty soup – a kind of variation on a classic fresh pea version – but using split peas means you can enjoy it all year round. Of course you could also make it in the summer when fresh peas are plentiful, which makes for a slightly lighter textured soup. If you make it ahead of time it will thicken up and you may like to thin it with a little extra stock or water before serving.

300 g green split peas

60 ml olive oil

I medium onion, finely sliced

I clove garlic, finely chopped

100 g butter or cos lettuce, roughly shredded

½ teaspoon dried mint

1½ litres vegetable or light chicken stock

½ cup fresh mint leaves, roughly chopped

salt and pepper

• Pick over the split peas and remove any stones, dirt and yellow peas.
• Heat the oil in a pan and add the onion, garlic and lettuce. Sauté gently for a few minutes, then add the dried mint and split peas. Stir well. Add the stock and bring to the boil. Then lower the heat and simmer uncovered for about 40 minutes, or until the peas are soft. Add the roughly chopped fresh mint and cook a further 3–4 minutes to soften.
• Taste and season with salt and pepper. Liquidise until very smooth, then strain to remove any bits.
• Garnish with Hot Mint Oil (page 170) and lightly whipped cream.
• Serves four to six.

Hot mint oil

A classic Persian recipe, hot mint oil is used a little like French pistou, for drizzling over all kinds of soups. You could also splash a little on fresh white cheese and eat it with hot, fluffy Turkish bread.

2 teaspoons olive oil

2 cloves garlic, finely chopped

1 teaspoon dried mint

• Heat the oil, then add the garlic and stir. Add the mint and immediately remove from the heat, as it burns quickly. Allow to infuse overnight. Sieve and use sparingly.

Minted cabbage salad

Cabbage salad is a popular Lebanese dish, often eaten as an accompaniment to kibbeh. This version includes both fresh and dried mint and is delightfully refreshing.

200 g Savoy cabbage, core removed
  and very finely shredded

⅓ cup watercress leaves

⅓ cup mint leaves

juice of 1 lemon

1 large clove garlic crushed with
  1 teaspoon salt

50 ml extra-virgin olive oil

1 teaspoon dried mint

salt and pepper

• In a large bowl, mix together the cabbage with the watercress and mint leaves. In a separate bowl, blend the lemon juice with the crushed garlic, extra-virgin olive oil and dried mint. Pour the dressing over the salad ingredients and toss lightly. To serve, twist small handfuls of the cabbage in the palm of your hand to form little turbans.

Hot mussel salad with fetta and fennel

This is a delightful salad full of clean, refreshing flavours like the salty fetta and aniseedy fennel. The juices from the mussels blend beautifully with the minty-lemon dressing, and make the whole dish taste of the sea. Eat as a salad with plenty of hot, crusty bread, or top each serve with a little turban of egg noodles, briefly sautéed in lemon butter.

1¼ kg fresh black rope mussels

2 tablespoons olive oil

1 onion, roughly chopped

1 celery stick, roughly chopped

2 cloves garlic, roughly chopped

100 ml white wine

1 large purple onion

250 g fennel

acidulated water

180 g good quality fetta cheese

⅔ cup watercress or parsley leaves

DRESSING

125 ml extra-virgin olive oil

juice of 2 lemons

1 clove garlic crushed with
   1 teaspoon salt

1 teaspoon dried mint

black pepper

TO SERVE

360 g egg noodles

1 tablespoon butter

juice of ½ lemon

salt and pepper

- Scrub the mussels clean of any sand and dirt and pull away the beards. In a heavy-based pot heat the olive oil and sauté the onion, celery and garlic. Add the wine and mussels. Cover and steam on a high heat for 3 minutes. Uncover and stir them around well, then steam for a further 2 minutes. Remove from the heat and leave covered to steam for another minute of so. Then strain off the liquor, reserving for future use. Discard the aromatics and any unopened mussels.
- Slice the whole onion into rings as finely as possible, then rinse it under cold running water for about 4 minutes. This crisps it up and softens the sharp flavour. Slice the fennel in half, remove the core, slice it very thinly lengthways and cover it with acidulated water until it is required.
- For the dressing, whisk the oil and lemon together, then add the garlic paste, 2 tablespoons of the mussel liquor, the dried mint and a grind of black pepper.
- To serve, place the fennel, onions, crumbled fetta and watercress in a mixing bowl. Add the mussels and dressing and mix carefully.
- Cook and drain the egg noodles, then sauté them briefly in butter and add the lemon juice, salt and pepper. Use a fork to twist into six little turbans and arange on top of salad.
- Serves six as a starter or light lunch.

Olives and Olive Oil

OLIVES

We 20th century folk consider ourselves pretty clever, with the sophisticated food-processing techniques we have at hand to help us manufacture and manipulate all sorts of fancy new foodstuffs. And yet consider the miracle wrought by our forbears on one of the most ancient trees we know: it seems barely credible that primitive man was able to develop ways of extracting oil from the hard little fruit of the olive tree, let alone work out a way to make these same fruit edible.

The olive tree is inextricably entwined with the history and development of Mediterranean civilisations. The olive tree has been cultivated for over 6000 years, beginning in Palestine and Syria. It was here that the wild tree developed into a sturdy, compact, oil-rich variety which quickly spread westwards to flourish all around the rocky coastlines of the Mediterranean. The great ancient civilisations of Crete, Egypt, Greece and Rome revered the olive's oil. It was used in ritual and religion, to light their temples, to anoint their bodies and also to work a more mundane transformation on their daily bread. Through the ages the olive branch has become a symbol of peace, constancy and wisdom – one might almost say of civilisation itself.

It remains a mystery when the discovery was first made that the small, bitter berries of the olive tree could be made edible by a complex curing process. Soaking in lye, rinsing, salting and preserving in oil or brine with herbs and other aromatics results in a unique, complex taste sensation – at once salty, bitter and pungent, with a hint of ripe sweetness. It is hardly surprising that cured olives quickly became a staple of the Mediterranean and Middle Eastern diet.

Each olive-growing country produces its own style of olive, the variations depending on soil, climate and local tradition. Green olives are young fruit, harvested when they are still rock-hard and unripe. Left on the tree, they slowly ripen to a soft purple, and finally to rich black. From here, the curing process complete, there is a bewildering range of sizes, shapes, textures and flavours: big, juicy kalamata olives from Greece; small, intensely flavoured niçoise olives; garlicky, chilli-spiced olives found in the souks of Morocco: plump, almond-stuffed green olives from Spain.

Different regions also eat olives in very different ways. Countries to the east, such as Egypt, Greece, Turkey, Lebanon and Syria, don't really use olives in cooked dishes. They eat predominantly black olives as appetisers, side dishes, snacks and garnishes. In the west, countries like Morocco, Tunisia, Spain, Portugal, Italy and France make more use of green olives. They also like to use olives, both green and black, as an ingredient in many cooked dishes.

SELECTING AND STORING OLIVES

In the souks of the Middle East, you are absolutely expected to taste before you buy, and the best advice we can give for choosing olives anywhere in the world is to do just this. There are so many different sorts to choose from, and they vary in flavour and quality so much, that it really is important to taste them first. For these reasons too, it is much better to buy olives where they are sold loose rather than bottled.

As a very general rule, green olives tend to have a lighter, grassier flavour, with firmer flesh, which clings to the stone. Softer and juicier, black olives tend to have a stronger and more complex flavour. Olives are often sold flavoured with all sorts of herbs and aromatics – bay leaves, rosemary, fennel, lemon and orange peel are all popular.

Olives do not have to be kept refrigerated, as long as they are stored in an airtight container in a cool, dark cupboard. If you do prefer to keep them in the refrigerator, make sure you allow them to return to room temperature before serving, to bring out their flavour.

USING OLIVES

If you intend to use olives in cooking, you run across the unavoidable chore of having to stone them. It is a fiddly job, but has to be done. Ready-stoned olives tend to be poorer quality rejects which may have been damaged during the harvesting or curing process. As a rule, the soft, squishy black olives are much easier to stone than green olives, which often leave a lot of their flesh behind on the stone. The quickest, but least delicate, way of stoning them is to give them a good sharp bash with a rolling pin, which splits them open. It should then be quite easy to pull the stone away. If you want to do a neater job, then carefully slice them lengthways with a sharp knife, twist them apart and pry the stone out with your fingernails.

As a rule, it is best to add olives to hot dishes, like braises and stews, at the end of cooking. This will ensure that they retain their shape and texture, and that their strong, salty flavour doesn't overpower the dish.

OLIVE RECIPES

Coarse tapenade salad

A robust salad full of strong salty flavours. Serve it with grills of lamb or beef.

juice of 1 lemon

40 ml extra-virgin olive oil

200 g black olives, stoned and diced

50 kaiser fleisch, finely chopped and
  sautéed until crisp

1 small purple onion, roughly diced

1 clove garlic, finely sliced

1 red pepper, roasted, peeled and
  cut into 1 cm dice

6 anchovies, rinsed and cut into thirds

black pepper

1 tablespoon fresh thyme leaves,
  chopped

1 tablespoon baby capers, rinsed

1 bullet chilli, de-seeded and finely
  chopped

1 cup parsley leaves, shredded

• Whisk together the lemon juice and olive oil.
• Thoroughly combine all ingredients and serve.

Other olive recipes

Niçoise-Style Green Bean Salad, page 25
Spanish Chickpea and Potato Salad, page 58

Green olive and lentil dip

This sludgy green lentil dip is fabulous with garlicky pork sausages or smoked ham.
Serve it with a drizzle of extra-virgin olive oil.

100 g brown lentils

1 tablespoon brandy

125 g pitted green olives

1 tablespoon small capers

2 anchovies

2 cloves garlic

½ teaspoon chilli flakes

1 tablespoon dried oregano

juice of 1 lemon

3 tablespoons extra-virgin olive oil

salt

a grind of black pepper

• Cook the lentils in twice their volume of water, at a rapid boil for 30 minutes, then strain them, reserving half a cup of the liquid. Place the lentils in a liquidiser with the brandy and purée while warm.
• Cover the olives in warm water and soak for 20 minutes, then drain. Rinse the capers and anchovies. In a heavy saucepan cook the olives, garlic, chilli and oregano with the reserved cooking liquid and boil for 5 minutes until the liquid has evaporated.
• Purée with the capers, anchovies and lemon juice. With the motor running add the oil very slowly, then tip into the lentil mixture and fold in well.
• Check seasoning, adding salt and pepper if needed.

Black olive cream

Light, lemony and with a sweet honey undertone, this delicate cream is delicious with any robust white fish. Serve a big blob of it, with grilled or sautéed snapper or John Dory. It is also good swirled into thick pulse-based soups. Choose a good flavoured fleshy olive, such as kalamata.

90 g black kalamata olives, stoned

40 ml olive oil

150 ml thickened cream

zest of ½ lemon

1 teaspoon honey

• Place the olives in a saucepan with the oil, cream, lemon zest and honey. Bring them to the boil, then lower the heat and simmer for 15 minutes. Remove them from the heat and allow them to cool completely.
• Purée. Chill.

ABOVE:
Chicken in parchment with
Moroccan aromatics and lentils
(recipe page 164)
BELOW:
Hot mussel salad with fetta
and fennel (recipe page 171)

Natural oysters with parsley–bastourma salad (recipe page 191)

OLIVE OIL

We are essentially a butter-free household, not only because Greg has to be careful with his cholesterol levels, but because we both prefer the underlying flavour olive oil imparts to many dishes. We use olive oil to cook with and as a condiment at mealtimes. In our view, there is virtually nothing which is not improved by a splash of fruity extra-virgin olive oil, whether it be a rich soup, a simple pasta, steamed crisp vegetables, grilled meats, chicken and fish, or a few humble leaves of lettuce.

Olive oil is the universal cooking medium of the Middle East and Mediterranean, and there is a wealth of literature praising its nutritional virtues, which we briefly touch on here. Beware of fanaticism, though; some dishes simply have to be made from butter. In Middle Eastern cooking these tend to be elaborate dishes like pastries, biscuits and cakes, which are eaten sparingly on special occasions.

Choosing a good extra-virgin olive oil has become a little like choosing a fine wine. Whether you choose a peppery Tuscan oil, a sweet, fruity Spanish, a bold, pungent Greek, a lighter floral French or a boutique Australian oil will depend on your personal preference. It makes sense to experiment and try all kinds of different oils.

OLIVE OIL AND CHOLESTEROL

It is universally acknowledged that replacing part of the animal fat content of our diet with olive oil can radically reduce levels of cholesterol. Current research centres around two main types of lipoproteins: low-density lipoproteins and high-density lipoproteins. The low-density ones (the 'baddies') move cholesterol around the body and leave deposits in the arteries and body tissue. They increase with our consumption of saturated animal fats. However, high-density lipoproteins (the 'goodies') have actually been shown to eliminate cholesterol from cells.

Polyunsaturated fats (found in sunflower and vegetable oils) have been shown to reduce both kinds of lipo-protein, whereas only monounsaturated fats reduce the level of the 'baddies', and actually increase the 'goodies'. Oils such as canola, peanut, sunflower and nut oils do all contain varying small levels of monounsaturated fats, but olive oil has the highest percentage of all, by far (55–83 per cent).

As well as being good for the heart, olive oil also contains small levels of a range of other nutrients and antioxidants, which are thought to play a part in reducing the risk of developing cancers. Extra-virgin olive oil, the purest form, has the widest range of all these.

A word of caution, however: despite its good qualities, olive oil is still a fat, and therefore high in calories. If you are concerned about your weight, it makes sense to limit your consumption of all oils and fats. However, you might choose to use extra-virgin olive oil, as its stronger flavour means that you will be inclined to use only small amounts.

SELECTING AND STORING OLIVE OIL

Light olive oil
This is not light in terms of calories, as the labelling might lead us to think, but rather in terms of flavour. This type of oil is a blend of lesser quality oils, which have been refined to give a mild, neutral flavour.

'Pure' olive oil
This is blend of refined oils with lesser quality unrefined virgin olive oil to give it some flavour. It is best used for general cooking purposes

Virgin olive oil
Virgin olive oil is extracted from the fruit by means which do not alter it in any way. This essentially means that no solvents and only minimal heat are used in the extraction process. The oil is not refined in any way and is not blended with other oils. Virgin olive oil is graded by its acidity – the lower the better. Less expensive virgin olive oils have an acidity of 1.5–3 per cent

Extra-virgin olive oil
This is the purest form of the oil, with the best flavour and lowest levels of acidity (below 1 per cent). It is also the most expensive. Some extra-virgin

olive oils are labelled 'first pressed' or 'cold pressed', which means little when used by the big brand-name commercial manufacturers – most olive oil these days is extracted using mega-presses, which extract the maximum amount of oil from just one press.

Small estates that press their own extra-virgin olive oils are a different matter. They fall under the same classification system, but are hugely superior. These oils may be extracted from organically grown olives using old-fashioned stone-milling techniques and minimal filtering. If they are labelled 'cold pressed' it really does mean that no heat has been used to enhance the extraction process. 'First pressed' means that the bottle contains only oil from the initial pressing.

When buying extra-virgin olive oils, there are all manner of fancy-shaped bottles and names to choose from, particularly in trendy food stores and delicatessens. In Australia we are lucky enough to have a small range of locally produced single-estate Australian oils which are excellent, as well as a large range of imported oils from small producers in Italy, France, Spain and Greece. These can be very pricey, but the aroma, depth and complexity of flavour will knock your socks off!

It is best to buy expensive oils in small quantities, so experiment and choose a different one each time. Olive oil deteriorates with age and in light, so store it in a cool cupboard or larder, and try to use it within a year of purchase.

USING OLIVE OIL

For all-purpose frying and cooking it is best to choose a mild-flavoured good quality 'pure' olive oil, and this is what we mean in all recipes when we refer to 'olive oil'. Most supermarkets sell their own house brands as well as a range of imported Spanish, Greek and Italian oils. As a rule, most major brands will have a consistent and reasonably acceptable flavour.

Extra-virgin olive oil – especially the really expensive stuff – is better used in dishes in which you can appreciate its fine flavour. Use it liberally as a condiment: drizzle onto soups or braised dishes just before serving; sprinkle over your favourite pasta dish; brush it on grilled fish, poultry and meats; make a little well in the surface of dips and purées, and fill with oil; always dress salad leaves with a home-made olive oil dressing: and splash it about over fresh sun-ripened tomatoes with freshly torn basil leaves.

Olive oil is a very good choice for fried dishes. You might think that it is more expensive than a polyunsaturated oil such as corn or sunflower oil, but these can only be used once. Leading Australian nutritionist Rosemary Stanton says that olive oil may be used up to 40 times, if strained after each use, whereas polyunsaturated oils develop dangerous chemical compounds if reheated. She also advocates using olive oil for deep-frying, as food which is deep fried at hotter temperatures actually absorbs less fat than food that is shallow fried.

Other olive oil recipes

Coriander and Soft-Boiled Egg Vinaigrette, page 82
Whole Roasted Snapper with Walnut-Coriander Dressing, page 85
Cumin Rouille, page 98
Eggplant Tonnato, page 114
Pickled Eggplants with Walnuts and Chillies, page 115
Andalusian White Soup, page 127
Parsnip Skordalia, page 130
Hot Mint Oil, page 170
A la Grecque Dressing, page 246
Soused Zucchini and Eggplant, page 296

OLIVE OIL RECIPES

Preserved lemon oil

The variety of flavoured oils is really only limited by your imagination. Preserved lemon oil is a firm favourite of ours. It should be used to add flavour to dishes, not for frying or cooking. It makes a surprising tangy change in vinaigrettes and salad dressings. Or drizzle it straight onto fish or poultry after grilling.

2 preserved lemons, skin only

2 lemons, cut into quarters

1 teaspoon coriander seeds, crushed

½ teaspoon black peppercorns, crushed

250 ml olive oil

• Scrape the flesh out of the preserved lemons and discard. Finely dice the skins and place into a 500 ml jar with the fresh lemon quarters, the coriander seeds and the black peppercorns. In a saucepan, gently warm the oil to blood temperature and pour over the lemons. Seal the jar tightly and allow to sit, undisturbed, for 3 days.

• Strain the oil through a tea-towel – allow it to drain naturally. Don't be tempted to push it through, as this will cloud the oil. Pour it into a sterilised bottle, reseal and use as desired.

• This infused oil will keep up to a month in a cool dark cupboard.

Green olive mayonnaise

2 egg yolks

1 teaspoon Dijon mustard

1 teaspoon white wine vinegar

250 ml olive oil

juice of ½ lemon

1 tablespoon green olives, chopped very finely

1 tablespoon baby capers

salt and pepper

• Whisk the egg yolks with the mustard and vinegar until they are light and creamy. Gradually add the olive oil, drop by drop, ensuring each amount is incorporated before adding more. When about half has been added you should have a very thick, glossy paste. Loosen the mixture with the lemon juice and then continue to add the olive oil in a slow trickle.

• Mix the olives and capers and add to the mayonnaise, taste and adjust seasoning and serve.

Orange-Blossom Water

A few years ago we spent an enchanted late-summer holiday pottering around Andalusia in southern Spain. We were there to explore the rich cultural heritage of the Moors – in the region's architecture, its gardens and, naturally enough, its cuisine. During those two weeks a benign sun shone down on us from a brilliant blue sky and, wherever we went, from the sun-dappled elegant city squares of Jerez to the shady, winding alleyways of Seville's Jewish quarter, the scent of orange blossom enveloped us, perfuming the air with its heady magic.

When Moorish invaders conquered Spain in the eighth century, they planted their new lands extensively with citrus trees from Persia, at the eastern end of their empire. In Andalusia's southern cities they constructed grand mosques, each of which had a *patio de los naranjos* alongside, the fragrant orange trees planted in austerely elegant lines. These were the bitter Seville oranges we favour today for jams and marmalades. The Arabs loved them not just for their bitter–sweet fruit, but also for their fragrant blossoms, leaves and twigs.

For many thousands of years, Persian and Arabic cooking has made liberal use of flower waters, such as rose petal and orange-blossom. A splash or two in an elaborate meat and fruit khoresht will lift it to another dimension. Orange-blossom water is frequently added to thirst-quenching fruit syrups and cooling sharbats, or sprinkled over simple summer fruit salads.

In Morocco too, they love the complex perfume of orange-blossom water, and sprinkle it over the traditional salad of grated carrot, which is served in just about every Moroccan restaurant to cleanse the palate after a rich tagine. All across the Maghreb and Levant, and even in parts of

Provence, a few drops of orange-blossom water flavour cookies and cakes, almond pastries and sweetmeats, milky puddings and refreshing fruit salads. It seems only natural that orange-blossom water should have a particular affinity with orangey things – and indeed just about any sweet orange dish, from a simple dish of sliced oranges to orange jellies, mousses, cakes and biscuits, is enhanced by a drop of its flower water.

In Lebanon orange-blossom water is even added to sweetened boiling water to make 'cafe blanc'. This has nothing at all to do with coffee beans, but is a soothing, fragrant digestive drink, often enjoyed at bedtime to ensure a sound night's sleep.

SELECTING, STORING AND USING ORANGE-BLOSSOM WATER

Orange-blossom water is made from the distilled flowers of orange trees. In the Middle East and North Africa you can often find concentrated floral essences, which are far stronger than the diluted flower waters available to us here. You will probably have to go to a specialist Middle Eastern or Asian grocer to find orange-blossom water. We use the Lebanese Cortas brand from choice.

Orange-blossom water has a fairly intense perfume and taste – too heavy a hand will result in food tasting of soap! Start with just a few drops – some people don't like their food overly perfumed, although they are happy with the gentlest suggestion of fragrance.

ORANGE-BLOSSOM WATER RECIPES

Perfumed pumpkin couscous

This is an oven-baked couscous dish with a surprise hidden layer of sweetly spiced pumpkin. It is good served with rich braises or stews.

120 g couscous

180 g butternut pumpkin, peeled and cut into 1 cm dice

1 teaspoon melted butter

salt and pepper to taste

¼ teaspoon cinnamon

20 g currants, soaked in water for 10 minutes

1 tablespoon water

½ tablespoon butter

orange-blossom water for sprinkling

• Prepare the couscous according to the instructions on the box, or use the quick-cook method on page 88.
• Steam the pumpkin for 5 minutes and then drain well. Brush a 16 cm × 26 cm baking dish with the melted butter and line the bottom with the pumpkin. Season lightly with salt, pepper and cinnamon.
• Sprinkle the currants over the pumpkin and then cover them with a layer of couscous. Lightly pack down and smooth the surface. Again, season lightly with salt and pepper. Drizzle a tablespoon of cold water around the edge of dish and dot a few knobs of butter over the top of the couscous. Cover with foil and bake in preheated 200°C oven for 15–20 minutes. Remove and sprinkle with orange-blossom water to serve.

Orange-blossom clotted cream

This perfumed cream is delicious served alongside almond, orange and lemon cakes, or with hot fruit tarts, roasted peaches or even Sweet Nut-Stuffed Quinces (page 225).

250 ml pure cream

50 ml sour cream

2 tablespoons mild-flavoured honey

zest of 1 orange, finely grated

1 teaspoon orange-blossom water

• Combine all the ingredients in a saucepan and very, very slowly bring them to the boil. As soon as the cream boils, lower the heat and keep it at a low simmer for 5 minutes. Tip it into a glass bowl and leave it overnight, outside the refrigerator, wrapped in a blanket.
• Refrigerate until required.

Orange-blossom tart

This sweet citrussy tart makes a pleasing change from plain lemon, once in a while. Orange-blossom jam is available from Middle Eastern grocers. The quantities below are enough to line one deep 20 cm tart ring, or one shallow 23 cm tart ring.

PASTRY

125 g plain flour

50 g castor sugar

70 g butter, chilled

zest of ½ orange

zest of ½ lemon

1 egg, chilled

1–2 tablespoons cold milk

FILLING

3 eggs, plus 1 yolk

90 g castor sugar

juice and zest of 1 orange

juice and zest of 1 lemon

½ teaspoon orange-blossom water

½ tablespoon orange-blossom jam

300 ml pure cream

• Place the flour, sugar and butter in the bowl of your food processor. Place the whole thing, blade too, in the freezer for 10 minutes. Remove and quickly pulse the ingredients to the texture of fine sand. Add the orange and lemon zest and the egg and pulse in quick bursts. Then add 1 tablespoon of the milk and pulse, adding the second if required. The mix will probably still look like buttery crumbs, but if you squeeze a little in your hand it should come together as a dough. Tip it out of the bowl and shape into a round. Wrap it in clingfilm and refrigerate for an hour.

• After an hour, roll out the pastry fairly thinly on a well-floured work surface and lift it onto a well-greased tart tin. Trim the edges and return it to the refrigerator for another hour. When you are ready to blind-bake the tart, preheat the oven to 180°C. Line the tart with foil, fill with beans and bake for 10 minutes. Then remove the foil and beans and cook for a further 10 minutes, or until the pastry has turned a pale golden.

• To make the filling, whisk the eggs and egg yolk with the sugar until they are combined. Add the juice and zest, the orange-blossom water and orange-blossom jam and stir. Pour in the cream and whisk together to incorporate.

• When you fill the tart, don't take it out of the oven – pull out the oven tray halfway and carefully pour the filling straight into the tart tin. Gently push the shelf back in and bake for 30–40 minutes, or until the filling is just set.

• Allow the tart to cool, and serve with slices of chilled fresh mangoes or peaches and a dollop of crème fraîche. Serves six.

Middle Eastern lemonade

This is an extremely simple lemonade, requiring no sugar syrup. The gritty action of sugar against the lemons' skins releases the essential oils. They should then be left to infuse for as many hours as you can wait. Make sure you use unwaxed fruit if possible, or at the very least scrub them well before you start. Serve the lemonade with plenty of crushed ice in tall glasses, with a drop of orange-blossom water to taste. Mixed with vodka and a few shredded mint leaves, this lemonade also makes a delicious cocktail for a hot summer's day.

5 whole lemons

I cup castor sugar

800 ml water

orange-blossom water to taste

• Wash the lemons very well, then cut them into eighths and place them in a large mixing bowl. Pour the sugar over the top and massage the lemons. The idea is to rub the sugar into the skins, as the abrasive action releases the lemon oils, and at the same time squeeze out as much juice as possible from the flesh. After about 5 minutes the sugar should have dissolved into a thick sticky syrup.

• Cover the bowl with clingfilm and chill in the refrigerator for 4 hours or so.

• Then add the water and return the bowl to the refrigerator to chill overnight.

• Strain and serve with lots of crushed ice and a few drops of orange-blossom water.

Other orange-blossom water recipes

Apricot and Orange-Blossom Cream, page 12
Cardamom Honey-Glazed Roast Duck, page 40
Cardamom-Orange Wafers, page 41
Honey-Roasted Pear and Walnut Salad, page 140

Parsley

Parsley is such a familiar and universal ingredient that even the most timid cook is happy to fling it about with gay abandon. We debated whether to include it in this book as it is so commonplace – that is to say, its distinctive, vital flavour is included in just about every savoury recipe you can think of, in many different cuisines. But just because something is commonplace doesn't mean it is not worth a mention!

Herbs have always been everyday ingredients for everyday folk – and not just in the kitchen either. As many as 5000 years ago the Sumerians and then the Egyptians were using them to concoct healing potions and remedies. Greek, Roman and Arab civilisations all contributed to the large body of herbal literature. Even today, a strong interest in herbalism and the healing power of plants persists. But on the whole, the medical and magical uses of herbs have dwindled and their main role is to brighten up our food with their pungent, lively flavours.

Of all the herbs, parsley is probably the favourite, loved the world over for its abundant, vivid green leaves and its vigorous, almost peppery flavour. In classical French cuisine parsley stalks are the backbone of the bouquet garni (with thyme and a bay leaf), which is used to flavour stocks, soups and casseroles. Finely chopped, its flavour is restrained enough to be used as a garnish for all kinds of savoury dishes, either on its own, or combined with equal quantities of finely chopped chervil, chives and tarragon to make fines herbes. Italian cooks sprinkle it over pasta and risotto dishes and combine it with lemon zest and garlic to make gremolata, the classic zesty garnish for rich, sticky osso buco and other hearty soups and stews. It tempers the stronger salty flavours of anchovy and capers in salsa verde, which accompanies poached chicken, fish and offal or boiled meats such as the favourite bollito misto.

Middle Eastern food is almost unthinkable without parsley. All sorts of dips and mezze dishes are garnished with roughly chopped parsley – never finely chopped, as in classical French cooking. The raw leaves are torn and tossed through countless refreshing salads – not just the ever-popular tabbouleh and fattouche. Parsley is often combined with lemon juice and garlic in dressings and marinades, which work particularly well with grilled poultry. It may also be combined with garlic and onion and other spices as a base for minced meat dishes such as kifta, or rice stuffings for vegetables.

SELECTING AND STORING PARSLEY

Large bundles of flat-leaf parsley look look a bit daunting next to those neat little posies of the curly sort, but the latter is barely known in the Middle East. Flat-leaf or Continental parsley has a much better flavour than the curly type. It is stronger and sweeter and perfectly suited to scattering around salads. Thankfully, these days it is widely available all year round.

Parsley is one herb which is totally unsatisfactory when dried. You really have to buy it fresh, but it keeps pretty well in the refrigerator. We store it in the refrigerator in a jug of water, with its head neatly tucked away in a plastic bag. If you remember to change the water every now and then, parsley lasts like this for up to a week. Alternatively, you can strip the leaves off, wash and dry them carefully, and keep them in a plastic container in the refrigerator.

USING PARSLEY

There is often grit and sand sticking to parsley leaves and stalks, so it is a good idea to wash it at least twice before picking the leaves from the stalks. A salad spinner is useful for drying them.

Parsley can be added to, and will improve just about every dish imaginable, so don't reserve it for use as a garnish. Middle Easterners buy herbs such as parsley in such dauntingly large quantities because they recognise the need to use lots and lots, not just a few dainty sprigs. Remember this particularly when it comes to making herb butters and sauces, which should be bright green and thick with the herb, not pale and speckled.

PARSLEY RECIPES

Preserved lemon gremolata

Gremolata is traditionally used to finish off the Italian dish osso buco, adding a sharp tangy counterpoint to the marrow-rich sticky dish. It can be used equally well with wintry braises and stews.

1 Preserved Lemon with Honey
  (page 155), skin only, finely chopped

1 cup parsley leaves, finely chopped

1 teaspoon sumac

2 cloves garlic, finely chopped

• Mix all the ingredients together and use as soon as possible for freshest flavour.

Other parsley recipes

Coarse Tapenade Salad, page 175
Fattouche, page 261

Natural oysters with parsley-bastourma salad

Bastourma is a Turkish air-dried beef, which has first been rubbed with fenugreek, chilli and sugar. You can find it at Turkish butchers and some Continental delicatessens. It is strongly flavoured and pungent, and very more-ish. Slivers of the beef with vital, metallic parsley work as a terrific counterfoil to the briny tannin flavours of natural oysters.

6 ripe tomatoes

50 g sugar

12 teaspoons water

30 ml olive oil for sautéing

200 g bastourma, thinly sliced then cut into 3 mm batons

1½ cups parsley leaves, shredded

100 g artichoke leaves

100 ml red wine vinegar

1 clove garlic, finely minced

100 ml extra-virgin olive oil

salt and black pepper

36 oysters, freshly opened

- Cut the tomatoes in half and scoop out the flesh and seeds.
- In a heavy pan, dissolve the sugar in 6 teaspoons water. Once it is fully dissolved simmer gently for 8 minutes, or until the syrup turns a deep-golden colour. Add 6 further teaspoons of warm water, stir and bring back to a simmer for 2 minutes more until the caramel thickens.
- Place the tomatoes on a rack, skin-side down, and drizzle the caramel over them. Leave them to dry in a preheated 140°C oven for 6–8 hours.
- Heat the olive oil in a heavy-based pan and sauté the bastourma over a high heat until it is crisp (around 3–4 minutes).
- Cut the caramelised tomatoes into thick strips. In a large bowl, mix together the tomatoes, bastourma, parsley, artichoke leaves, red wine vinegar, garlic and extra-virgin olive oil. Season lightly.
- For each person, arrange 6 oysters in their shells on a plate, and place a heaped spoonful of the parsley salad on top of each oyster.
- Serve straight away to six people as a starter.

Parsley salad with parmesan-crumbed brains and a tomato-pomegranate dressing

This makes a lovely light lunch for six people. The creamy brains in their crunchy crumb are perfectly offset by the peppery, bitter leaves and tangy sweet-sour Tomato-Pomegranate Dressing (page 218).

6 sets lamb's brains, cleaned and soaked overnight in milk

½ lemon

I cinnamon stick

½ onion, quartered

½ celery stick, roughly chopped

I bay leaf

salt and pepper

20 g grated parmesan cheese

80 g fresh breadcrumbs

flour for dusting

I egg

200 ml canola oil for shallow-frying

SALAD

1½ cups parsley leaves

1½ cups watercress sprigs

I head radicchio, leaves roughly torn

I purple onion, sliced finely

pepper

6 small rashers bacon, cut into batons and fried crisp

150 ml Tomato-Pomegranate Dressing (page 218)

• Rinse the brains and place them in saucepan. Cover them with cold water and add the lemon half, juice squeezed in first, with the cinnamon, onion, celery and bay leaf. Bring slowly to the boil, then lower the heat and simmer for 3 minutes. Remove from the heat and allow the brains to cool down in the poaching liquor.

• Dry each set of brains and cut it into quarters. Lightly season with salt and pepper. Combine the parmesan with the breadcrumbs and begin to flour, egg and crumb each portion of brain. Heat the oil in a wok, which is ideal for shallow-frying. Fry 6 pieces at a time for about 5 minutes, or until golden-brown.

• To assemble the salad, combine the parsley, watercress and radicchio leaves in large bowl with the onion and bacon. Season lightly with pepper and add half the Tomato-Pomegranate Dressing. Toss the leaves gently. Mound a portion in the centre of each plate and carefully arrange 4 pieces of crumbed brains on the top. Drizzle extra dressing around and serve straight away.

Prawns wrapped in almond kataifi (recipe page 199)

Sambusek (recipe page 200)

Pastry

Most people go somewhere romantic for their honeymoon: Fiji, Venice or Paris all fit the bill nicely. We, on the other hand, went to Beirut, better known in recent years for kidnapping, bullets and bombs! But so much for preconceived notions and worries. Beirut, and indeed the rest of Lebanon, proved to be a constant delight and endless fascination during our two-week stay.

Despite the ravages of seventeen years of civil war, one thing which has survived miraculously intact is the overwhelming warmth of Arabic hospitality. Every home we visited seemed to be mysteriously prepared for guests – their coffee tables were always set with little dishes of pistachio nuts, Turkish delight or other exotic sweets. Our arrival would cause a flurry of excitement, kisses and questions and, of course, instant refreshments. As if from nowhere, cardamom-scented coffee would appear, poured from exquisitely engraved brass pots into tiny cups, always accompanied by sweet nut-stuffed biscuits or elaborate sticky pastries.

Both the Arab and Ottoman empires excelled in the art of making pastries, cakes and biscuits. Their influence can be seen right across the Mediterranean in an endless variety of sweet and savoury pastries, ranging from the universally popular baklava and kataifi to savoury filo pies, such as Greek spanakopita and bisteeya, the extraordinary cinnamon-spiced pigeon pie from Morocco, to Lebanese filo 'cigars', Turkish boreks, and Tunisian briks à l'oeuf.

SELECTING, STORING AND USING PASTRY

Many of the Middle Eastern style recipes that follow both sweet and savoury, require special kinds of pastry which are virtually impossible to make at home. What a bonus for the weary home cook!

There are many different brands of commercially available filo, and a few of kataifi, many of which are frozen. However, quality is variable, and they are often not stored well, which means you can end up with a packet of torn, sticky filo sheets, with crumpled corners, or kataifi which is too crushed to unravel. If you buy your pastry frozen, do not refreeze it, but wrap and seal it carefully and store it in the refrigerator where it will keep for a few days. If you have the inclination, it is worthwhile tracking down good quality Greek or Lebanese freshly made versions.

As far as preparation goes, the same rules apply for filo and kataifi, in both savoury and sweet dishes. Only take from the packet as much pastry as you think you'll need. Carefully wrap and seal the remainder and put it back into the refrigerator. These pastries really must be used immediately, as they dry out and harden surprisingly quickly in the air. If you are assembling individual pastries, one at a time, place one sheet of filo or a small bundle of kataifi on the work surface and cover the rest with a damp cloth. Both filo and kataifi need to be liberally brushed with butter or ghee to get the required golden crunchiness. This is no time to be worrying about cholesterol!

Techniques for other home-made pastry doughs are explained as appropriate.

SAVOURY PASTRY

Savoury pastries are enormously popular throughout the Middle East. As with their sweet cousins, there is a huge and varied repertoire of different shapes, sizes and fillings found all around the Middle East and eastern Mediterranean. They are believed to have been spread by the Arabs and Ottoman Turks, and are also a specialty of the Sephardic Jewish tradition, probably learned in Spain under Moorish rule.

Each region, community and family has its own favourites. Pastries can be made from crisp, wafer-thin filo, or a flaky type of puff pastry, or a denser yeast dough. They can be deep fried or baked. Fillings can be anything from spicy minced meat, poultry or offal to lemony spinach, meltingly soft eggplant or tangy, salty cheese. Some are tried-and-tested combinations, while others are just a good way of using up left-over bits and bobs. Favourite shapes are little triangles, cigars, crescents, rectangular parcels and little round raised pies.

Smaller pastries such as Lebanese fatayer, Syrian sambusek, Tunisian briks, Turkish boreks or even Spanish empanadas, are eaten as snacks or as part of a mezze selection. Other larger pies, such as the Greek spanakopita or Moroccan bisteeya, can be more substantial dishes.

Overall, savoury pastries are an important part of the mezze culture. This idea is central to the Arabic tradition of hospitality, friendship and generosity. A mezze selection can be as simple as a dish of olives and some freshly cut up vegetables and dips, or it can be a range of elaborately made bite-sized morsels which tempt the eye far beyond the stomach's capacity. If you are ever lucky enough to be invited to an Arabic home for a special occasion, you will almost certainly not have enough room left for the main course once you have succumbed to the temptation of tasting every mezze dish on the table.

Many of these little parcels can be fairly labour-intensive and time-consuming to prepare, especially in the large quantities which are required for special occasions and parties. There is still a tradition among some of our Egyptian friends and our Lebanese in-laws for several generations of women to get together to make big batches of little savoury pies like sambusek for a family party.

Savoury Arabic pastries make a deliciously different starter, or the perfect light lunch accompanied by a simple green salad. They make a terrific alternative to the various quiche-type of savoury tarts, and can be very easy to make. After all, the concept is pretty straightforward – crisp pastry parcels with some kind of tasty filling. The options are endless.

SAVOURY PASTRY RECIPES

Tunisian briks with brains

Briks are probably the best known Tunisian snack food, and are sold just about everywhere in Tunisia. They are traditionally made from the same type of paper-thin pastry as the warka pastry used in bisteeya. This is often sold as 'brik' pastry, but is hard to find, and filo will do just as well, or at a pinch, Chinese spring-roll wrappers. The fillings are numerous, but mashed tuna fish, spinach and cheese or creamy brains are favourites. Briks nearly always include an egg, which is broken onto the filling. The pastry is then carefully wrapped up and the whole parcel quickly deep fried. The idea is to eat them immediately, so the egg yolk is still runny when you bite into the crispy pastry.

6 sets of lamb's brains, cleaned and soaked overnight in milk

½ lemon

1 stick cinnamon

½ onion, quartered

½ stick celery

a few parsley sprigs

1 bay leaf

salt and pepper

50 g melted butter

6 sheets of filo pastry

12 large mint leaves

3 teaspoons Chermoula (page 67)

6 egg yolks

• Soak the brains overnight and when you are ready to cook, rinse them well and place them in a saucepan. Cover with cold water and add ½ lemon – squeeze in juice first – the cinnamon stick, onion, celery stick, parsley and the bay leaf. Bring the water slowly to the boil, then lower the heat and simmer for 3 minutes. Remove the pan from the heat and allow the brains to cool down in the poaching liquor. When they are completely cold, remove the brains from the liquor, pat them dry and lightly season them with salt and pepper.

• Take a round soufflé or ramekin dish (8 cm diameter) and brush inside with melted butter. Take one sheet of filo pastry and brush it with melted butter. Fold it in half and brush it with butter again, then fold it in half again. Carefully place the filo pastry square inside the ramekin so that it covers the base and comes up the sides.

• Lay a mint leaf on the bottom and place one set of brains upside down, on top. Carefully smear a scant teaspoon of Chermoula over the surface and then gently spoon an egg yolk into the hollow at the centre of the brains. Season lightly with salt and pepper, then lay a second mint leaf over the top of the egg yolk and fold the pastry sides up and over to completely cover the filling.

- Repeat for the remaining 5 briks.
- Bake in preheated 220°C oven for 8 minutes, or until the briks are golden-brown. Remove from the oven and carefully turn the brik out. Put back into the ramekin, right side up, and return to oven for another 4–5 minutes at 200°C or until the top is golden brown.
- Serve straight away.
- Makes six briks.

Coriander and prawn briouats

Serve these deliciously flaky fragrant pastries with a blob of Preserved Lemon Guacamole (page 156), a splash of Green Harissa (page 82) or even a creamy Coriander and Soft-Boiled Egg Vinaigrette (page 82).

240 g raw prawn meat

I tablespoon olive oil

2 shallots, finely sliced

I tablespoon Chermoula (page 67)

½ cup fresh coriander, roots removed
and roughly chopped

½ cup fresh mint leaves, roughly chopped

I egg yolk

salt and pepper

3 sheets filo pastry

egg wash made from I egg and I teaspoon water

200 ml vegetable oil for shallow frying

• Peel the prawns and chop into smallish pieces, about ½ cm.
• Heat a tablespoon of olive oil in a frying pan then add the shallots and Chermoula and stir for a minute to bring out the flavour of the spices. Remove from the heat and add to the prawn meat. Then add the coriander, mint and egg yolk, season with salt and pepper, and mix together lightly.
• Lay a sheet of filo out and cut it into thirds lengthways. Each strip makes one briouat. Take one strip and brush with egg wash. Place 1 tablespoon of prawn mixture across the corner of one end. Fold this corner up and over on the diagonal, to make a triangle shape. Fold the triangle over, and continue in this fashion all along the pastry strip. Trim any extra little pieces of pastry. You should end up with a nice triangle-shaped pastry parcel. Seal any open edges with egg wash. Repeat to make 7 more pastries.
• Shallow-fry these pastries – a wok is ideal – two at a time until they are golden-brown. It should take about 2 minutes on each side. If they brown too quickly then lower the temperature, wait a few minutes and try again.
• Remove them from the oil and drain them on absorbent paper.
• Serves four people (two each) as a starter.

Prawns wrapped in almond kataifi

Don't think that kataifi is used only for sweet pastries. It works just as well for many savoury pies. Serve these as a spectacularly simple starter, with a sprinkle of Preserved Lemon Gremolata (page 190), a drizzle of extra-virgin olive oil and a big dollop of Saffron-Yoghurt Cheese (page 289).

12 king prawns

salt and pepper

1 preserved lemon

½ packet kataifi pastry

150 g butter

75 g flaked almonds fried in
   20 ml olive oil

1 tablespoon Preserved Lemon
   Gremolata (page 190)

extra-virgin olive oil

100 g Saffron Yoghurt Cheese
   (page 289)

- Remove the body shells and legs from the prawns, keeping the heads and tails intact. Cut carefully along the back and remove any black intestines. Lightly season with salt and pepper. Scrape away the flesh from the preserved lemon and cut the skin into 3 mm strips. Lay a strip of lemon along the groove in each prawn's back.
- Carefully unfold the kataifi pastry into one 'skein' and ease away one half. (Return the rest to the packet, seal tightly, and refrigerate or freeze for future use.)
- Trim the pastry to 20 cm, and carefully divide it into 12 long sections. Take one section (cover the rest with a damp tea-towel), bunch the strands together tightly and lay out in a strip along the work surface. Brush all down the length of the pastry strands with melted butter and then sprinkle with the flaked almonds.
- Lay the prawn, head-touching-tail, at one end of the pastry, and roll it up tightly to make a fat pastry cocoon around the body. Trim so any excess pastry is tucked underneath the prawn. Repeat with the remaining prawns. Cover them with a damp tea-towel and refrigerate for at least half an hour before baking.
- Preheat the oven to 180°C. Place the prawns on an oven tray lined with baking paper, and cook until the pastry is golden-brown and crisp.
- Serves six people (two each) or four hungry people (three each)!

Sambusek

These crescent-shaped pastries are very similar to Turkish boreks. Our Egyptian friend Denise and her mother Rachel make a version which is legendary among her friends. She uses ordinary cheddar cheese for a filling, which sounds banal, but they are absolutely delicious. This version, however, uses the classic Middle Eastern combination of spinach (you could also use silverbeet) and cheese, lifted with a dash of pomegranate essence. The crunch comes from hazelnuts, although traditionalists would probably use pine nuts, which are pricier. Serve them as party nibbles or as a mezze dish. Sambusek are also good as a starter drizzled with a tangy Avgolemono sauce (page 157) or the creamy Coriander and Soft-Boiled Egg Vinaigrette (page 82).

The dough for sambusek is easy to make – we favour a mixture of oil and butter and self-raising flour. To make the little crescent shapes, pinch off a walnut-sized piece of dough and roll it to a thin round circle (approx 8 cm diameter) using a well-oiled glass bottle. Place a heaped teaspoon of your choice of filling into the middle, fold the dough over and shape the pie into a crescent. Traditionally the edges are then pinched and twisted to seal.

PASTRY

200 g self-raising flour

30 g butter, chilled

¼ teaspoon salt

a pinch sugar

50–100 ml warm water

FILLING

30 ml olive oil

2 shallots, finely chopped

1 clove garlic crushed with 1/4 teaspoon salt

2 bunches spinach, leaves picked and washed twice

100 g toasted hazelnuts, skin rubbed away

50 g fetta cheese

• Place the flour, chilled butter, salt and sugar into a food processor, and whiz until the mixture is the consistency of fine breadcrumbs. Gradually add enough lukewarm water for the mixture to just come together in a dough. Allow to rest for half an hour before using.

• Heat the oil in a pan and sauté the shallots and garlic for 3–4 minutes until they have softened. Throw in the spinach leaves, turning them as they wilt down. When all the spinach has collapsed and softened, tip it into a colander and press out the moisture well.

• Lightly crush the hazelnuts in a mortar and pestle.

• Put the spinach into a mixing bowl and add the hazelnuts, fetta, allspice, lemon juice and zest, hazelnut oil and pomegranate molasses and mix together thoroughly.

¼ teaspoon ground allspice

juice and finely chopped zest of
   I lemon

I tablespoon hazelnut oil (or any
   other nut oil)

I teaspoon pomegranate molasses

egg wash made from I egg and I
   teaspoon water

• Preheat the oven to 200°C. To make the sambusek, roll out the pastry on a floured surface to around 3 mm thickness. Cut out pastry circles using an 8 cm pastry cutter and brush half with the egg wash. Place a tablespoon of the mixture into the centre of the circle. Fold the pastry over to make a half-moon shape and pinch or crimp the edges to seal. Brush with more egg wash and place the pastries on a non-stick baking tray.
• Bake it on the middle shelf for 10 minutes or until golden-brown.
• Makes around 15 sambuseks.

Other savoury pastry recipes

Grilled Haloumy Tart with a White Winter Salad, pages 46–47
Figs Wrapped in Prosciutto and Kataifi, page 121
Spinach, Pecorino and Potato Pie, page 257

SWEET PASTRY

In the Middle East desserts tend to revolve around fresh fruit. Sweet pastries are considered something of a luxury and are reserved for special occasions and entertaining. There are countless varieties of these honeyed golden pastries with all sorts of suggestive shapes and names – ladies' fingers, sweethearts' lips, lovers' navels, to name a few! Many of these appear all around the Middle East and eastern Mediterranean sporting different names and slightly different fillings, depending on the region.

Sweet pastries are part of the Arabic tradition of hospitality and friendship. A beautifully wrapped box of these sweetmeats is quite the correct gift to take when visiting and, in turn, no self-respecting Arab housewife would be without a selection of goodies in her pantry to offer guests. However, most Middle Eastern housewives no longer have the time to spend making their own pastries – except, maybe, for a family celebration or party. These days, they are more likely to buy their selection from a specialist pastry shop which bakes its own, where the variety can be mind-boggling, and where they can be assured of excellent quality.

Of the huge range of Middle Eastern pastries, baklava are probably the best known to us in the West, as they are served in just about every Greek and Lebanese restaurant around the world. These are the small lozenge-shaped pastries made from layers of filo pastry, which sandwich a filling of ground pistachio nuts, walnuts or almonds, perhaps flavoured with a touch of cinnamon, and are drenched in an orange-blossom syrup.

Kataifi (or konafi) are the pastries made from the special dough which looks remarkably like shredded wheat. They too are made with a range of different fillings, such as walnuts, pistachios or even soft cream cheese. Then there are the long cigar-shaped pastries, or the snail-like spirals, or the ones which look like little bird's nests – the list goes on and on!

The recipes below are decidedly non-traditional. For authentic Middle Eastern pastries we suggest you do what most Middle Eastern housewives would do, and seek out a really good Middle Eastern pastry shop. This will allow you to sample many more pastries than you could ever make at home.

SWEET PASTRY RECIPES

Caramel pear kataifi with pine nut praline and ginger cream

These are warm, rich flavours for the autumn: sticky caramelised slices of pear, buttery crisp 'bird's nests' of pastry and a spicy whipped Ginger Cream (page 136).

8 William pears

150 g castor sugar

100 g melted butter

¼ cup apple juice

½ packet kataifi pastry

Ginger Cream (page 136) to serve

½ cup Pine Nut Praline (page 210)

• Peel the pears, cut them in half and remove the core. Then cut each piece into 1 cm slices. Place the sugar in a pan and heat gently until it dissolves and just begins to colour. Add the pears and 2 tablespoons of the butter. Sauté until the pears are well coated with caramel. Add the apple juice and cook for another minute until the caramel thickens.

• Unravel the kataifi into a straight long piece and divide it into 8 equal portions. Keep the remaining portions covered as you work. Take one section and curl it into a 6 cm pastry cutter to form a perfectly round 'bird's nest'. Lift the cutter away and drizzle the pastry with melted butter. Repeat with remaining sections. Brush a baking tray with butter and gently place the nests on the tray. Bake them in a preheated 200°C oven for 6–8 minutes until they are golden–brown. Remove them from the oven and dry them on kitchen paper.

• When ready to serve, place a kataifi nest in the centre of each plate. Spoon the pears on top, then a dollop of the Ginger Cream and a sprinkling of the Pine Nut Praline. Place another kataifi nest on the top and sprinkle extra praline around the plate. Drizzle extra caramel around.

• Serves eight.

Honey-curd pies with rose-scented figs

These little raised pies are made from fresh curd cheese, flavoured with honey, orange zest and sherry-soaked currants. They are similar to many Jewish cream-cheese desserts, but not nearly as sweet as you might imagine. Serve them with rose-scented fresh figs, fresh white peaches in caramel, mixed summer berries, or simply a drizzle of maple syrup.

225 g fresh curd cheese (such as Whitelaw Top Paddock)

2 tablespoons currants, soaked for 10 minutes in 2 tablespoons sherry

4 tablespoons flaked almonds

zest of 1 lemon, finely chopped

1 teaspoon cinnamon

1 egg

4 tablespoons mild honey

30 g butter

6 sheets filo pastry

12 fresh ripe figs

6 teaspoons rosewater

200 g castor sugar

2 kg ice-cubes

icing sugar to dust

• Preheat the oven to 200°C.
• In a large bowl, mix together the cheese, currants and any excess sherry, almonds, zest, cinnamon, egg and 1 tablespoon of honey until they are well blended. Melt the butter.
• Lay a sheet of filo on your work surface and brush it with melted butter and fold. Repeat the folding and brushing twice more. Place a heaped teaspoon of the cheese mixture in the centre of each pastry square. Brush the sides with more butter then gather up the corners and sides over the mixture, and flatten slightly to form a little ball-shaped pie. Repeat with the remaining pastry and filling to make a total of 6 pies.
• Place the pies on a lightly greased baking sheet, brush them all over with butter and cook them on the top shelf of the oven for 8–10 minutes until they are golden-brown.
• Meanwhile, cut the figs in half and lay them, cut side up, in a flat dish. Sprinkle each fig with the rosewater and sugar. Then pour ice-cubes into a deep metal tray and lay the dish of figs on top of them (this ensures the figs don't cook through). Place the tray under a very hot preheated grill for 1–2 minutes until the figs caramelise.
• To serve, remove the pastries from the oven and dust them with a little icing sugar. Serve immediately with the rose-flavoured figs and cream.
• Serves six.

Arabic pancakes with fresh mangoes and orange-blossom clotted cream

These are thick, fluffy little pancakes, closer to a dropscone or pikelet than a thin French crêpe. They are traditionally made with a yeast batter. If you want a lighter, airier version you can use baking powder to raise them or, as in this recipe, egg whites. Like their counterparts in the West these pancakes are a great favourite all over the Middle East, where they are often bought ready-made from the bakery and stuffed with Arabic clotted cream (eishta) chopped pistachios and rose-petal jam, and drizzled with syrup. The following pancakes are a lighter version, delicious on their own with whipped cream or butter and maple syrup. But layered with slices of luscious mango and rich Orange-Blossom Clotted Cream, they are out of this world!

3 egg yolks

60 g castor sugar

200 g self-raising flour

zest of 1 orange, finely chopped

2 drops vanilla essence

250 ml milk

3 egg whites

2 mangoes, cheeks sliced off, peeled and cut into thick slices

200 ml Orange-Blossom Clotted Cream (page 185)

• Whisk the egg yolks with half the sugar. Mix in the flour, orange zest and vanilla, and then add the milk slowly, ensuring their are no lumps. The batter should be like a thick pouring cream.

• Whip the egg whites with the remaining sugar until they form soft peaks and carefully fold them into the batter. Fry spoonfuls of batter in a non-stick pan.

• Serve layered with slices of mangoes and Orange-Blossom Clotted Cream or drizzle over a little caramel or maple syrup, or a little dried-lime sugar-syrup (page 284).

• Makes around 12 pancakes.

Other sweet pastry recipes

Toffeed Fig Tart, page 123
Orange-Blossom Tart, page 186

Pine Nuts

On warm summer days, when the heady aroma of basil perfumes the air, many a young cook's fancy turns to pesto. If you have experienced the pleasure of making your own home-made vivid-green pesto sauce, you will have also experienced the pain associated with the pine nut's hefty price tag.

These tiny golden kernels come from the cones of the stone pine tree, which is native to the southern Mediterranean. Their harvest is a long and labour-intensive business, and the yield is proportionally extremely small. But their rich, creamy texture and sweet, piney flavour make them well worth the effort.

All around the Mediterranean and in the Middle East, the legacy of the Arabs is clearly visible in the number of different dishes which combine pine nuts with fruit, such as currants or raisins, often in a tangy sweet–sour base. Spinach salads with pine nuts and currants can be found in many different Mediterranean regions, from Portugal and Spain through to Provence and Italy. In Sicily they are crushed into a kind of sweet–sour salsa, also with currants, and served as an accompaniment to grilled sardines. In fact there are countless dressings and sauces made thick with crushed pine nuts, of which the best known is undoubtedly the Genovese favourite, pesto. In Lebanon, pine nuts are often ground with bread, lemon juice and olive oil to make the dressing called 'tarator'.

Pine nuts are also dearly loved for the flavour and crunch they add to many dishes, ranging from hot savoury pilafs and rice stuffings to refreshing cool salads. They are also used in more extravagant sweet biscuits and cakes as a special treat.

SELECTING AND STORING PINE NUTS

The most readily available pine nuts in Australia are imported from China. These are the ones you will find in little plastic packets in supermarkets. Harder to find, but far superior, are the long elegant Lebanese pine nuts. You will probably be able to find them in a specialist nut shop or Middle Eastern store, and they are well worth tracking down for their creamy soft texture, and buttery flavour with more complex piney overtones.

Like all nuts, pine nuts are high in fat (mostly unsaturated), which means they should be stored in the refrigerator and used quickly.

USING PINE NUTS

Many dishes around the Middle East and Mediterranean use pine nuts as a pleasing crunchy garnish for salads and rice dishes. As with most nuts, toasting or frying intensifies and mellows their flavour. But watch them carefully so that they don't burn. It is probably wise to toast them in a dry frying pan, rather than roast them in the oven, as this gives you far greater control. It only takes a few minutes of gentle tossing over a low to medium heat. Don't get impatient and leave them to sit still, as they burn surprisingly quickly.

Like many other nuts, pine nuts are also a sublime ingredient in confectionary, and are a firm favourite in Mediterranean countries. The Italians make them into a praline, croccante di pignoli, which is often scented with lemon or orange peel, and they work equally well in buttery sweet biscuits and in almondy tarts, such as the provençal tarte aux pignons.

PINE NUT RECIPES

Fried pine nut gnocchi

Finely ground semolina is used in Middle Eastern countries, particularly for sweet desserts. Here it is cooked a little like an Italian polenta, and enlivened with cheese and a pine nut crunch. You can make these gnocchi a day ahead.

1 litre milk

200 g fine semolina

2 egg yolks

50 g butter

50 g parmesan cheese

180 g pine nuts, fried in oil until golden brown

1 teaspoon salt

½ teaspoon pepper

flour for dusting

vegetable oil for frying

• Bring the milk to the boil, the slowly add the semolina, whisking as you go, until it is all incorporated into a stiff paste. Lower the heat and cook at a gentle bubble for about 15–20 minutes, stirring from time to time. When cooked, the semolina grains should have dissolved into the paste. The best way to test this is to taste a little – if the mix feels grainy in your mouth it needs further cooking.

• Remove the pan from the heat and add the egg yolks, butter, cheese and fried pine nuts and season with salt and pepper. Pour into a buttered tray (approximately 28 cm × 24 cm and at least 3 cm deep) and smooth the surface with a spatula. You should then allow the mix to rest and cool completely, for a minimum of 6 hours – or even a day.

• When you are ready to cook, turn the slab out onto a work surface and cut it into desired shapes with wet knife. These can be any shape you like, but shouldn't be too big – around 5 cm × 5 cm is about right. Dust the shapes lightly in flour and deep-fry them in oil heated to 180°C for 4 minutes or until they are golden-brown. They can also be shallow fried – it will take about 3 minutes on each side for them they colour evenly.

Pine nut wafers

Surely nothing could be simpler than these cheesy little wafers. They keep for 2–3 days in an airtight container and are delicious served with pre-dinner drinks – a good chilled amontillado sherry would be ideal – or as an accompaniment to a Preserved Lemon Guacamole with Smoked Eel (page 156). This quantity will make about a dozen wafers.

100 g pine nuts, roughly chopped

100 g parmesan cheese, grated

1 teaspoon fennel seeds, roasted and lightly crushed

- In a mixing bowl, combine the ingredients well.
- Line a baking tray with baking paper and sprinkle the mixture into circles, about 7 cm in diameter and 1 mm thick – use an egg ring or pastry cutter as a mould if you have one.
- Bake them in a preheated 180°C oven for 8–10 minutes.
- Remove them from the oven and allow them to cool on the baking tray, then using a metal spatula, carefully remove them to a cake rack until they are completely cold.
- Store them in an airtight container.

Pine nut praline

Praline has endless uses in desserts and cakes. It works with all flavours from chocolate to fruits, and is particularly useful for adding a bit of textural crunch to creamy smooth desserts. Don't think of it just as a garnish, to sprinkle over desserts, but fold it into whipped cream to accompany rich chocolate cakes, or mix it into all sorts of ice-creams, custards and mousses to add sweet crunch. This recipe will make a good cup of praline.

150 g sugar

2 tablespoons water

200 g pine nuts

• Place the sugar and water in a saucepan and heat slowly to dissolve the sugar. Bring to the boil and cook for about 5 minutes until the syrup reaches the thread stage (when a drop of the syrup falls from a wooden spoon in a long thread) at about 110°C.

• Stir in the pine nuts, which will make the sugar mixture crystallise as the oils come out of the nuts. Don't panic! Turn the heat down a little and stir gently until the crystallised sugar redissolves to a caramel. This will take 10–15 minutes.

• Carefully (as it's hot) pour the syrup onto a baking tin lined with baking paper or greased tin foil. Smooth it with the back of a fork and allow it to cool down and harden.

• When it is completely cold, bash it with a rolling pin to break it into chunks and then pound it to crumbs in a mortar and pestle. The praline should be the consistency of coarse breadcrumbs. It can be frozen and used as required.

Pine nut praline ice-cream

This is made using the Italian method rather than the French custard-based method. It is quick and easy, virtually fool-proof and results in a luscious, creamy ice-cream. To make airy, velvety-smooth ice-cream at home, you really do need an ice-cream machine. Making it in the freezer compartment of the refrigerator requires constant stirring and scraping, and the result is a hard, solid block rather than the soft, airy creaminess we all love.

200 ml water

250 g sugar

1 vanilla bean, split lengthways
and scraped

8 egg yolks

800 ml thickened cream

½ cup pine nut praline

• Put the water, sugar and vanilla bean in a saucepan and bring to the boil, stirring so the sugar is fully dissolved. Lower the heat and simmer for 5 minutes.

• Meanwhile, place the egg yolks in a electric mixer and whisk for about 5 minutes until they are light and fluffy. Reduce the speed of the whisker and pour the the boiling syrup in. Add the cold cream, whisking quickly to incorporate, then turn off the motor.

• Allow the mixture to cool for about 5 minutes, then pour it into your ice-cream machine and churn according to the manufacturer's instructions. Just before it is ready to be transferred to the freezer, add the pine nut praline and let the machine work it through the mixture. Move it to the freezer and let it firm up before serving.

• Serves four to six.

Other pine nut recipes

Pigeon Stuffed with Cracked Wheat Pilaf, pages 33-34
Smoky Eggplant Salad, page 112
Honey Mousse with Pine Nut Praline, page 143
Marinated Baby Lamb with Lebanese Nut Rice, page 150-151
Lebanese Pizza with Pine Nuts and Pomegranate, page 219

Pistachios

We are all familiar with the pistachio nut, lightly roasted and salted, as a stylish pre-prandial nibble. When we visit Greg's family, there is always a huge dish of pistachios on offer, which everyone from the youngest child to the oldest grandparent eagerly scoops up by the handful. And then begins the fun of prising open the polished shells – some stubborn ones need to be carefully cracked between teeth – to get at the tasty morsel within.

The pistachio tree is thought to be a native of Persia, and its name derives from the Persian word 'pesteh'. In their homeland, pistachio nuts grow into plump beauties with a delicious sweet flavour – worlds away from the older shrivelled up little nuts we are more familiar with here. In autumn, however, freshly harvested pistachios are available here – although you will have to hunt them out. These boast a vivid reddy-pink skin (which fades to a duller brown with age) around a bright-green juicy nut.

Sweetened and ground to a paste pistachios impart a delicate pastel hue to ice-creams. Studded into galantines, pâtés and terrines, they add a delightful visual surprise and pleasing textural counterpoint. Finely chopped and sprinkled over Middle Eastern pastries they add a gaudy, almost vulgar final touch.

SELECTING AND STORING PISTACHIOS

Roasted, salted pistachio nuts should be reserved for nibbles and snacks. For cooking always buy unsalted pistachios, which can be bought ready shelled, but will usually still be shrouded in their rough reddy-brown skin. The older they are, the darker the skin will be – fresh pistachios have a vibrant blushing-red skin. Regardless of age, the nuts need to be soaked for 5–10 minutes in boiling water – or longer for older nuts – and the skin should then slip off easily. Always ensure that they are well dried before use or storage. The simplest way is to scatter them on a baking tray and dry them in a cool oven for 10 minutes or so.

USING PISTACHIOS

Cut into slivers, or finely chopped, pistachio nuts are used around the Middle East as a garnish for both savoury and sweet dishes. They are a key addition to many Persian pilafs, and other Middle Eastern rice dishes, and are also delicious in meat dishes. Mixed with rice and herbs, for example, they can be stuffed into a whole boned chicken, which is then roasted and sliced to reveal the bright-green nuts within.

Naturally, their delicate sweetness makes them ideal for desserts and pastries. Coarsely ground pistachio nuts are a popular festive stuffing for special-occasion sweet pastries such as baklava, or the Easter biscuit, ma'amoul. Chopped pistachios are also used to garnish numerous different types of creamy desserts and rice puddings, usually with a drizzle of flowery sugar syrup. Even a humble fresh fruit salad will benefit from a sprinkling of pistachio dust, made by crushing the nuts finely in a food processor and mixing them with icing sugar, and perhaps a splash of lemon or lime sugar syrup.

Other pistachio recipes

PISTACHIO RECIPES

Squid stuffed with pork and pistachios

Ideally, you need fresh medium-sized squid tubes for this dish. Stuffed with a spicy pork-mince filling, studded with pretty green pistachios, they make an attractive and very tasty starter. Serve with a handful of salad leaves and warm crusty bread.

4 medium squid tubes, about 60 g each

40 g pistachio nuts, shelled and soaked
in cold water for 5 mins

320 g pork mince

1 clove garlic, finely chopped

1 shallot, finely chopped

1 teaspoon sweet paprika

½ teaspoon ginger powder

1 large green chilli, de-seeded and finely shredded

1 tablespoon extra-virgin olive oil

1 egg

salt and pepper

1 tablespoon olive oil

1 lemon, cut into 4 wedges

• Clean the squid tubes thoroughly and pat them dry.

• Soak pistachios in cold water for 5 minutes to get rid of any extra salt. Mix the pork, nuts, garlic, shallots, spices, chilli, extra-virgin olive oil and egg until they are thoroughly combined. Preheat the oven to 200°C.

• Stuff a quarter of the stuffing into each tube, making sure you work it right down to the very bottom and that no air is trapped inside. Leave about 1 cm at the open end. If you like, use a piping bag for this bit. Close the ends with a toothpick. Lightly season the tubes with salt and pepper.

• Heat a tablespoon of olive oil in an oven-proof pan and sear the squid tubes on medium–high heat, rolling them around like sausages, until they are a nice golden colour all over.

• Move the pan to the middle shelf of the oven and cook for 12 minutes.

• Remove the squid tubes from the oven and allow them to rest for a couple of minutes on a wire rack until ready to serve.

• Slice each tube into 4 even pieces and arrange them on a plate. Drizzle a little extra-virgin olive oil over the top and serve with lemon wedges.

Lamb rump with pistachios and peppercorns

This is a great way of jazzing up lamb rumps or lamb rounds. To serve, slice each rump into 3 thick slices and accompany with a big bowl of Goat's Cheese Mashed Potatoes (page 49), cheesy Pease Pudding with Goat's Cheese (page 48), garlicky Parsnip Skordalia (page 130) or a robust Coarse Tapenade Salad (page 175).

50 g unsalted, shelled pistachio nuts

30 g white peppercorns

10 g whole allspice berries

100 g fresh breadcrumbs

4 lamb rumps (250 g portions)

1 tablespoon grainy mustard

salt and pepper

• In a spice grinder or mortar and pestle, grind the pistachio nuts then the peppercorns and the allspice berries, and then mix them together with the breadcrumbs.
• Brush each lamb rump evenly with a little mustard and then roll in the crumbing mixture.
• Preheat the oven to 200°C and roast the lamb rumps for 12 minutes for medium–rare or a little longer for medium. Remove them from the oven and allow them to rest for another 12 minutes in a warm place.
• Flash in a hot oven for 1–2 minutes when ready to serve.

Dried fig and pistachio chocolate truffles

Squidgy, fudgy and chocolatey, with a pleasing crunch from the nuts, these chocolate goodies are irresistible. This makes quite a large quantity, but they freeze well and will keep for 3–4 weeks in the refrigerator, although it is unlikely they will last that long!

200 ml condensed milk

500 g good quality dark chocolate

1 tablespoon vanilla extract

1 cup dried figs, finely diced

2 cups unsalted, shelled pistachio nuts

best quality cocoa powder for dusting

• Melt the condensed milk, chocolate and vanilla over a pan of simmering water.
• Mix in the figs and pistachio nuts and pour into a tin lined with greaseproof paper. Leave to set, then turn out, cut into squares and dust with cocoa powder.

Pomegranates

One of nature's most challenging fruits, for many people pomegranates fall into the 'too hard basket'. However, all you really need is a good sharp knife, and maybe a little patience, to pierce the leathery skin and pry loose the delicious seeds lodged in the thick, creamy membrane. But it's well worth the effort – gloomy winter days are immeasurably cheered by these glorious ruby-red seeds, bursting with sour–sweet juice.

In many cultures, pomegranates are considered a symbol of fertility and abundance – no doubt due to their prolific number of seeds. At Jewish New Year, traditionalists will set out a dish of pomegranates as an omen for fertility. In Greek legend the pomegranate is forever linked to the change of seasons – Persephone, daughter of Demeter, the goddess of agriculture, was condemned to spend half the year in the underworld because she ate six seeds of the fruit!

In the Middle East, where they are believed to originate, pomegranates are consumed avidly. The refreshingly tart–sweet juice is squeezed into both savoury and sweet dishes, and its jewel-like seeds add a divinely opulent touch when sprinkled like sparkling rubies over a humble dish of baba ghanoush, the odd salad or even rice dishes.

Despite their glossy beauty, few of the imported pomegranates available to us here warrant the effort in terms of flavour. They may certainly be used as an exotic addition to fancy flower arrangements and table decorations, but they are likely to be a big disappointment on the culinary front. If you also believe that life is too short to spend digging away at pomegranate seeds, you could consider pomegranate molasses. We are big fans of this lusciously dark and mysterious syrup. It is very concentrated, and shouldn't be substituted directly for fresh pomegranate juice without being diluted, or it will overwhelm a dish with its heavy, sticky sweetness. But used with a light touch, pomegranate molasses adds that exotic sweet–sour tartness so favoured in many Persian and Arabic dishes.

SELECTING AND STORING POMEGRANATES

Choosing fresh pomegranates can be a bit of a hit-and-miss affair, and the rather insipid ones we get here in Australia are really only likely to be useful for their decorative little seeds – many of them seem to have no juice at all inside. The usual rules apply, though: select fruit which appear to be unblemished – in the case of pomegranates, this means a smooth, dusky, golden-red skin. If they feel heavy for their size, this is a good sign. They are more likely to be fresher and juicier. Pomegranates can be stored at room temperature for a couple of weeks before they dry out.

USING POMEGRANATES

To remove the seeds from their creamy, pithy cocoon requires a little patience. Cut the fruit in half, and using a teaspoon or a very small skewer, dig out the top layer of seeds. A more brutal approach involves whacking the back of the fruit with a rolling pin a few times, which can dislodge more seeds. Do this over a bowl to avoid making a mess.

If you are lucky enough to get a juicy pomegranate, you can squeeze the fresh juice out using a normal lemon squeezer. Be warned though, it will take several pomegranates to obtain a decent amount of juice. Far better, we think, to buy a bottle of Middle Eastern pomegranate molasses, which will give you the desired ruby-red juice (when diluted with water) with no effort at all.

Other pomegranate recipes

Parsley Salad with Parmesan-Crumbed Brains and a
Tomato-Pomegranate Dressing, page 192

POMEGRANATE RECIPES

Oysters with tomato-pomegranate dressing

Pomegranate molasses adds an indefinable tart sweetness to a vinaigrette, when used instead of balsamic vinegar. This dressing works well with cooked vegetable salads such as spinach, zucchini or eggplant, as well as salad leaves, and is good drizzled over barbecued fish or poultry. It works brilliantly with creamy offal such as the Parsley Salad with Parmesan-Crumbed Brains (page 192). We love it spooned on natural oysters as a change from all those Thai-inspired dressings and dipping sauces.

I teaspoon pomegranate molasses

4 shallots, finely chopped

I clove garlic, finely chopped

juice of I lemon

2 ripe tomatoes, de-seeded and cut into ½ cm dice

180 ml extra-virgin olive oil

salt and pepper

24 freshly shucked oysters

• Place all the ingredients except for the salt, pepper and oysters in a bowl and whisk well. Season with salt and pepper.
• Spoon a little dressing onto each oyster and serve.
• Serves four (six each) as a starter.

Pomegranate butter

Use discs of this tangy butter on top of all kinds of grilled and barbecued dishes, or stuff it under the skin of a whole chicken before roasting.

175 g softened butter

I teaspoon pomegranate molasses

½ teaspoon sumac

2 shallots, very finely chopped

½ clove garlic, very finely chopped

zest of ½ lemon

• Add all the ingredients to the softened butter and mix thoroughly.
• Shape into a rough sausage shape and place onto a square of greaseproof paper. Roll to a smooth log and then wrap in clingfilm and refrigerate until needed. It will keep in the freezer for 3–4 weeks.
• Cut off discs and use as required.

Lebanese pizza with pine nuts and pomegranate

A splash of pomegranate molasses added to all kinds of minced meats will lift them to another dimension. These Lebanese 'pizzas' are a firm favourite. Serve them hot from the oven with a squeeze of lemon juice and, if you like your food spicy, a sprinkling of dried chilli flakes.

PIZZA DOUGH

6 teaspoons dried yeast

1 1/4 cups water, room temperature

200 g high-protein bread flour

2 teaspoons extra-virgin olive oil

2 teaspoons salt

extra flour

MEAT TOPPING

40 ml olive oil

40 g pine nuts

1 small onion, finely chopped

1 clove garlic, finely chopped

180 g minced lamb

1 tomato, de-seeded and finely chopped

1 teaspoon pomegranate molasses

1/2 teaspoon allspice

1/2 teaspoon cinnamon

1/4 teaspoon black pepper

1/2 teaspoon salt

1/2 teaspoon sumac

• Mix together the yeast, water and flour. Knead on a lightly floured surface for about 5 minutes until the dough becomes firm and elastic as the gluten develops. Cover and allow to rest for 30 minutes in a warm place. Tip into an electric mixer and while beating with the dough hook, add oil, salt and a further tablespoon of flour to make a stiff dough. Beat on medium speed for 5 minutes. Tip the dough into a bowl, cover with a damp cloth and allow it to prove in a warm, draught-free spot for an hour.

• Fry the pine nuts over a medium heat until they are golden-brown, then remove them and drain them on kitchen paper.

• Fry the onion until it is soft and then add the garlic and mince. Cook until the mince is browned all over. Add the pine nuts, tomato, pomegranate molasses and spices and stir well. Remove from the heat and check seasoning.

• Preheat the oven to 200°C and heat a heavy baking tray. Divide the dough into 6 equal portions and roll them into circles about 1/2 cm thick. Spread a portion of the topping on each. Bake the pizzas for 10 minutes, or until the pastry is a nice golden-brown.

• Serve hot from the oven with a squeeze of lemon and a big dollop of yoghurt.

Quinces

The quince is a strange old-fashioned kind of a fruit, with a delightful sibilant name. Its fall from grace in our kitchens is something of a mystery, as despite its ordinary appearance, rather like an overgrown apple, it is deliciously fragrant. A bowl of quinces will perfume a whole house – well, a small one like ours, anyway. Even more bewitching is the transformation of its flesh, on cooking, from an unremarkable pastry white into a beautiful rosy-amber hue.

According to American food writer Waverley Root, a key reason for the demise of the quince is its startlingly astringent flavour. He suggests that because sugar is now such a dominant flavour preference in western diets we reject foods which lack it. Less prosperous regions like the Middle East or the southern Mediterranean are traditionally more dependent on natural sweeteners such as honey, date syrup and fresh fruits rather than bland old sugar cane. Their palates are more likely to accept sour, tart and bitter flavours than our lazy western ones!

However, the quince in this country is a very different fruit to that of the hotter countries of the Middle East, where it has been widely cultivated for over 4000 years. In those climates, the fruit becomes softer and juicier and can even be eaten raw. Quince trees do not fruit as well in more temperate climates, where the lack of enough sunshine means the fruit has a disappointing tendency to rot on the tree rather than ripen.

As they have a very high pectin content, the most obvious use for quinces is to make jams, jellies and pastes. French cotignac, Italian cotognata and Spanish or Portuguese marmelado are all different sorts of quince paste, the latter in fact being the origin of our English word 'marmalade'. The curious word 'quince' is itself derived from a French word, 'coing', after the ancient city of Kydonia on Crete, where the best quinces were said to grow in ancient times.

In Middle Eastern countries like Iran, Syria and Turkey, quinces are commonly used in both sweet and savoury dishes. They make a delicious fruit compote, poached with a little honey and lime syrup and served with whipped cream or yoghurt. They can be stuffed with a mixture of chopped nuts and spices, and slowly oven-baked until their aroma fills the kitchen. Other Persian recipes favour stuffing them like a vegetable, with a mixture of minced meat and split peas. They are also the fruit par excellence to use in a Moroccan lamb tagine, enlivened with paprika, saffron and ginger.

SELECTING AND STORING QUINCES

In terms of finding quinces, you have to seize them when you can. If you know someone with a quince tree in their garden, make sure you become their best friend! The season for quinces is startlingly short (May–June) and they are not really grown commercially in Australia. However, they are becoming a more common sight in specialty greengrocers and markets, and, a true sign of increased acceptance, stewed quinces are returning to the breakfast menus of lots of chic little bistros, while quince paste has become almost a common accompaniment to many a cheeseboard.

Choose fruit which are firm and free from wrinkly bits and insect damage. The colour of the fruit will give some clue to its ripeness – as quinces mature they lighten from a sharp, pale-green to a Golden Delicious yellow. Fully ripe quinces are a deeper, brighter yellow, and the real giveaway is the bewitching honeyed fragrance which is at its most intense in the ripe fruit. Don't reject the less ripe fruit though. They have a higher pectin content, which makes them ideal for making jams and jellies. Riper fruit is better suited to poaching or baking.

Quinces should not be kept in the refrigerator. They have a naturally long shelf life and are very slow to rot. But more obviously, one of the very best things about quinces is their extraordinary scent – leave them in a bowl on the kitchen table and allow them to work their magic!

USING QUINCES

To prepare the fruit for poaching, it first needs to be well washed to get rid of the grey down on its skin. Then comes the hard work. Quinces are usually rock-hard, so use a very strong knife to cut, core and peel them. Include the cores and peelings with the slices of fruit as they also contribute flavour, especially when making jellies or pastes. A great deal of the fruit's pectin is to be found in the skin and the pips

Like apples, quinces discolour very quickly, which may or may not matter to you, and will in most cases depend on the recipe you are using. Some people recommend dropping them in acidulated water until you are ready to cook, which will certainly slow the browning process. However, quinces undergo a fairly dramatic colour change on cooking – poaching them transforms them to a glowing pink, and if you are simmering the fruit for a long time to make jam or jelly, then the individual slices will collapse down to a deep-amber hue, and a little surface discolouration won't really matter.

When poaching quinces, the key thing to remember is that they take a long, long time – sometimes as much as an hour, or even more, to soften to an acceptable texture. As they are very tart, they require a lot of sugar, especially in sweet dishes. They also benefit from the addition of a vanilla pod, or some orange, lemon or even lime zest to the cooking syrup.

A few wafer-thin slices of quince added to an apple pie will impart a delicious scent to the whole dish. You might also like to develop an eastern theme by adding a few grains of cardamom.

QUINCE RECIPES

Spiced quinces

Quinces, with their aromatic tart–sweet perfume, are the ideal fruit to balance rich fatty cuts of lamb in a Persian or Moroccan braise. Many traditional recipes are overly sweet to western palates, though, and the addition of even one quince will easily sweeten an entire dish. If you are partial to savoury-sweet combinations, add a few slices of these pickled quinces to a spicy lamb tagine, or serve them with terrines and pâtés and cold meats such as honey-roasted ham or even left-over slices from the Sunday roast.

4 quinces, peeled, cored and cut into 8 pieces

250 ml white wine or cider vinegar

500 ml water

6 tablespoons mild honey

I teaspoon black peppercorns

I teaspoon coriander seeds

I teaspoon cardamom seeds, crushed and sieved

½ teaspoon allspice berries

½ teaspoon whole cloves

I cinnamon stick

2 bay leaves

• Place the quinces in acidulated water until you are ready to cook – you do not want them to discolour.

• Place them in a large pan and cover with the liquids, honey and spices. Bring slowly to the boil, stirring gently to ensure the honey dissolves. Then lower the heat and simmer for 25–45 minutes until they are soft and tender. Be careful not to overcook them or they will start to disintegrate.

• Using a slotted spoon, carefully lift the quince slices into warm sterilised jars and pour the poaching liquor over them so that the fruit is completely covered.

• Seal and store in a cool dark place for at least 4 weeks before using.

Quince Turkish delight

There are many types of quince paste or cheese to be found all around the Mediterranean. These are delicious eaten as a sweetmeat, or as in Spain with a slice of Manchego cheese. Softer versions are delicious spread on toast like jam, or as a glaze for grilled meats. The idea inspired Greg to use quince as a flavour for Turkish delight, finding out only later that old traditional recipes used it as well. The tart–sweet quince flavour is a thrilling change from the very sweet rosewater and vanilla versions usually on offer in Middle Eastern stores and restaurants.

Turkish delight is time-consuming to make, requiring plenty of patience and a strong arm for stirring. It is a fickle sweet, and the addition of different fruits requires constant slight variations to the basic recipe. The recipe below is a simple adaptation, using shop-bought quince paste to provide the flavour and colour.

4 cups castor sugar

1¼ litres water

1 teaspoon lemon juice

1 cup cornflour

1 teaspoon cream of tartar

200 g quince paste, cut into ½ cm dice

200 g icing sugar

80 g cornflour

• Place the sugar in a heavy-based pot with 375 ml of the water and the teaspoon of lemon juice and bring to the boil.

• In a separate bowl, gradually mix together the cornflour and cream of tartar with the remaining water, ensuring there are no lumps. As soon as the syrup reaches 116°C on a sugar thermometer, quickly pour in the cornflour mixture, stir well and lower the heat to a bare simmer.

• Cook on this very gentle heat for about 2 hours, stirring constantly so that it does not stick to the bottom of the pan and burn. The mixture will gradually thicken, become transparent and deepen in colour to a soft amber hue.

• Eventually the mixture will be thick enough for you to draw a distinct channel across the bottom of the pan with your spoon. At this point, add the diced quince paste and stir in evenly.

• Quickly pour into a deep baking tray, 30 cm × 25 cm × 3 cm, lined with greaseproof paper. Allow to cool overnight, but do not refrigerate.

• Turn out and peel away the greaseproof paper. Cut into 2 cm cubes and roll them in a mixture of the icing sugar and cornflour before serving with strong black coffee.

Honey-curd pies with rose-scented fresh figs (recipe page 204)

ABOVE:
Lamb rump with pistachios and
peppercorns (recipe page 215)
BELOW:
Kataifi pastry

Sweet nut-stuffed quinces

Oven-bake quinces as you would apples. Stuff them with a buttery mixture of chopped toasted nuts and honey and serve them with Burnt Honey Ice-Cream (page 142), Ginger Cream (page 136), Orange-Blossom Clotted Cream (page 185) or generous dollops of softly whipped cream.

NUT STUFFING

30g ground almonds

30g unsalted pistachio nuts, finely chopped

¼ teaspoon cardamon seeds, ground

60 g soft brown sugar

50 g butter

2 large or 4 small quinces

2 tablespoons honey

40 g butter

juice and zest of 1 orange

zest of ½ lemon

½ vanilla bean, split and scraped

100 ml water

- Combine ingredients to make nut stuffing and reserve.
- Cut the quinces in half and hollow out the core. Pack the quinces, cut side up, into a lightly buttered gratin dish. Drizzle with the honey and add the remaining ingredients.
- Bake in a preheated 180°C oven for 1–2 hours until the quinces are tender. About 20 minutes before the end of the cooking time, stuff the central hollows of the quinces with the nut mixture. Raise the heat to 200°C and return to the oven until the nut topping is golden-brown.
- Serve with plenty of softly whipped cream.

Rice

In the West – by which, rather ethnocentrically, we mean Australia, North America, England and most of western Europe – people traditionally have not eaten much rice. Rice is, at best, a starchy stomach-filling accompaniment to Chinese or Indian takeaways and, at worst, bland, pappy baby food.

Almost unfathomable then, is the fact that rice is the main sustenance of nearly three-quarters of the world's population, largely because of economic necessity but also, curiously, through choice. All around West Africa, India, China and South-East Asia people have developed a fierce devotion to this grain, each community preferring their own particular local variety, for its unique texture, aroma and flavour – differences which most of us in the West would be hard pressed to distinguish. But even those Mediterranean countries which grow their own small (in world terms) rice crops prefer the home-grown variety: for northern Italians there is only Arborio, ideally a superfino such as Carnaroli or Vialone Nano; for Spaniards a paella can only be made with their very own arroz de Valencia.

In the Middle East, rice is also a serious business. Like bread, it is often referred to as 'aishi' (the Arabic word for 'life') and forms the basis of most daily meals. However, it is not native to the Middle East. The first grain of choice in this region was wheat, which originated and flourished in the area between the Tigris and Euphrates rivers known as the 'Fertile Crescent'. The origins of rice are somewhat less clear. Primitive strains of numerous different varieties are believed to have evolved independently all through Asia, but its earliest cultivation is thought to have centred around the hot, humid foothills of the mountainous region between China and India. Its spread from there was comparatively slow, for rice cultivation requires sophisticated farming and irrigation techniques.

Rice is though to have reached ancient Persia via northern India about 2000 years ago. The Persians, with their farming know-how and advanced irrigation systems, farmed it quite happily for several hundred years. It was virtually unknown in Europe, though, until the Arabs started cultivating it in their new territories. They took it with them as they forged a trail west from Persia, introducing it on the way to Turkey, Sicily and Spain, until by the tenth century the secrets of irrigation and rice cultivation were known throughout the Muslim world, and began to influence local cuisines in ways that endure to this day.

SELECTING, STORING AND USING RICE

There are many thousands of different varieties of rice cultivated around the world. If you would like to know more about rice, *The Rice Book* by Sri Owen (see the bibliography at the end of this book for publication details) makes compelling reading. On the whole, though, Middle Easterners use long-grain rice, unless making a stuffing or puddings, in which case short-grain rice is preferred.

Below is an overview of the three broad types of rice: long-, medium- and short-grain.

Long-grain

As a general rule, long-grain rices are the least starchy, so the individual grains remain separate, dry and fluffy after cooking. For this reason they are ideally suited to savoury dishes and pilafs. Good quality long-grain rices include the aromatic basmati rice and fragrant jasmine rice, although the latter's very distinct flavour is probably better suited to Thai dishes. For many Middle Eastern rice dishes we use a good basmati rice, which swells up to three times longer on cooking, but retains its elegant slimness.

Medium- and short-grain

Medium-grain rices are plumper and shorter than long-grain varieties, and are ideal for the Chinese style of cooking. Short-grain rices are the plumpest and shortest of all, and tend to be starchier and quite sticky when cooked. They are good for Middle Eastern stuffing mixtures and other dishes for which the rice is required to clump together, such as Japanese sushi and Spanish paella. Their propensity to break down to a soothing, creamy mass also makes short-grain rices perfect for puddings.

Risotto rice, known as 'Arborio', is probably better defined as round-grain. Its grains are larger, with a firm, chalky centre. Risotto rice is never washed before cooking, as the lovely, smooth, surface starchiness is essential for making creamy rich risottos. Our favourite risotto rices are Vialone Nano and Carnaroli.

Other rice

Other varieties of rice, outside the scope of this book, are South-East Asian varieties such as glutinous rice and black rice. Then there is red rice from the Camargue in France, and brown rice which has its bran still attached and is enjoyed by the virtuous and nutrition-conscious. Wild rice is not rice at all, but the strong-flavoured grain from a species of North American wild grass.

As far as storing rice goes, the same rule applies to them all: once opened, the packet should be kept it in an airtight container. The general consensus is that most refined rices available in the West keep fairly well for up to three years, although aromatic rices gradually lose their fragrance. Cooked rice has a surprisingly short life span. Harmful bacteria will grow very quickly above 4°C, and will even grow slowly in the refrigerator. Cooked rice should therefore be refrigerated and eaten within two days.

USING RICE

In the Middle East rice cooking is almost an art form and different regions and even different families swear by their own particular method. At its most straightforward, long-grain rice (which is preferred for most occasions) is cooked by a simple absorption method, so that each perfect spoonful is light and fluffy, never sticky, each grain firm and separate.

From here the variations are endless – some people like to sauté the rice in a little oil or butter first, others add this afterwards. Some people soak, others don't even wash the rice first. Many people cover the rice with a tight-fitting lid, others only partly cover the pan. Even the amount of cooking water used and the cooking time will be endlessly disputed.

We have included in this book a number of risotto dishes, which are of course not at all Middle Eastern! Greg spent part of his training in Italy, where he cooked risotto every day. As a result he is quite passionate about it – he always includes a risotto dish on his menus and we cook it at home as a regular treat. They work beautifully with many Middle Eastern ingredients and make a terrific accompaniment to many Middle Eastern and Mediterranean dishes.

RICE RECIPES

Risotto – the basic principles

To make risotto, the first thing to know is that you should never wash the rice – you definitely want all the starchiness you can get. There is nothing hard about making risotto; it simply requires supervision and constant stirring to create the proper creamy texture. Risotto is ready when the individual grains are tender but with some residual bite. The overall consistency of the dish should be a little like a porridge – creamy and starchy, and definitely not swimming in liquid. One other thing: risotto is not for those watching their cholesterol and calories. The final compulsory touch is a healthy handful of grated parmesan and a big nob of butter – these help to thicken the final dish, enrich it and add a lovely glossy sheen.

Following is a basic 'four-stage technique'. Stock is added in three stages to make a base, with a little reserved until the fourth stage. Other ingredients are added halfway through the third stage. In the fourth stage the risotto is enriched with butter and cheese.

60 ml olive oil

1 small onion, quartered

400 g Vialone Nano rice

Up to 1 litre chicken stock, simmering

100 g butter, chilled and cut into
   small cubes

60 g parmesan cheese

salt and pepper

Stage 1
• Fry the onion for a few minutes to flavour the oil, then discard it. Add the rice and stir for two minutes to coat each grain of rice with the oil. Next, add enough hot stock to cover the rice by a finger-width. Cook on medium heat, stirring with wooden spoon from time to time, until most of the stock has been absorbed.

Stage 2
• Add the same quantity of stock. Again, cook on medium heat, stirring with wooden spoon from time to time, until most of stock has been absorbed.

Stage 3
• Add a third amount of stock (reserving 100 ml for the last stage) and when half the liquid has been absorbed, add your choice of vegetables, spices etc. Stir gently until the stock is absorbed.

Stage 4
• Stir in the butter and parmesan and season with salt and pepper. Add the last 100 ml of stock and stir until the butter has been incorporated. Cover and allow to rest off the heat for a minute.

Risotto with zucchini, prawn and preserved lemon

This is a brightly coloured flavourful risotto which makes an ideal light lunch with a simple salad.

2 large zucchini

240 g raw prawn meat

60 ml olive oil, flavoured with
   I small onion, quartered

400 g Vialone Nano rice

Up to I litre chicken stock, simmering

100 ml olive oil

2 shallots, finely sliced

I clove garlic, finely sliced

salt and pepper

I preserved lemon, skin only,
   washed and diced small

100 g butter, chilled and cut into
   small cubes

I tablespoon parsley, chopped

- Shred zucchini into small batons. Shell and clean prawns.
- Prepare risotto according to basic four-stage method.
- Meanwhile, in a separate frying pan, heat 50 ml oil until it is smoking hot. Throw in the zucchini and shallots. Do not stir, but let sit for 30 seconds. Then stir well, remove from the heat and drain in a colander or sieve. Place the frying pan back on heat, add the remaining 50 ml oil and heat again until it is smoking hot. Throw in the prawns and again, do not stir, but let sit for 30 seconds. Then add the garlic, season with salt and pepper and stir well. Remove the pan from the heat.
- Halfway through the third stage of making the risotto, add the prawns, zucchini and preserved lemon dice with the cold butter. Add the last 100 ml stock and stir well until the butter is incorporated. Cover and let sit for a minute. Adjust seasoning.
- Scatter with parsley and serve.

Broad bean pilaf – Lebanese-style

Beans and rice are an almost universal favourite. This is an adaptation of two traditional Lebanese dishes – rice with beans and rice with chicken. It is quite rich and, served with a bitter-leaf salad, makes an ideal lunch or supper dish.

60 ml olive oil

½ small onion, finely chopped

200 g minced chicken

salt and pepper

½ teaspoon allspice

400 g basmati rice

160 g fresh broad beans, blanched and peeled

80 g pumpkin, cut into ½ cm dice

600 ml chicken stock, simmering

1 clove garlic crushed with ½ teaspoon salt

juice of 1 lemon

½ cup fresh coriander leaves

• Heat the oil in a pan and sauté the onion for a few minutes until it has softened. Add the chicken mince and cook on high for 2–3 minutes until the juices start to run out. Season with a little salt and pepper and the allspice. Then add the rice, broad beans, pumpkin and chicken stock. Turn the heat low, cover and cook for 15 minutes without disturbing.

• Turn off the heat and fork through a mixture of the garlic paste and lemon. Cover again and rest for a further 5 minutes. Turn out onto a large shallow dish and garnish with coriander.

• Serve with dollops of satiny-smooth yoghurt.

Spring vegetable paella

This paella is cooked more like a risotto so the rice becomes creamy. It has no cheese, though, in order to maintain the fresh intense flavours of the vegetables.

60 ml olive oil flavoured with I small onion, quartered and 2 cloves garlic

400 g Vialone Nano rice

Up to I litre chicken stock, simmering

120 g shelled peas, blanched for 2 minutes

120 g fresh broad beans, blanched and peeled

8 artichokes cooked à la niçoise (page 17), or good quality purchased artichokes, preserved in oil.

15 saffron strands, roasted and crushed to powder

2 medium tomatoes, de-seeded and diced

2 small red peppers, roasted, skinned and diced

100 g butter, chilled and cut into small cubes

salt and pepper

- Prepare the risotto according to the basic four-stage method.
- Prepare the peas and broad beans, and cut the artichokes in quarters.
- Halfway through the third stage add the blanched peas and beans, the artichokes and the saffron. Stir gently and then add tomato, red pepper, salt and pepper.
- Remove from the heat, cover the pan and let sit for 3 minutes. Return the pan to the heat and add the cold diced butter and the last 100 ml of stock and stir gently until the butter has been incorporated.
- Adjust seasoning and serve with a fresh green salad.

Rice and chorizo stuffing

Use this to stuff chicken or any other game birds. Rub the skin with crushed garlic, thyme and lemon zest, and roast. This quantity will stuff a size 20 chicken, roasted for 50 minutes at 190°C, or 12 quail, roasted for 15 minutes at 200°C.

1 tablespoon olive oil

1 shallot, finely chopped

1 small clove garlic, finely chopped

50 g semi-dried chorizo sausage, finely shredded

100 g medium-grain rice

200 ml stock or water, simmering

zest of 1 lemon, finely chopped

1 tablespoon parsley, chopped

1 egg yolk

• Heat the oil in a pan and gently sauté the shallot and garlic until they have softened. Add the chorizo and rice and stir well to combine ingredients. Add the simmering stock, cover and cook over a low heat for 12 minutes. Remove the pan from the heat but leave the lid on and allow to steam a further 5 minutes. Tip into bowl and allow to cool. Add the lemon zest, chopped parsley and egg yolk to bind.

Other rice recipes

Fried Almond Risotto, page 4
Lebanese Nut Rice, page 150
Mjaddarah, page 163
Chicken and Pistachio Dolmades, page 279
Koussa Mahshi, page 294

Rosewater

Roses have been enjoyed since ancient times for their beauty and perfume – from the lush gardens of Persia where they were first cultivated to Roman times when they were strewn extravagantly about the floors and tables at banquets and used to scent bathing water. Early civilisations macerated rose petals in hot oil to make pomades, which were used for anointing the body as a kind of primitive perfume. But it was not until the tenth century that the Arabic doctor Avicenna discovered the process of extracting the rose's essential oil by distillation. The intensely concentrated perfume could then be diluted to make rosewater, for use in medicine, perfume and cosmetics and even cooking.

With their heady sweet fragrance it is hardly surprising that rose petals and rosewater were also enjoyed by the ancients in their food, as indeed they are today in parts of the Eastern world. Iranian cooks like to sprinkle crushed dried rose petals onto rice pilafs or deserts, and add them to complex spice mixes, to which they contribute a musty-sweet undertone. Nearly all Middle Eastern and eastern Mediterranean countries have a tradition of rose petal preserves, which are eaten as jam with bread for breakfast, or enjoyed as spoonfruit, eaten in tiny spoonfuls as an accompaniment to a cup of strong black coffee and a glass of icy-cold water.

At the other end of the Arab world, the Maghreb countries of North Africa also use rosebuds in cooking. Huge sacks of tiny dried rosebuds are to be found in every spice shop in Morocco. They are mixed with other sweet spices like cinnamon to add an exotic dimension to both sweet and savoury dishes. They are also a common ingredient in stronger North African spice mixes, like the Moroccan ras el hannout or the Tunisian 'four spice' mix.

Rosewater, too, is used at mealtimes all around the Middle East – both as a perfumed hand wash and to add a touch of edible luxury to nearly every dessert and sweet pastry imaginable. It is used to flavour honey and sugar syrups, and poured lavishly over all kinds of sweet pastries. Rosewater is used to flavour buttery ground-almond cookies and to moisten delicate nut pastes for stuffing into little shortbready biscuits, like ma'amoul. Creamy milk puddings, thickened with ground rice, cornflour or ground almonds are a favourite dessert treat in Middle Eastern countries. These too are nearly always enhanced with a few drops of fragrant rosewater or orange-blossom water.

Rose petals and rosewater featured quite largely in the cooking of medieval England. They were used extensively in candies and preserves, desserts and syrups, as well as more exotic game and fish dishes, but by the nineteenth century had fallen from favour. It is true that, used with too heavy a hand, flower waters can become cloying and overpowering, yet a delicate touch can add an exotic dimension to many European desserts too. Rosewater can be added to cakes and biscuits, splashed into sorbets and ice-creams, mousses, fools and cooked creams or even added to a humble rice pudding for an exquisitely different sweet flavour.

Rosewater marries particularly well with fresh fruit. A favourite Moroccan dessert, for instance, is devastatingly simple – fresh orange segments are dusted with cinnamon and sugar and then sprinkled with rosewater. At home we often drizzle a little rosewater over fresh strawberries or a mixed-berry compote and serve them with thick creamy yoghurt for a deliciously easy summer dessert.

SELECTING, STORING AND USING ROSEWATER

Rosewater can be found in Middle Eastern and Indian stores, and in some upmarket food shops and delicatessens, but usually in a diluted form compared with the full-strength distillations available in Asia. Our favourite is the Lebanese Cortas brand, but there are several other Lebanese, Syrian and even Indian varieties available.

Rosewater and orange-blossom water are often used interchangeably, particularly in sugar syrups which are poured over fresh fruit salads, sticky pastries and almond-thickened milk puddings. However, rosewater tends to be less overpowering than orange-blossom water. Surprisingly, it is also quite robust and, contrary to all expectation, can be heated quite happily without an alteration in its flavour.

ROSEWATER RECIPES

Persian-style rose-scented plum jelly

We have a relentlessly productive plum tree in our garden and created this gorgeous jewel-like jam as a way of using up the summer's glut of fruit. Plums are high in pectin, and this jelly practically makes itself. It is good on fresh white bread with lots of butter, but we like it particularly on nutty whole-wheat or even savoury rye toast.

2.5 kg plums

50 ml rosewater

sugar

- Place the plums in a large heavy-based pan and boil for about 10 minutes until they are soft and pulpy and have released a lot of juice.
- Strain them overnight through a jelly-cloth (a piece of muslin or cheesecloth, or even an ordinary kitchen cloth like a Chux will do just as well). Do not force them through as this will make the jelly cloudy, but allow them to drip through naturally. The amount of juice yielded will vary, depending on the fruit, but you should have about 2 litres.
- Pour the juice into the pan and for every 600 ml add 500 g sugar. Stir well over a low heat until the sugar has completely dissolved, then bring to the boil.
- Boil for 20–25 minutes, until the jelly reaches the setting point. To test, spoon a small amount onto a cold plate and place it in the refrigerator to cool. The jelly is at setting point if it forms a skin which wrinkles when you push your finger through. When it reaches the setting point, remove the pan from the heat and skim the froth from the surface.
- Stir in the rosewater and then carefully ladle the jam into sterilised jars and seal with preserving wax.

Rose-flavoured berry fool with mascarpone

2 punnets strawberries, hulled
  and halved

2 punnets blueberries

2 punnets raspberries

(Reserve a few of each berry to garnish)

100 g coffee crystals

30 ml rosewater

100 g sugar

120 ml cold water

200 ml pure cream

200 g mascarpone

sprinkling of Pine Nut Praline (page 210)

• Make a berry purée using 1 punnet of each of the fruits. Cook with the coffee crystals for 10 minutes, and then allow to cool and pass through a sieve to remove the seeds. Stir in half the rosewater and allow to cool.

• Heat the sugar with 60 ml of the cold water until the sugar is dissolved. Bring the water to the boil, then lower the heat and simmer until it thickens and darkens to a caramel. Remove it from the heat and add the remaining cold water. Stir in well and allow it to cool down.

• Whip the cream with the mascarpone and remaining rosewater until stiff. Loosely fold in the whole berries with half the purée and half the caramel to give a marbled effect.

• Place a big blob on each plate and swirl with extra purée and caramel.

• Garnish with the fresh whole berries and a sprinkling of Pine Nut Praline.

Apple-rosewater sorbet

This fragrant sorbet makes a lovely light dessert. As the apples discolour slightly on cooking, the purée needs a splash of colour to give it a rosy blush – add a few puréed raspberries, a drop of ribena or grenadine syrup or even beetroot juice!

6 green apples, peeled, cored and diced

250 ml apple juice

juice and zest of 1 lemon

100 g castor sugar

125 g glucose

1 stick cinnamon

3 juniper berries

2 cloves

½ litre water

2 teaspoons rosewater

1 teaspoon grenadine (optional)

• Gently simmer the apples in the apple juice with the lemon juice and zest until they are soft and starting to collapse down.

• Place the sugar, glucose, cinnamon stick, juniper berries and cloves in a pan with the water and bring to the boil. Lower the heat and simmer for 5 minutes to make a syrup. Allow to cool a little and then strain to remove the cinnamon stick, cloves and juniper berries.

• Purée the apple mixture and then pass it through a sieve. Allow it to cool and then add the rosewater and grenadine. Mix together the syrup and apple purée, pour into an ice-cream machine and churn according to the manufacturer's instructions.

• Serve with fresh berries or other fresh fruits.

Other rosewater recipes

Watermelon Sorbet, page 283
Watermelon Salad with Cherry-Vanilla Ice-Cream, page 285

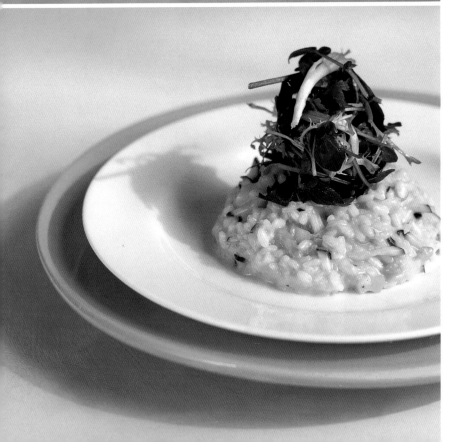

ABOVE:
Pomegranate
BELOW:
Risotto with zucchini, prawn and preserved lemon (recipe page 231)

Grilled seafood bouillabaisse (recipe page 247)

Saffron

A rummage for saffron in our kitchen cupboard at home revealed the following: one plastic sachet of fake 'saffron' threads purchased for novelty value from the souks of Marrakesh (it is really safflower); one small square glass bottle of La Mancha saffron threads brought back from a holiday in Spain; and one tiny pot of brick-red, ferociously expensive saffron powder from Iran. Neither versions of the real thing look like much for the money, but even the tiniest pinch results in an explosion of bright-yellow sunshine through your food, and contributes an indescribable bitter–sweet flavour that leaves you longing for more.

True saffron threads are the orangey-red stigmas of a type of crocus flower (*crocus sativus linnaeus*) which is thought to be native to the Fertile Crescent. Archaeological remains in Sumerian burial grounds, suggest that saffron was used as a natural yellow dye as early as 5000 BC. The yellow colour comes from crocin, an intensely potent natural pigment – one part crocin will turn 150,000 parts of water bright yellow! This characteristic meant it was much in demand in ancient times as a dye for textile and carpet weavers.

Saffron has always been adored by the aristocracy as a symbol of opulence and refinement. The Greeks and Romans used it to dye their clothes and to tint their bathing water. They believed it had cleansing qualities, and used it to perfume their houses and public meeting places. Saffron was also used medicinally, to relieve depression and as a tonic for the heart, while stuffing it in bedding was thought to aid sleep. In the kitchen, saffron was used to gild all manner of pastries, meat and seafood dishes, as well as contributing its own indefinable flavour.

The Romans spread saffron all around their empire – even as far west as England, but with the decline of their empire, trading networks in Europe collapsed and the supply of spices from the East dried up. The violent peoples responsible for the chaos of Europe's Dark Ages had no interest in subtlety and refinement – least of all in their food – so it was not until the emergence of the Arab empire in the eighth century that relative calm returned to the region. Gradually, the Arabs re-emerged as a significant trading power. Many spices were re-introduced to European cities, and refinement returned to local customs and in particular foods. The word for saffron in most European languages is strikingly similar, and they all derive from the Arabic (from 'sahafarn', meaning 'thread', and 'za'faran', meaning 'yellow').

The use of saffron in many cuisines can be traced back along common cultural threads. In Spain, for instance, the Arabs planted fields both of rice and saffron – the ingredients for the best known Spanish dish, paella. Saffron is also added to rice dishes in countries as far apart as Iran, Turkey, the Balkan countries, Lebanon, Syria, Italy and Morocco. Another significant cross-cultural use of saffron is in the baking of special cakes and breads for religious celebrations.

Saffron adds a magic touch to both savoury and sweet dishes. It is often combined with seafood, as in the classic Mediterranean bourrides and bouillabaisse, and adds a spicy pungency to Moroccan tagines. Saffron also works in sweet dishes, transforming milky custards, brûlées and ice-creams. In northern Europe it is favoured in baking and yeast cookery, tinting breads and tea cakes, batters and pastries a glorious yellow.

SELECTING AND STORING SAFFRON

The rule with saffron is that if it isn't expensive, it probably isn't real saffron, and you should give it a miss! This rule applies particularly if you are a traveller in a strange land. In Morocco, for instance, many vendors in the spice markets offer vividly appealing mounds of a deep orange-yellow powder which they insist is saffron. In fact it is turmeric (often called 'Indian saffron'), which is not at all the same thing. Turmeric is used a great deal in Moroccan cooking to add colour, but it has nothing like the pungent, distinctive flavour of real saffron, and the two are certainly not interchangeable. At other stalls, you might be offered 'saffron' threads, which look genuine and are again offered at an enticingly cheap price. This, too, is likely to be an imposter, probably tasteless safflower or, worse still, shredded marigold petals. There is no getting away from the fact that because of the labour-intensive process of its cultivation and harvest, real saffron is expensive – and the better the quality, the costlier it will be. But, the rewards are great and the impact is huge relative to the amount needed.

On the whole, we recommend using saffron threads rather than saffron powder, as the latter is too easily adulterated (although there are exceptions, like the very pricey powder from Iran). Here in Australia, however, you are most likely to buy saffron from an upmarket food store or delicatessen. They pretty much only have the real thing, imported from Spain, Iran, Turkey or Greece, reassuringly packaged in neat little containers and often sealed with a label giving information about brand name, packing date, weight and even quality.

Good quality saffron threads should be densely entwined, long, fine filaments of a deep orangey-red hue. Most will probably also contain a small number of whitish-yellow styles – which are removed from the top-grade stuff – but they don't affect the aroma or flavour. Top-quality saffron powder usually comes in sachets or tiny plastic pots, and should be as dark as brick-dust. It is also more expensive than the whole threads, as the moisture is extracted before it is ground to a fine powder. Having spent so much money, you will naturally want to store your saffron correctly – away from the light in a cool dry cupboard, where it should last for 3–5 years.

USING SAFFRON

When using saffron, the first thing to work out is how much to use. Many recipes are decidedly unhelpful, suggesting only a vague 'pinch'. Weighing saffron is nigh impossible, given the tiny quantities used. In our view, it is more appropriate to count out the threads on a per-person basis. You will probably find that once you start using saffron and become used to its bewitching flavour, you will want to use more and more, but a good starting point is to use four threads per person, plus a few for luck. In other words, for four people, use 16–20 threads.

Saffron needs to be 'heat-activated' before use, or its impact will be disappointing. One option is to dry-roast saffron threads gently and grind them to a powder before use (bought powder has already undergone this process). The alternative is to make a saffron infusion in a hot liquid, which should be made ahead of time and added during the cooking process. Some cuisines employ a combination of these techniques, gently roasting the saffron threads before infusing.

To roast saffron, toss the threads in a totally dry pan over a moderate heat, for around 30 seconds. The last thing you want to do is burn them, but they must be completely dry before grinding. Once they have crisped up and begun to release their pungent aroma, tip the threads into a mortar, and allow them to cool before crushing them with a pestle.

To make an infusion of saffron, measure out the threads and dry-roast them if desired. Next, place them in a cup and add just enough hot water to cover them – start with a tablespoon. The threads will immediately start to release their colour into the water, and this will deepen and intensify over time. A minimum infusing time of 30 minutes is essential, but the saffron will continue to develop for about 12 hours. Some people like to store a saffron infusion in a tightly sealed jar for use over several weeks, in which case you should infuse them in boiling water.

When using saffron, either as a powder or as an infusion, the general rule is that you add it at the start of the cooking process for maximum colour, and at the end for maximum flavour. Some people like to have the best of both worlds by adding it early and reserving a little to add at the very last minute before serving.

SAFFRON RECIPES

Golden mussel chowder

In this glorious, creamy soup plump, salty mussels and sweet, candied bacon rub up against soft, starchy potato in a golden broth. It needs only hot crusty bread to make a satisfying luncheon dish, or a soul-restoring starter on a cold, grey day.

1 kg black rope mussels, de-bearded and scrubbed

1 onion, sliced

2 sticks celery, sliced

2 cloves garlic, chopped

30 ml olive oil

200 ml white wine

2 small leeks, steamed whole

2 medium potatoes, peeled, diced and steamed

200 ml thickened cream

10 strands saffron, roasted and crushed

1 tablespoon fresh thyme leaves

2 medium tomatoes, de-seeded and diced small

pepper

4 small bacon rashers

soft brown sugar

• In a heavy-based pot sauté the onion, celery and garlic in 30 ml olive oil for about one minute. Then add the wine and the mussels. Cover, turn the heat up high and steam for 3 minutes. Turn the mussels well, replace the lid and steam a further 2 minutes, or until the mussels have opened.

• Remove the pot from the heat and allow to steam a further minute before taking off the lid and straining the liquor through a fine sieve to catch any dirt. Reserve the liquor. Throw any unopened mussels back into the pot and steam for another minute or two. Any which stubbornly refuse to open should be discarded. Allow the mussels to cool and then remove them from their shells and cut them in half.

• Steam the whole leeks and diced potatoes for 10–15 minutes, until they are tender. Remove them from the heat and allow them to cool a few minutes. Split the leeks in half lengthways and then cut them into 1 cm slices.

• Return the mussel liquor to the pot, add the cream and bring it to the boil. Add the potatoes and leeks, then the saffron and thyme. Heat thoroughly. Add the diced tomatoes and mussels and warm through for a few moments. Season with pepper.

• To candy the bacon, sprinkle the rashers liberally with soft brown sugar and grill them until they are golden-brown. Shred and sprinkle them on the soup.

• Serves four to six.

A la grecque dressing

Greg's all-time favourite, this is a fantastically versatile saffron-infused dressing which spreads a flood of sunshine on your plate and an explosion of flavour in your mouth.

10 strands saffron, roasted and crushed to a powder

80 ml white wine vinegar

40 ml white wine

1 teaspoon honey

5 shallots, evenly and finely diced

2 cloves garlic, finely chopped

1 bullet chilli, finely chopped

2 sprigs fresh thyme, leaves picked

1 teaspoon coriander seeds, roasted and crushed

½ teaspoon white peppercorns, roasted and crushed

½ teaspoon fennel seeds, roasted and crushed

juice of 1 lemon

250 ml extra-virgin olive oil

salt and black pepper

• In a saucepan, mix the saffron with the vinegar, white wine and honey. Warm the pan gently to dissolve the honey and add the shallots, garlic, chilli and thyme leaves. Pour into a large mixing bowl and allow to cool.

• Roast and grind the coriander, white peppercorns and fennel seeds. Add them to the dressing, then whisk in the lemon juice and the olive oil.

• Taste for seasoning and add salt and freshly milled black pepper as required.

Other saffron recipes

Pigeon Stuffed with Cracked Wheat Pilaf, pages 33–34

Little Pigeon Bisteeya, page 74

Cumin Rouille, page 98

Green Lentil Soup with Saffron-Scrambled Eggs, page 162

Spring Vegetable Paella, page 233

Saffron-Yoghurt Cheese, page 289

Grilled seafood bouillabaisse

In traditional bouillabaisse recipes the fish are cooked in the broth as a fish stew. Here they are grilled separately and placed in the soup as it is served. This means that oily fish like salmon may be included, and each fish retains its colour and texture. You can use any white reef fish, such as garfish, snapper, or black bream.

CRAB STOCK

2 kg crab, reserve claws for garnish

150 ml olive oil

4 sticks celery, roughly chopped

2 medium onions, roughly chopped

4 cloves garlic, roughly chopped

1/2 teaspoon fennel seeds, roughly chopped

1 can crushed tomatoes (400 g)

125 ml sherry

peel of 1 orange

15 strands saffron, roasted and crushed

2 whole bay leaves

12 stalks thyme

4 litres water

BOUILLABAISSE

3 large waxy potatoes, peeled and sliced thickly

3 leeks, sliced 2 cm thick on the diagonal

2 medium fennel bulbs, cored, removed and cut into 8 wedges

4 tomatoes, de-seeded and diced

salt and pepper

1.5 kg black mussels

750 g salmon fillet, skinned and cut into thick slices

750 g white fish fillets

12 king prawns (2 per person)

- Remove the underbody of the crab and pull away the dead men's fingers. Cut the body in half and bash the shell and remaining claws into largish pieces. In large heavy pot heat the olive oil to smoking point. Throw in the crab and sauté it briefly over a high heat. Add the celery, onion, garlic and fennel seeds and sauté for a further 2 minutes. Then add the tomatoes, sherry, orange peel, saffron, bay leaves and thyme. Add the water and bring it to the boil, then skim. Lower the heat and simmer uncovered, for an hour, skimming from time to time. Strain, and reserve the stock.
- Parboil the potato slices in half the stock, then add the leek pieces and fennel wedges and cook for 4 minutes. Add the tomato dice, taste and season lightly with salt and pepper. Remove the pan from the heat and keep to one side.
- Steam the mussels in half a cup of the stock, until all have opened. Meanwhile grill the salmon, white fish and prawns. To serve, pour the broth into a bowl with the vegetables. Pile the seafood on top, arranging the mussels around the side.
- Serve with Cumin Rouille (page 98) and crusty bread.
- Serves six hungry people.

Sesame Seeds

Sesame seeds are as familiar to us as the story of Ali Baba and his cave of treasure. They were cultivated and traded as a precious commodity by ancient civilisations, who mixed them with other grains to make a coarse flour, or crushed them for their oil. Not only was sesame oil one of the first oils used in cooking around Egypt, the Middle East and Indus Valley and the Mediterranean, it was also in huge demand for lighting, as an emollient and for use in ancient medicine.

Today we tend to associate sesame oil mainly with Asian cooking, where a few drops add a unique nutty flavour to many stir-fried dishes. In the Middle East and eastern Mediterranean they use mainly sesame seeds. These are added to spice mixes such as dukkah, sprinkled as garnish onto salads and vegetable dishes, and added to all manner of breads, biscuits and cakes. When Greg and I were honeymooning in Lebanon and Syria we often ate crunchy sesame-encrusted bracelets of bread, known as 'kahk', for breakfast. Similar versions of these biscuit-like breads are sold by street vendors all around the region, from Lebanon and Syria to Egypt, Greece and Turkey.

No self-respecting Middle Eastern home would be without a jar of tahini in the refrigerator. Made from crushed sesame seeds, tahini looks a little like a smooth, rather oily peanut butter, and has a strong earthy, nutty flavour. Tahini is used as a base for Arabic dips, like hummus and baba ghanoush. Thinned down, it is also served as an accompaniment to baked fish.

Sesame is also a favourite ingredient in confectionary. The whole seeds are used to coat sticky sweets and to make crunchy toffee brittles, while ground to a fine powder they add flavour to the mysterious, sand-coloured sweet known in the Middle East as 'halawa', or in Greece as 'halvah'.

SELECTING, STORING AND USING SESAME SEEDS

Sesame seeds come in two colours – black and white, although the white seeds are far more widely available. White sesame seeds may be purchased hulled or unhulled – in the latter case they are actually a dull-beige colour. These may be used interchangeably, although some Asian and Middle Eastern cooks prefer the flavour of the unhulled seeds. Black sesame seeds are used for their dramatic visual effect on flat breads. They are oilier and have a more intense flavour.

Regardless of colour, the flavour of all sesame seeds is greatly improved by dry-roasting. They need only a few moments gentle tossing over a medium heat, which will send them popping all around the pan. Roasting brings out a lovely toasty aroma, and turns the seeds a shade or two darker. They can be stored quite well for several weeks after toasting, although that just-roasted nutty quality fades slowly over time. The dry-roasted seeds can also be given a quick whiz in a spice grinder, to make a thick coarse paste to thicken sauces, dips and dressings.

Tahini is used with gay abandon in the Middle East. Don't confuse it with the Chinese and Japanese sesame pastes – these are made from roasted sesame seeds and are darker and stronger than tahini. Tahini may taste almost bitter straight from the jar, but diluted with lemon juice and water and whisked to make a dressing or sauce, it has a smooth creaminess and an incomparable nutty flavour.

You will probably find that your tahini separates out in the jar, and that you have a thick layer of oil floating on top. This needs to be vigorously mixed back into the paste before use, which requires a certain amount of muscle. Once opened, tahini will keep for 4–6 weeks in the refrigerator.

Other sesame seed recipes

Artichoke Salad with Bacon and Eggs, page 18
Hummus Bi Tahini, page 56
Baba Ghanoush, page 113

SESAME SEED RECIPES

Egyptian eggs with dukkah

We were first introduced to dukkah by our Egyptian friend Denise. Dukkah is a coarsely ground mixture of sesame seeds, hazelnuts and heady cumin and coriander. It is delicious eaten on oil-dunked bread for breakfast or as a snack. In recent years it has also become fashionable in trendy restaurants, which offer little bowls of it for pre-prandial snacking. These deep fried Egyptian eggs are delicious but for a simpler dish, sprinkle dukkah on soft-boiled eggs and eat with hot buttered toast.

DUKKAH

8 tablespoons sesame seeds

4 tablespoons coriander seeds

3 tablespoons cumin seeds

50 g hazelnuts

I teaspoon salt

½ teaspoon pepper

4 eggs

plain flour for dusting

vegetable oil for deep-frying

• For the dukkah, roast each ingredient separately, and rub away as much of the brown skin from the hazelnuts as you can. Pound the seeds using a mortar and pestle or whiz them carefully in a spice or coffee grinder. When you grind the sesame seeds and hazelnuts be careful not to overgrind them or they will disintegrate into an oily paste. Combine the nuts and seeds with salt and pepper, and keep in an airtight jar in the refrigerator.

• Soft-boil the eggs for 3 minutes. Cool them down under running water and peel them carefully. Dust them in plain flour and then deep-fry each egg for 1–1½ minutes, or until they are golden-brown. Remove them from the oil and immediately roll them in dukkah.

• Eat them straight away as a snack or as a light lunch with hot buttered toast. Or serve them with a salad such as the Artichoke Salad with Bacon and Eggs (page 18) as a starter.

Chicken livers pressed with dukkah

Ghee or clarified butter is used rather than normal butter in this recipe. Butter contains milk solids and water, which can seep out and spoil the texture of the terrine. Ghee also has a nice nutty, buttery flavour that marries well with the dukkah and richness of the livers.

300 g ghee or clarified butter

1.25 kg chicken livers, cleaned of
   sinews

salt and pepper

100 g dukkah

½ tablespoon fresh thyme leaves

2 large leeks, trimmed to the size of
   the terrine mould, steamed until
   soft

• Line a terrine mould completely with four layers of clingfilm – a 30 cm Le Creuset cast-iron terrine mould is ideal. In a large, heavy-based pan heat 2 tablespoons of ghee until it is almost smoking. Add a third of the chicken livers, sealing both sides to a good colour, and seasoning with salt and pepper. The livers should be cooked medium, for no more than 2 minutes. Remove them immediately onto a wire rack and repeat the process with the remaining two-thirds of the livers, using 2 tablespoons of ghee each time.

• Pack half the livers into the bottom of the terrine mould, sprinkle them with a tablespoon of the dukkah and half the quantity of fresh thyme leaves. Then pour 2 tablespoons of fresh melted ghee over the top. Next season with salt and pepper and place the 2 leeks down the centre of the terrine, one on top of the other, flattening and pressing slightly into the livers. Cover with the remaining chicken livers and sprinkle with more dukkah and the remaining fresh thyme. Pour over the remaining ghee (100 ml) and fold over the clingfilm to seal.

• Cut out a piece of polystyrene, or a few thick pieces of cardboard just smaller than the mould, and place them so they fit inside the terrine, directly on top of the livers. Press with 4 kg weight and refrigerate for at least 6 hours.

• After 6 hours remove the weight. When you are ready to serve, unwrap the terrine and cut it into 2 cm slices. Make a tangy dressing using 150 ml extra-virgin olive oil, 50 ml champagne vinegar, a touch of honey and a splash of pomegranate molasses. Brush the slice of terrine with the vinaigrette and serve with some lightly dressed salad leaves and slices of toasted buttery brioche.

• Makes ten to twelve portions.

Tahini whipped with yoghurt

This is makes a light creamy dressing, combining the nuttiness of tahini with the tang of lemon juice and yoghurt. It is delicious with falafel and fish.

150 g yoghurt

3 tablespoons tahini

1 clove garlic crushed with
  ¼ teaspoon salt

juice of 1 lemon

½ teaspoon pepper

• Combine all the ingredients in a bowl and whisk thoroughly. Taste and adjust seasoning if required.

Sesame-honey wafers

Buttery, crisp and golden, these wafers use the classic combination of honey and sesame. Eat them with all sorts of ice-creams and creamy desserts – or just on their own with a cup of strong coffee.

125 g butter

200 g castor sugar

4 teaspoons honey

100 g plain flour

½ teaspoon ginger powder

2 egg whites

100 g sesame seeds

• In your electric mixer, cream the butter and sugar at high speed. Add the honey, flour and ginger powder. When they are fully blended, add the egg whites and mix until they are well combined.
• Line a baking tray with greaseproof paper and smear the mixture into circles about 1 mm thick – a wet finger is ideal for this! Sprinkle the circles liberally with sesame seeds, pouring off any excess.
• Preheat the oven to 160°C, and bake on the middle shelf for 7–10 minutes, or until they are golden-brown.
• Cool them down on a wire rack and store in them in an airtight container.
• Makes about 30 wafers.

Silverbeet and Spinach

From a very young age children are exhorted to eat their greens by well-intentioned adults. Naturally, this 'it's good for you' approach leaves most children cold – especially when greens such as silverbeet and spinach can be strong-flavoured or even bitter, and cook down to a distressing sliminess.

With age, of course, comes a little wisdom, and eventually most of us make that wonderful discovery that greens really are delicious. Yes, they are full of fibre, vitamins and minerals, but instead of that being their main selling point, it becomes merely a bonus. What is more, that detested slipperiness is what suddenly makes them so desirable – steamed or braised to a luscious glossy silkiness, or conversely adding a crunchy vitality to raw salads.

Silverbeet, spinach and many other wild greens are found throughout the Mediterranean and Middle East, where they are hugely popular. Of the two, silverbeet (or Swiss chard, as it is also known), is thought to have been cultivated since Neolithic times, and was certainly known and loved by the ancient Greeks and Romans. Silverbeet is actually a type of beet, but the leaves have been developed rather than the root. In France and Italy they tend to use the stalks – the chards – which are sliced out and braised or gratinéed separately, rather like celery. Middle Easterners prefer the leaves, which are sturdy enough to be stuffed, or can be shredded into soups, stuffings and pies or braised with garlic, lemon and allspice for a cold mezze dish.

Spinach, on the other hand, seems to have been unknown to the Greeks and Romans. Native to Persia, it is yet another vegetable that was carted west by the Arabs. By the Middle Ages spinach had become popular in Spain, Italy, France and even England. Its European names all derive from the Arabic 'sapanekh', which comes itself from the Persian word 'espenaj'.

Spinach is rather more delicate than silverbeet. It needs only the briefest of cooking (or can even be eaten raw), and lends itself generously to other stronger flavours: garlic, lemon-juice and chilli all complement it superbly. The Arabic legacy can be seen all around the southern and eastern Mediterranean, where there are countless recipes for spinach mixed with chickpeas or lentils – often garnished with currants and crunchy pine nuts. Spinach works equally well, of course, with the smooth, softening influence of cream, yoghurt, cheese or eggs.

SELECTING AND STORING SILVERBEET AND SPINACH

Silverbeet is a surprisingly popular home-grown vegetable. It is easy to grow and its season is almost never-ending. Its crinkly leaves can be a deep, glossy green or brightly hued red, orange or yellow. When buying silverbeet from the market or supermarket, choose small bunches, as the leaves are likely to be younger and more tender. Silverbeet should be firm and vital, not soft and wilted. The leaves should be glossy, without too much sun damage, and the long stalks should be crisp and white.

Spinach comes in large bundles or in convenient ready-washed loose leaves. Again, choose bunches which look vibrant and healthy, not withered and drooping. If you can, select smaller leaves and avoid any which are yellow, slimy or torn. Spinach often comes with a generous covering of mud which needs to be washed off very thoroughly.

The stalks should be torn off at the base of the leaf – the whole central stem does not need to be removed, as it does with silverbeet.

Frozen chopped spinach is an adequate substitute for fresh spinach in soups or stuffing mixes where the texture is less important. But if you want to serve spinach as a vegetable dish or salad, then really only fresh will do.

USING SILVERBEET AND SPINACH

For most Middle Eastern dishes, only the silverbeet leaves are required. After washing thoroughly, carefully slice out the stalks (they can be blanched and refrigerated for use in other recipes, if desired). If the leaves are to be used whole, they should be blanched for a few minutes and then refreshed in cold water. Otherwise they may be steamed until tender for around 6 minutes and tossed in butter or olive oil. Silverbeet leaves are also good braised in olive oil with garlic, lemon juice and a pinch of allspice.

Spinach may be steamed in its rinsing water in a large pot – it needs to be turned constantly so that the bottom leaves don't burn and the top leaves get their turn close to the heat. As soon as all the leaves have wilted down, the spinach must be very well drained and all that is required then is a large knob of butter and a seasoning of salt and pepper. Or they may be sautéed in hot olive oil with a little garlic, or even blanched, a handful at a time, in lots of boiling salted water. Each little bundle should then be plunged into a sink of cold water and then tightly squeezed of its water. This method is often better when the spinach is not to be eaten straight away as a simple accompaniment. The leaves will be drier, so are better for stuffing mixes, or for salads. The blanched leaves can even be very carefully unfurled and stuffed themselves, as a change from vine leaves.

SILVERBEET AND SPINACH RECIPES

Silverbeet stewed with Tunisian spices

Silverbeet braised with lemon juice and topped with caramelised onions is a traditional Lebanese favourite. Here, in place of the usual allspice, we raise the heat level with a touch of fiery tabil, a Tunisian spice mix.

TABIL

1½ cups fresh coriander, roots removed

1 tablespoon caraway seeds, roasted and crushed

½ head garlic, cloves peeled

1 red pepper, roasted and peeled

6 bullet chillies, de-seeded, scraped and finely chopped

80 ml olive oil

80 ml olive oil

2 onions, sliced

1 teaspoon red wine vinegar

1 leek, finely diced

1 bunch silverbeet, stems removed and roughly chopped

1 clove garlic crushed with ½ teaspoon salt

juice of 1 lemon

salt and pepper

1 teaspoon tabil

- To make the tabil, whiz all the ingredients together, slowly adding the oil to make a smooth paste.
- Heat half the oil in a heavy-based pot and sauté the onions over a low heat for 10–15 minutes until they are darkly caramelised. Stir in the vinegar and remove the onions to a bowl.
- Heat the rest of the oil and sauté the leek for a minute until it has softened, then add the silverbeet and garlic. When this has wilted, add the lemon juice and season with salt and pepper. Cover, lower the heat and braise for 10 minutes. Then raise the heat, remove the lid and stir in the tabil. Remove from the heat and serve in a bowl with lemon wedges and the caramelised onions piled on top.
- Serves four to six.

Spinach, pecorino and potato pie

Pecorino is a sharp Italian cheese made from sheep's milk. It works beautifully with the Middle Eastern combination of spinach and allspice with cubed waxy potatoes in these pies. Serve them as a starter or light lunch dish with a salad, or as an accompaniment to roast lamb or other barbecued meats.

60 ml olive oil

3 shallots, finely sliced

I clove garlic, finely chopped

I small bullet chilli, de-seeded, scraped and finely shredded

200 g spinach, destalked and finely shredded

I large waxy potato, peeled and cut into I cm dice

¼ teaspoon allspice

salt and pepper

200 ml stock or water

40 g pecorino cheese (or parmesan or grana), grated

4 sheets filo pastry

20 g melted butter mixed with 20 ml olive oil

• Heat the olive oil in heavy-based pot. Add the shallots, garlic and chilli and stir over a medium heat for 30 seconds. Add the shredded spinach and stir for a further minute until it collapses and softens slightly. Then add the potato dice, allspice, salt and pepper and stock and bring to the boil. Cover the pot, lower the heat and simmer for 4 minutes over a gentle heat. Then raise the heat and cook uncovered for an additional 4 minutes, to let the liquid evaporate. Remove from the heat and tip into a sieve to allow any excess moisture to drain away. Stir in the grated cheese and allow the mixture to cool.

• Preheat the oven to 200°C. To make the pies, lay a sheet of filo out widthways and brush one half with the melted butter mixture. Fold this half over the other. Turn this smaller rectangle through 90° so it is again widthways in front of you, and brush half with the butter mixture. Again fold it in half. You should then have a rectangle of about 14 × 20 cm. Trim off 6 cm from one side to make a 14 cm square. Brush with butter. Heap a quarter of the silverbeet mixture into a high mound in the centre of pastry. Fold the pastry sides up and over the filling and flatten them slightly to form a raised pie. Brush the pastry edges with melted butter to help them stick together and then carefully turn the pie over. Flatten and smooth the top slightly and then use the palms of both hands to shape into a neat round pie. Brush the surface with butter and cook for 8 minutes on a tray lined with baking paper.

• Remove the tray from the oven and turn the pie over. Return the tray to the oven and cook a further 4 minutes until the pie is a golden-brown all over.

• Remove it from the oven and serve it immediately.

Moorish spinach and almond salad

Versions of this cooked spinach salad are popular throughout Portugal and Spain. The sweet–sour dressing and fruit-and-nut combination reveal its Moorish origins!

2 bunches spinach, picked over and well rinsed

4 shallots, finely sliced

2 teaspoons currants

60 ml sherry

¼ teaspoon allspice

¼ teaspoon cinnamon

30 ml sherry vinegar

50 ml extra-virgin olive oil

salt and pepper

60 g flaked almonds, fried in olive oil until golden brown and crisp

• Blanch small batches of the spinach in plenty of boiling, salted water for 10 seconds. Refresh in cold water and then squeeze out as much moisture as possible.

• Soak the currants in the sherry. Mix the shallots with the sherried currants in a large mixing bowl.

• Gently pull the clumps of spinach leaves apart and place in the bowl with the spices, vinegar and oil. Generously season with salt and pepper and sprinkle the fried almonds over the top.

Other silverbeet and spinach recipes

Sambusek, pages 200–201

Sumac

When it comes to food, a defining characteristic of Middle Easterners is their love of sour flavours. Lemons, pomegranates and sumac are all used extensively to add a refreshing tartness to dishes. Of these three, sumac, which has a lovely lemony flavour and is a pretty dark-red colour, is virtually unknown outside the Middle East.

Sumac is usually purchased as a coarse powder. It is ground from the dried berries of a shrub which grows widely all around the Middle East and eastern Mediterranean. Sumac is particularly popular in Lebanon and Syria, but it is also used in Iran, Iraq and Turkey and other Middle Eastern countries.

In Iran and Iraq sumac is used mainly as a tangy seasoning for sprinkling over kebabs – Iranian restaurants will nearly always set it on the table as a condiment to accompany grilled meats. Elsewhere, sumac is used in marinades – its tangy flavour works well with grilled meats, poultry and fish. It is often added to vinaigrettes and other dressings, or added to salads such as the refreshing bread salad fattouche. In Lebanon, sumac's greatest use is in the ubiquitous spice mix za'atar (page 265), in which it is combined with thyme and sesame seeds and used as a topping for fabulous freshly baked breads.

SELECTING, STORING AND USING SUMAC

You will have to visit a specialist Middle Eastern grocer to find sumac, but it is worth tracking down. Compared with other spices and herbs it is sold in confusingly large quantities (usually 250 g) but it is far from being expensive and keeps very well in an airtight container in a cool, dark cupboard.

Sumac is a pretty deep red-brown colour, rather like rich loamy soil, with a sour, salty flavour. When you use it in Middle Eastern recipes, it is often a good idea to wash it in a little water first – heap it into a tea-strainer and run it under the cold tap for a few minutes. This helps to intensify the flavour even further.

Other sumac recipes

Lebanese Bread with Za'atar, page 267
Slow-Cooked Salmon with Arabic Spices, page 268
Soused Zucchini and Eggplant, page 296

SUMAC RECIPES

Fattouche

Fattouche is a simple garden salad, and a handy way to use up stale pieces of Arabic bread. It is most delicious when the bread pieces are fried, but for a healthier option you can toast or grill them.

2 teaspoons sumac

¼ teaspoon allspice

¼ teaspoon pepper

I medium purple onion, sliced

4 cos lettuce leaves washed and dried

2 tomatoes, ripe but firm, roughly diced

2 Lebanese cucumbers, cut into
   chunky dice

½ cup parsley leaves, roughly chopped

⅓ cup mint leaves, roughly chopped
   leaves (or I tablespoon of dried mint)

½ cup purslane (if available)

I piece Arabic bread

60 ml olive oil

60 g butter

I clove garlic crushed with
   I teaspoon salt

juice of I lemon

40 ml extra-virgin olive oil

½ tablespoon balsamic vinegar

• Soak the sumac in cold water for a few minutes and remove any husks or uncrushed berries which float to the top. Add the sumac, allspice and pepper to the sliced onion, and rub it in well. Cut the cos leaves crossways into 3 cm strips. Place them in a large salad bowl with the tomatoes, cucumbers and all the herb leaves.

• Split the bread open and cut it into rough 2 cm triangular shapes. Melt the butter and oil in a frying pan until they are foaming and fry the bread in two batches until it is golden-brown, remove it with a slotted spoon and drain it on absorbent kitchen paper. Mix the garlic paste with the lemon juice. Whisk together the extra-virgin olive oil and balsamic vinegar.

• When you are ready to serve, add the spiced onions to the other salad ingredients, add the lemon–garlic mix and stir well. Finally, pour over the dressing, add the pieces of fried bread, mix everything together gently and serve straight away.

• Serves six.

Quail escabèche with Middle Eastern spices

Escabèche is a traditional Spanish and Portuguese dish, using fish or little game birds like quail and partridge. These are fried or poached, then cooked and allowed to cool in a spicy marinade for 24 hours or so. They are served at room temperature as a tapas dish or as a light meal. The sourness of sumac works really well with the tangy lime marinade. Serve with warm crusty bread as a starter or a light lunch.

4 jumbo quail

2 cloves garlic

½ teaspoon salt

2 tablespoons Ras El Hanout (page 73)

100 ml olive oil

2 onions, finely sliced

1 large green chilli, de-seeded, scraped and finely shredded

2 medium ripe tomatoes, skinned, de-seeded cut into large dice

juice of 2 limes plus the zest of 1

2 teaspoons sumac

salt and pepper

- Cut the quail in half and trim off excess fat.
- Crush garlic with the salt and add 1 tablespoon of the Ras El Hanout and 2 tablespoons of the oil. Rub this mixture all over the quail pieces and let them sit for 1–2 hours.
- Heat the remaining olive oil in a heavy-based pan and place the quail pieces in, skin side down. Cook on a medium heat for about 5 minutes, until they become golden. Turn them and cook a further 5 minutes. Remove the quail from the pan with a slotted spoon.
- Lower the heat and add the onions, chilli, tomatoes and lime juice and zest. Allow to sweat gently until the onions become very soft and translucent (about 10–15 minutes). Place the quail back on top of the onion mix and cook on the same low heat for a further 8–10 minutes.
- Place the quail in a serving dish and pour hot marinade over the top.
- Allow to cool, then cover and refrigerate overnight. Allow to return to room temperature before eating.

Salmon grilled with sumac and fennel crumbs

These days salmon has lost its cachet as a true gourmet food as it is widely farmed, relatively cheap and readily available. Sadly though, the farmed variety lacks the flavour of its wild cousins, and we are always looking for interesting ways to liven it up. As salmon is a dense, oily fish it benefits from being matched with robust flavours. Baking salmon medallions in this tangy crumb is surprisingly simple and effective. Serve them with a big bowl of Goat's Cheese Mashed Potatoes (page 49) and salad leaves dressed with a sour-sweet Tomato-Pomegranate Dressing (page 218).

CRUMBING MIX

1 tablespoon sumac

1 tablespoon fennel seeds, roasted and crushed

zest of ½ lemon

½ cup fresh breadcrumbs

4 salmon medallions, skinned (160 g portions)

¼ teaspoon salt

pepper

40 ml olive oil

1 teaspoon Dijon mustard

• Preheat the oven to maximum heat. Mix the sumac, fennel seeds and lemon zest with the breadcrumbs and set aside.
• Lightly season the salmon medallions all over with salt and pepper. In a heavy-based oven-proof pan, heat the olive oil and sauté the salmon pieces (skin side up) for 30–40 seconds, moving them constantly so they don't stick. Turn them over and sauté for a further 30 seconds, still moving them around the pan.
• Remove the pan from the heat, brush the salmon with the mustard and sprinkle over a ½ cm layer of the crumbing mix, packing it on neatly.
• Place the pan on the top shelf of the oven and cook for 3 minutes for medium–rare, or longer as desired.
• Remove from the oven and allow to rest in a warm spot for 4–5 minutes.

Thyme

The heady fragrance of thyme wafts through the sun-warmed air above countless rocky hillsides around the Mediterranean and in the Middle East. But it is a hardy, tenacious little plant and grows just as well in cooler climates, even thriving as far north as Iceland!

Thyme is a well-known herb due to its inclusion in those dusty little bags of herbes de Provence, and it is also one of the three essential herbs in a bouquet garni, used to make stocks, soups and all kinds of slow-cooked savoury dishes in classical French cooking. It has a special affinity with rabbit – bunnies that have fed on wild thyme are said to be particularly delicious – as well as game birds such as quail, pigeon, guinea fowl and even partridge. Even simple lamb cutlets acquire a lovely savoury flavour when grilled with a few sprigs of thyme, or when brushed with a honey–thyme glaze. Interestingly, the magical alliance between honey and thyme was even remarked by Virgil – the bees which make the legendary Greek Hymetus honey have been gathering their nectar from tiny thyme flowers for centuries.

Fresh or dried, thyme is dearly loved in the Middle East for its lively savoury flavour. The fresh leaves are stripped from their stalks and scattered into salads and salad dressings. The dried leaves retain their intense flavour and are often combined with cheese dishes. Shankleish – golf-balls of chalky-dry yoghurt cheese – are often rolled in thyme with a little chilli and then marinated in olive oil.

In many Middle Eastern countries the most common use of thyme is in the aromatic mixture za'atar, which is eaten on a daily basis throughout Lebanon. 'Za'atar' is the Arabic word for both thyme the herb and the seasoning mix made with dried thyme, sour red sumac berries and sesame seeds. When we travelled through Lebanon a few years ago our favourite breakfast was mankoushi, a flat round bread rather like a pizza, thickly spread with za'atar and eaten hot from a wood-fired oven. The aroma of this bread fills the streets early in the morning, and is quite irresistible. At home we make our own instant version by mixing za'atar with a little olive oil to make a paste which is quite delicious spread on toast.

SELECTING AND STORING THYME

There are many different varieties of thyme but the only two you are likely to find in the shops are common thyme and lemon thyme. They are quite different and should, therefore, be used differently. Lemon thyme really does have distinct lemony overtones, and works well with poultry, veal or baked fish dishes. Common thyme is spicier, with a strong savoury flavour, and is better suited for seasoning heavier dishes like rich stews, soups or even stuffings – either on its own or as part of a bouquet garni.

Thyme is a perennial, and is readily available all year round, either picked from your own herb patch, or in little twiggy bundles from greengrocers and most supermarkets. Fresh thyme is a hardy herb and will keep happily in the refrigerator for at least a week. Dried thyme lasts several months before losing its potency.

USING THYME

Carefully wash and dry the herb before you start on the fun task of stripping the tiny little leaves from thyme's woody stalks. Then scatter them liberally over grills, toss them through salads or mix them into stuffings. Some resourceful people keep a little bunch of thyme to use as a handy brush for dousing olive oil and flavour directly onto grilling meat.

Some recipes specify dried herbs. Thyme dries particularly well, retaining much of its flavour for several months. Ideally you should hang your bunch upside down, in a dry airy place for 2–3 weeks, until it is completely dry.

To make the Lebanese mix za'atar you need to buy a bag of sumac and a bag of za'atar from a Middle Eastern grocer. Keep them separately, stored in an airtight container, until you want to make up the mix. It is best to make za'atar in fairly small quantities to ensure that the flavours stay fresh and zingy. The proportions are three of za'atar to one of sumac (start with a tablespoon measure). Combine the two loosely together and then drizzle in enough oil to make a loose paste. No, it doesn't look very exciting – but just wait until you taste it!

THYME RECIPES

Lebanese bread with za'atar

Bread making often ends up being much less of a chore than you anticipate. If, like many of us, you are totally sick of focaccia, then try making these stubby little bread sticks for a change. This quantity makes 20 sticks, which might seem like a lot, but somehow they always seem to disappear quite swiftly.

BREAD DOUGH

500 g plain flour

20 g salt

30 g fresh yeast

20 g white sugar

1½ cups warm water

LEBANESE SPICED OIL

3 tablespoons za'atar

1 tablespoon sumac

100 ml olive oil

• Place the flour and salt in your electric mixer. In a separate bowl whisk together the yeast, sugar and water to a smooth, creamy liquid and add it to the flour. Mix with the dough hook for 5–10 minutes until the ingredients form a smooth, glossy dough. Cover the dough with a cloth and place it in a warm place to prove for around an hour.

• For the Lebanese spiced oil, mix the za'atar, sumac and olive oil.

• Knock the dough back and roll it out on a floured work surface to an 80 cm × 25 cm rectangle, about 1.5 cm thick. Brush it with the Lebanese spiced oil and sprinkle it with a little salt. Then cut it into sticks about 2.5 cm wide. Place them on a baking tray and leave them to prove in a warm place for a further 10 minutes.

• Preheat the oven to 180°C and bake for about 10 minutes until the sticks are golden-brown.

Slow-cooked salmon with Arabic spices

These days it is very fashionable to grill or fry salmon quickly, so that the outer edges cook to a neat little border around a bright pink – often raw – centre. This recipe is the complete antithesis, and is pleasurably simple to make. The slow-cooking merely sets the salmon's firm oily flesh to a gelatinous, almost buttery soft wobble! The spices are a good way of livening up farmed salmon's predictable flavour. Serve with a tangy sauce, like Avgolemono (page 157), or with Soused Zucchini and Eggplant (page 296) or even with crunchy croutons spread with a little Black Olive Cream (page 176).

I tablespoon za'atar

I teaspoon sumac

I teaspoon fresh thyme leaves

4 salmon medallions, skinned
   (160 g portions)

60 ml olive oil

salt and pepper

• Preheat the oven to the lowest possible heat. Mix the za'atar, sumac and thyme together. Brush the salmon pieces generously with the oil. Lightly season with salt and pepper and then sprinkle the herb mixture all over the salmon, so pieces are completely covered. Line a heavy baking tray with baking parchment (this helps slow heat conduction from the metal tray to the fish).

• Place the salmon on the tray in the centre of the oven. Leave for 15 minutes and then check that it is not cooking too fast (if opaque milky liquid has started to ooze from the fish, then the oven is too hot). If necessary, leave the oven door ajar while cooking a further 20 minutes. When it is ready the salmon should look opaque and almost gelatinous.

Garfish grilled with thyme

zest of 2 limes, finely grated

1 tablespoon fresh thyme leaves,
    chopped

1 teaspoon sumac

8 garfish, cleaned and filleted into
    butterflies, so that the two halves
    remain attached to each other

salt and pepper

60 g olive oil

• Dry the lime zest overnight, or for about ½ hour in a very low oven.
• Mix the lime zest with the thyme leaves and sumac.
• Open out the garfish and fold them in half widthways, to form a fattish rectangle. Sprinkle with salt and pepper and a little of the lime–thyme–sumac mixture. Heat the olive oil and cook the garfish, head end down, until nicely coloured. This will take about a minute on high heat. Turn the fish over and sprinkle with more of the spice mix. Cook for another minute and then remove from the pan.
• Serve straight away with Baba Ghanoush (page 113) and Parsley Salad (page 192).
• Serves four (two garfish each).

Other thyme recipes

Coarse Tapenade Salad, page 175
Portobello Mushrooms Baked Between Vine Leaves, page 280

Turkish Coffee

Café culture in the Middle East is largely men's business. Anyone who has ever visited this region, where alcohol is often prohibited, will be aware of how central cafes are to men's daily lives. They spend many long hours sitting at tables – alone or with friends – sipping small cups of fierce black coffee, puffing on water pipes, playing backgammon or cards, arguing, reading the papers, watching the telly or listening to the radio. Any excuse to linger will do, at any time of day of night!

Hospitality in the home is also unthinkable without coffee. A visitor's arrival is the cue to prepare fresh coffee, which is then brought to the guest and poured with much ceremony from elegant long-handled pots into tiny china cups. Coffee is always drunk very strong, usually sweet, and often flavoured with cardamom seeds or orange-blossom water. When coffee is served the goodies come out also – no self-respecting Arabic housewife would be without a tin of buttery little raybeh biscuits, or perfumed, nut-stuffed ma'amoul, and of course on special occasions there is always a huge range of sticky sweet pastries to be sampled.

If you are lucky, when the coffee is finished someone will suggest a reading of the cups. The empty cups are turned over and the dregs allowed to trickle down the insides and dry. The resulting patterns usually predict imminent romance, vast wealth, or hordes of children, depending on one's circumstances!

Originating in Ethiopia, the wild coffea arabica bush is believed to have been cultivated by African tribesmen from the sixth century AD, where it was enjoyed for its stimulating properties – rather in the same way that we enjoy it today! It is likely that at first the berries were just chewed, and then later on they were crushed to a wet paste and infused with water.

Later still, a more sophisticated coffee drink was made by fermenting the juice from the ripe berries. However, the modern drink, as we know it, was not invented until the thirteenth century, when beans were cleaned and roasted before infusing. Despite all manner of fancy coffee-making contraptions which litter our kitchens nowadays, in Middle Eastern households they still make coffee by pulverising the roasted beans to a powder and combining it with boiling water to make the strong infusion we call Turkish (or Arabic) coffee.

From Ethiopia, the use of coffee spread across the Red Sea to Aden in Yemen and its popularity swept rapidly through Arabia. By the sixteenth century, its consumption had become fashionable in Mecca, Damascus and Constantinople, where the first true coffee house was established in 1554. It is not hard to see why coffee was such an immediate hit in these intensely religious Muslim lands where alcohol was forbidden. In fact, our word 'coffee' comes from the Turkish word 'kahveh', which itself comes from the old Arabic word for wine, 'kahwah'. Denied the real thing, Muslims had to invent a new drink! Coffee was so popular in Constantinople, according to the French food writer Alexander Dumas in his *Dictionnaire de Cuisine*, 'that the imams complained their mosques were empty while the coffee houses were always full.'

SELECTING AND STORING TURKISH COFFEE

Chez Malouf, we are just as likely to enjoy a cup of instant coffee or to jiggle a tea-bag in a mug, but as a special treat Greg will make Turkish coffee. We buy a popular Lebanese blend – from a Middle Eastern grocer – which is already flavoured with cardamom seeds. However, there are many different types of Turkish and Arabic coffees available, and it is a good idea to try different ones to find the brand you like. Otherwise, any dark roasted coffee beans will be quite acceptable (perhaps Mocha beans from Yemen for the sake of authenticity) and additional flavourings (like cardamom or cinnamon) can be added later on.

If you prefer to let the store grind the coffee beans for you, then make sure you ask for the very finest grind possible – it should end up being closer to a fine powder than the coarser grind we use for European methods of coffee-making. One thing to avoid above all, though, are the instant powdered versions of so-called Turkish coffee available from supermarkets. They just don't come anywhere near the real thing!

As with all good quality coffee, the oil content means that it will deteriorate over time. Coffee beans and ground coffee should be stored in the refrigerator or in the freezer.

Chicken livers pressed with dukkah (recipe page 251)

Turkish coffee ice-cream (recipe page 274)

TURKISH COFFEE RECIPES

Turkish coffee

Turkish or Arabic coffee is best made in small quantities in the traditional long-handled pot called a 'rakweh', but a very small saucepan will just about do. The whole process is extremely simple, but like so many things, tends to be shrouded in mystique, everyone having their own particular method for making plenty of the desirable golden froth. Each family, too, tends to have its own little traditions and rituals – the Maloufs, for instance, favour tapping the side of the pot with a spoon at various points of the procedure. Nobody quite knows why – it's just something they do!

Various aromatics may be used to flavour the coffee. The Lebanese and Syrians like to add a few cracked cardamom pods, or a pinch of ground cardamom to the pot. In the Gulf states they add splash of rosewater, or occasionally even saffron. In North Africa they enjoy cinnamon and sometimes coriander seeds, while in Yemen they favour ginger and cloves.

6 small cups of water

3 heaped teaspoons dark-roasted, plain
   Turkish coffee, finely ground

2 teaspoons sugar

3 cardamom pods, lightly crushed

- Bring the water to the boil and add the coffee, sugar and cardamom pods. Bring the mixture back to the boil and, as soon as the froth begins to rise, remove the pot from the heat.
- Once the froth has settled, return the pot to the heat and repeat the process twice. Serve the coffee straight away, taking care to give everyone a share of the froth. Let it settle in the cup for a minute or two before sipping.
- Serves six.

Turkish coffee ice-cream

Turkish coffee makes a simply superb ice-cream. Rich, smoky and very adult, it is delicious with a steamed chocolate pudding, a hot chocolate soufflé, roasted pears or hazelnut Florentine biscuits. Even a simple mix of summer berries works beautifully.

200 g castor sugar

½ cup water

100 g liquid glucose

3 cardamom pods, cracked

100 g dark-roasted, plain
   Turkish Coffee, finely ground

60 g best quality dark chocolate

12 egg yolks

¼ cup Tia Maria

1 litre thickened cream

• Place the sugar, water, glucose, cardamom and coffee in a pan and slowly bring to the boil, making sure the sugar dissolves completely. Simmer for 5 minutes then pour over the chocolate and stir until it melts.

• Whip the egg yolks at high speed until they are light and fluffy. Strain the coffee-chocolate mixture though a coffee filter into the egg yolks and beat for 1 minute. Add the Tia Maria and cream and refrigerate for 1 hour. Pour into an ice-cream machine and churn according to the manufacturer's instructions.

• Serves eight.

Turkish coffee petits pots

50 g dark-roasted, plain Turkish coffee, finely ground

250 ml pure cream

I cinnamon stick

50 g best quality dark chocolate, grated

4 egg yolks

50 g castor sugar

• Moisten the ground coffee with warm water and tie it in a muslin square.
• Bring the cream to the boil with the coffee bag and cinnamon stick. Simmer for 5 minutes to infuse the coffee and cinnamon. Turn off the heat and squeeze the muslin bag to extract as much coffee flavour as possible. Add the grated chocolate and stir until it is completely melted.
• In a separate bowl, whisk the egg yolks with the sugar and then pour them over the hot cream mixture. Stir well and return to the saucepan. Stir over low heat until the mixture thickens to the consistency of custard. You should be able to draw a distinct line through the custard on the back of a spoon.
• Pour the custard into a glass bowl and immediately place it in a sink of cold water or crushed ice. Stir gently while the mixture cools down.
• Spoon into petit pots, or little ramekin dishes, and chill. Serve with a sprinkle of Pine Nut Praline (page 210), or Sesame-Honey Wafers (page 252).
• Makes around eight petit pots.

Vine Leaves

Over the last few decades Australia has become one of the most significant wine-producing countries of the world, and a sadly neglected by-product of all this excellent industry is the vine leaf! Throughout the Mediterranean and the Middle East, however, people make good use of vine leaves as a kind of edible wrapping paper. Grape vines grow wild throughout these regions, and many people have a handy supply of the leaves right outside their back door.

There can't be many of us who haven't tried stuffed vine leaves as part of a Greek or Lebanese banquet. Dolmades, as they are best known to us, can be served hot or cold, with slightly different, but equally delicious fillings. Cold, they usually have a rice stuffing, flavoured with subtle combinations of cinnamon, allspice and mint, and sometimes even enriched with the pungency of saffron. The flavours merge beautifully into the lemony backdrop provided by the vine leaf itself. Turkish and Iranian cooks also like to include pine nuts and currants, and yet another popular version uses dill.

Hot vine leaves are traditionally filled with minced meat – usually lamb – bulked out with rice and onion and flavoured with plenty of spices. They may not sound quite as exotic, but braised slowly they develop a lovely rich lemony flavour. Greg's mother, May, cooks her vine leaves on top of lamb ribs or shanks, with handfuls of garlic cloves, lots of lemon and fresh mint. In good one-pot-cooking style, the meat can then be enjoyed as a main meal after the vine leaves.

Vine leaves are not just used for making dolmades. Their chief attraction is the slightly tart, lemony flavour they impart, so they have a natural affinity with fish and poultry. A favourite Mediterranean cooking technique is to wrap vine leaves around small fish such as sardines and red mullet and chargrill or roast them. They not only look very pretty, but the vine leaves help protect the delicate flesh from the flames and keep the flesh moist, while adding a subtle hint of citrus. Meatier and oily fish, such as tuna and swordfish, and even poultry and game birds benefit from this technique. Brush the meat with a little oil and lemon juice first, sprinkle with oregano, wrap in a large vine leaf and bake in the oven.

SELECTING AND STORING VINE LEAVES

Even if you don't live next to a vineyard, vine leaves are still widely available. The leaves preserved in brine are perfectly acceptable, even if the process of buying them is not be quite as romantic as plucking them straight from the vine. If you can lay your hands on some fresh leaves, they can be frozen for future use. Small younger leaves are more tender, and have a more delicate flavour.

USING VINE LEAVES

Fresh vine leaves need to be blanched before using. Plunge them into boiling water and count to ten, then remove them and refresh them in cold water. Squeeze them dry before carefully unfurling and spreading them out on a benchtop ready to stuff.

Preserved vine leaves are stored in brine and need to be well rinsed in warm water before use.

VINE LEAF RECIPES

Goat's cheese baked in vine leaves

This is one of the most delicious starters we can imagine! It is a great way of using any dried-out ends of goat's cheese logs you might have in the refrigerator, but very young fresh cheese works well too. These fat little parcels should be served hot from the oven, all squelchy and lemony, with the hot tangy cheese almost bursting through the skins. Serve lots of warm crusty bread on which to smear the bubbling hot cheese.

100 g vine leaves, rinsed and drained

200 g goat's cheese (25 g per person)

extra-virgin olive oil

a pinch of dried mint

pepper

• If you use fresh vine leaves, quickly blanch them before use. The jars of brine-pickled leaves need to be well rinsed and dried first.

• Lay the vine leaf, vein side up (or two together if small) on a kitchen bench. Mould a portion of cheese into a small sausage shape and place across the base of leaf. Drizzle a little oil over the cheese and add a pinch of mint and grind of pepper.

• Roll the leaf over once, then fold the sides in and continue to roll it into a neat sausage shape. Brush it with a little oil and cook under a preheated hot grill for 4–5 minutes or until they start to colour and blister.

• This quantity will make eight little parcels to eat as a snack or quick and easy starter.

Chicken and pistachio dolmades

Shop-bought dolmades often have a nasty 'tinny' flavour, suggesting that the vine leaves have been used straight from a big commercial-sized tin, with barely adequate rinsing. The chicken and pistachios make these home-made dolmades more delicate than traditional lamb versions.

250 g vine leaves

100 g long-grain rice

200 g chicken mince

1/4 teaspoon allspice

1/4 teaspoon cinnamon

1/4 teaspoon black pepper

60 g unsalted, shelled pistachio nuts

zest of 1 lemon, finely chopped

pinch of salt

1/2 teaspoon pepper

4 tomatoes, sliced

4 cloves garlic, cut in half

1 bunch mint

1 litre chicken stock

juice of 1 lemon

• If you are using preserved vine leaves, soak them well, then rinse them and pat them dry. Fresh vine leaves should first be blanched. Wash the rice and mix it with the chicken mince, allspice, cinnamon, black pepper, pistachio nuts and lemon zest.

• Lay a vine leaf on the work surface, vein side up, and place a spoonful of filling across the base of the leaf. Roll it over once, fold the sides in and then continue to roll it into a neat sausage shape. The dolmades should be around the size of your little finger – don't roll them too tightly or they will burst during the cooking. Continue stuffing and rolling until the filling is all used.

• Line the bottom of a heavy-based casserole with vine leaves and a layer of sliced tomatoes.

• Pack the dolmades in tightly on top of the tomatoes, stuffing the halved garlic cloves in among them. Lay the bunch of mint over the top, then pour in the chicken stock and lemon juice. Cover with a plate and slowly bring to the boil. Once boiling, lower the heat and simmer gently for 45 minutes.

• Allow to cool, then turn out into a serving dish and serve hot, warm or even cold, with plenty of yoghurt.

• These quantities will make around twenty dolmades.

Portobello mushrooms baked between vine leaves

Portobello mushrooms are also known as 'Swiss browns', and are readily available from supermarkets. Tangy and fragrant with thyme, these meaty baked mushrooms are a lovely accompaniment to grilled meats. Or for a quick and easy light meal, they can be served with a small salad with plenty of bread to mop up all the lovely lemony, garlicky juices.

100 g vine leaves, rinsed well in cold water and dried well

80 ml olive oil

16 medium-size portobello mushrooms,

60 g shallots, sliced finely

1 clove garlic, sliced thinly

8 stalks fresh thyme

juice of 1 lemon

salt and pepper

• If you are using preserved vine leaves, soak them well, then rinse them and pat them dry. Fresh vine leaves should first be blanched and refreshed.

• Brush the base and sides of an ovenproof dish (28 cm × 20 cm, and 5 cm deep) with a little oil. Lay the vine leaves over the bottom of the dish and up around the sides, reserving enough to cover.

• Wipe the mushrooms and trim the stalks so they are flush with the base of the mushroom.

• In a large bowl, combine the mushrooms, shallots and garlic with half the remaining olive oil. Place the mushroom mix in the ovenproof dish, mushrooms with stalk side down, and scatter the sprigs of thyme over the top.

• Sprinkle with lemon juice, season with salt and pepper and cover with the remaining vine leaves, tucking them in around the side. Brush with oil and cook in a preheated 180°C oven for 30 minutes.

Watermelon

There is something childishly appealing about watermelons, with their vivid mouthwash–pink flesh, slick black seeds, stripy green skin and simple sweet flavour that satisfies our primitive desire for sugar. It is hard to retain a sense of dignity when you munch a big smiley slice of watermelon and feel the juice run down your chin!

Watermelons are believed to have originated in Africa. Their first recorded harvesting was nearly 5000 years ago in Egypt, where there are numerous paintings in Pharaonic tombs depicting their beauty. Watermelons still grow wild in desert watering-holes in some parts of Africa and one can only admire Mother Nature for her foresight in arranging for such a welcome source of liquid refreshment in harsh desert lands!

From Egypt, watermelons were spread along ancient Mediterranean trade routes by traders who carried the seeds in the holds of their boats. By the tenth century they had crossed the Middle East to reach China, and by the thirteenth century the Arabs had enthusiastically spread them around the rest of Europe, although they were not known in England until the end of the sixteenth century. The southern states of America took to the watermelon with as much alacrity as they did the African slaves who brought them. They seem to have been a particular favourite of that famous southern author Mark Twain, who wrote in 1894: 'When one has tasted it, he knows what the angels eat.'

For the hot and dusty countries of the Middle East and southern Mediterranean watermelons have long provided a welcome liquid relief to parched throats. Anyone who has visited Asia or Southern Europe during the hot summer months will recall the relief of spying a street vendor whose barrow was piled high with chilled watermelons. An icy cold wedge sliced from one of these monsters does more to slake one's thirst than any fizzy soft drink!

In the Middle East endless varieties of fruit are available during the summer, and an extravagant selection is always offered at the end of a meal. Melons and watermelons are great favourites and are always served chilled. Persians have known how to store winter snow and ice for use in the summer months for at least 2000 years, and it doesn't require much of an imagination to see how easily watermelons, with their crunchy, granular, almost icy flesh, could have been transformed, perhaps with the addition of a few drops of rosewater, into sweetly perfumed sherbet.

SELECTING AND STORING WATERMELON

Nowadays watermelons come in more manageable sizes. The Minilee, for instance, is closer in size and shape to a honeydew or Galia melon. This makes them much less daunting to the shopper, and far easier to cart home.

When purchasing, look for fruit which feels firm and heavy. Once cut, watermelons can be wrapped in clingfilm and kept in the refrigerator for up to a week. Instead of reaching for ice-blocks or cans of fizzy drinks on hot summer days, why not try a slice of delicious, thirst-quenching watermelon instead?

USING WATERMELON

In Middle Eastern and Mediterranean countries, watermelon is most often enjoyed as a thirst-quenching snack or as part of a dessert fruit plate, perhaps with a few slices of creamy halvah. Watermelons are ideal for making sorbets and, simpler still, only require a little mashing to make a granita.

With the large thick-skinned varieties of watermelon it is also possible to pickle the white layer of rind under the outer green skin. Watermelon pickles are a very popular condiment on Greek and Eastern Mediterranean tables, and are also much loved in the southern states of America. In France and Spain the rind is also popular candied and is often part of a glacé fruit selection. And then there are the seeds! In many Middle Eastern countries they are toasted, wrapped in little packages and sold as a popular street-snack.

WATERMELON RECIPES

Watermelon sorbet

Early Persian sherbets and iced fruit drinks must surely have made use of the icy-cold sweet watermelon. This sorbet is extremely simple to make. Enlivened with a splash of lemon juice and the merest hint of rosewater, it is quite delicious served with fresh berries and finely chopped mint leaves as a refreshing summer dessert.

800 g watermelon

200 g castor sugar

100 g glucose

200 ml water

juice of 2 lemons

splash of rosewater

- Remove the peel from the watermelon, chop the flesh into largish chunks and remove the pips. Whiz to a purée in a food processor and sieve.
- To make a sugar syrup, bring the sugar, glucose and water to the boil over a medium heat, then lower and simmer for 5 minutes. Mix the fruit purée with the syrup and allow to cool. Then add the lemon juice and rosewater. Pour into an ice-cream machine and churn according to the manufacturer's instructions.
- Serves four to six.

Watermelon with white port and pistachios

Served well chilled, this watermelon salad makes a lovely light ending to a meal and has an interesting alcoholic kick! Dried limes are a Persian speciality, available from Middle Eastern grocers. They need to be cracked with a heavy rolling pin and then infused to impart their musty citrussy flavour.

100 g castor sugar

100 ml water

1 stick cinnamon

peel of 1 lemon or 1 cracked dried lime (optional)

4 cracked cardamom pods

1 kg watermelon flesh

200 ml white port

80 g unsalted, shelled pistachio nuts

1 punnet blackberries

• Put the sugar and water in a pan and bring them slowly to the boil, making sure the sugar dissolves completely. Add the cinnamon stick, lime or lemon peel, and cardamom pods, lower the heat and simmer for about 5 minutes to make a syrup. Remove from the heat and allow to cool.

• Peel the watermelon into 2 cm thick triangles. Place them in a bowl, sprinkle them with port and macerate them in the refrigerator for an hour. Roughly crush the pistachio nuts and mix them with a tablespoon of the sugar syrup. To serve, stack the watermelon slices in the centre of the plate, sprinkle them with pistachio nuts and blackberries and douse the lot with syrup.

• Serves six.

Watermelon salad with cherry-vanilla ice-cream

100 g castor sugar

100 ml water

1 stick cinnamon

peel of 1 lemon or 1 cracked dried lime (optional)

4 cardamom pods, cracked

1 teaspoon rosewater

1 kg watermelon flesh

1 punnet raspberries

1 punnet blueberries

1 punnet blackberries

½ cup shredded mint leaves

CHERRY-VANILLA ICE-CREAM

8 egg yolks

200 g castor sugar

200 ml water

1 vanilla bean, split and scraped

600 ml thickened cream

500 g cherries (stoned weight)

½ cup castor sugar

50 ml water

juice of 1 lemon

- To make the ice-cream base, first whisk up the egg yolks in an electric mixer until they are light and fluffy. Bring the sugar, water and aromatic to the boil. Pour the boiling syrup over the whisked egg yolks, still whisking slowly. Then add the cream and turn off the beaters. Allow the mixture to cool down for a few moments. Tip it into ice-cream machine and churn according to the manufacturer's instructions.
- Place the cherries, sugar, water and lemon juice in a heavy pot. Stir gently to ensure the sugar dissolves, and slowly bring to the boil. Lower heat and simmer for about 5 minutes. Remove from the heat and purée in a liquidiser. Strain through a sieve to remove the skins.
- Put the sugar and water in a pan and bring slowly to the boil, making sure the sugar dissolves completely. Add the cinnamon stick, lime or lemon peel and cardamom pods, lower the heat and simmer for about 5 minutes to make a syrup. Remove from heat and allow to cool. Strain and add half the rosewater. Chill until needed.
- Cut the watermelon into small bite-sized pieces, and place in a large mixing bowl with the berries. Add the shredded mint leaves and pour over enough syrup to moisten, mix everything gently and then sprinkle with the remaining drops of rosewater.
- Allow to cool and stir in rosewater, if desired. Swirl the cherry purée into the ice-cream when you transfer it to the freezer.
- Serve the watermelon salad with a scoop of cherry-vanilla ice-cream.
- Serves six.

Yoghurt

Yoghurt is one of those foods which firmly divides people – you love it or loathe it! Greg, for instance, in true Lebanese style, will happily eat yoghurt as an accompaniment to just about every meal, and when he gets home from work late at night will open the refrigerator and eat great spoonfuls of icy-cold yoghurt straight from the tub. Luckily, although this drives me mad, I do share his enthusiasm. When I was seventeen, on holiday in the Greek islands, I survived for almost an entire month on yoghurt and honey, with the odd piece of fruit thrown in for dietary balance.

In Australia over the last 15 years or so yoghurt has come a long way. It used to be that the only yoghurt readily available was a gloppy, gelatinous substance, usually sweetened beyond belief and coloured pink (raspberry), yellow (banana) or even brown (chocolate). The so-called 'fruit' flavours had certainly never seen a real raspberry or strawberry. On the other hand, 'natural' yoghurt was something eaten only by earnest hippy-types and you either had to hunt it down in a health-food shop or make it yourself.

Yoghurt has now become very fashionable, and is just one product in an ever-expanding range of dairy desserts. Supermarkets stock dozens of exotic flavours, ranging from mango, guava and passionfruit to muesli and coconut. There are yoghurts made from cow's milk, goat's milk, sheep's milk and even buffalo milk. Fat contents range from nearly zero to as much as 8 per cent. The latest marketing idea for this ever-growing industry is that yoghurt is the key to eternal life! The current buzz-word is 'probiotic', and we are all getting used to hearing about the health-giving properties of lactobacillus-this, acidophilus-that and casei-Shirota-the other.

While laboratory research has shown that these new strains of bacterial cultures, such as the acidophilus, bifidus and casei strains, do promote the growth of 'good' bacteria in a test-tube, whether the benefits can be transferred to the human digestive system remains to be proven. If we are to believe the boffins, though, humble yoghurt can provide – if not exactly eternal life – help with digestive problems such as constipation and irritable bowel syndrome, as well as some allergies, and in counteracting the adverse side-effects of antibiotics.

The good news is, that regardless of all the pseudo-scientific guff spouted by the manufacturers, all yoghurts are protein- and calcium-rich and extremely delicious – something which Middle-Easterners have always known. The even better news is that yoghurt (although fat contents vary widely) is not nearly as high in fat as many ricottas, and all types of cream and mascarpone. Needless to say, the higher the fat content of the yoghurt, the more voluptuously rich and velvety smooth the result!

Yoghurt is enjoyed throughout the Arab world, although almost never as the oversweetened dairy dessert we know here in Australia. Middle Easterners would hardly recognise yoghurt in these forms, which bear so little resemblance to the refreshingly sour original. In hot, sunny countries it is enjoyed as a cooling drink or to dampen the fire of chilli dishes. It is used in soups, stews, marinades, pastries and cakes. It is served as an accompaniment to all kinds of savoury dishes. Hung in a bag until the whey drains away it thickens into a delectably creamy version which is delicious with a drizzle of honey, a sprinkle of cinnamon or mixed with summer berries. Longer straining – for up to three days – results in a very soft, slightly sharp fresh cheese, which may be flavoured with fresh herbs and served with crusty bread.

FAT CONTENT

Product	Fat content (%)	Product	Fat content (%)
Low-fat yoghurt	0.2–1	Light soured cream	18–25
Full-fat yoghurt	3.5–5.5	Soured cream	25
Fromage frais	4	Light cream cheese	32
Goat's milk yoghurt	7	Cream cheese	33
Sheep's milk yoghurt	7	Thickened cream	35
Buffalo milk yoghurt	8–9	Crème fraîche	min 35
Strained yoghurt	10	Mascarpone	40
Ricotta	8–15	Double cream	50
Low-fat cream	18	Clotted cream	min 55

SELECTING AND STORING YOGHURT

For cooking, always buy plain natural yoghurt. These days there are numerous brands and styles of yoghurt available. In particular there are some excellent European style and 'biodynamic' yoghurts which we use at home. It is worth experimenting to find out which style you prefer – a thinner, sourer type or the richer creamier 'Greek' style. The creamier and softer the flavour, though, the higher the fat content is likely to be. Yoghurts range from full-fat (4 per cent) to low fat (around 1 per cent).

It is sensible to buy yoghurt with the longest use-by date. Not just because it is perishable, but because the flavour sharpens over time (even when properly stored in the refrigerator). Most natural yoghurts contain live cultures, which continue to munch on the milk-sugars (lactose) and cause acidity levels to slowly increase. However, most very fresh store-bought yoghurts will keep perfectly well for up to two weeks after purchase.

USING YOGHURT

Straining yoghurt for a few hours in a muslin cloth gives a richer more concentrated product. It is delicious eaten like a very soft fresh cheese, lightly salted and drizzled with olive oil, and maybe flavoured with garlic and fresh herbs. Sweetened with one of the lovely floral honeys, or sprinkled with rosewater or orange-blossom water, chopped pistachios or fresh berries, yoghurt makes a luscious creamy dessert.

Watermelon salad with cherry-vanilla ice-cream (recipe page 285)

ABOVE LEFT: Cardamom pods ABOVE RIGHT: Pomegranate molasses and rosewater
BELOW LEFT: Amardine (dried apricot sheets) BELOW RIGHT: (from left) Jordanian za'atar, sumac and dukkah

YOGHURT RECIPES

Saffron-yoghurt cheese

The basic method described here works without the saffron too. It is equally delicious plain or swirled with a variety of different flavourings. Try adding a spoonful of spicy harissa, smoked paprika or purées of fresh herbs such as basil, oregano or dill. Swirl into the yoghurt and strain as outlined below.

Rosewater also adds an exotic dimension. Salt and drain the yoghurt and, when ready to serve, form into smooth round balls or quenelle shapes using spoons. Make an indentation in the top and fill with rosewater and a big drop of extra-virgin olive oil. Serve it with Seven Vegetable Couscous with Onion Jam and Green Harissa Broth Tagine (page 92).

For a sweet treat, beat 2 tablespoons of honey and 1 capful of orange-blossom water into the yoghurt, sprinkle in the lightly crushed seeds from 4 cardamom pods and drain for up to 48 hours. Serve with fresh strawberries or as accompaniment to syrupy cakes or puddings instead of cream.

1 kg natural yoghurt (sheep's milk for a richer result)

1 clove garlic crushed with 1 teaspoon salt

10 saffron strands, lightly roasted and crushed

• Scoop the yoghurt into a clean muslin square, cheesecloth or tea-towel. Mix in the garlic paste, then sprinkle the saffron over the top and swirl it in roughly. Tie the four corners of cloth together to form a hanging bag and suspend it from a wooden spoon over a deep bowl. Allow it to drain in the refrigerator for 48–72 hours (the longer the time, the firmer the result).

• Use the 48-hour soft cheese as an accompaniment for spicy dishes such as tagines, Indian curries or most rice dishes. Or drizzle with extra-virgin olive oil and eat with crusty bread and a dish of olives. At the end of 72 hours you will have a very firm lump of fresh cheese.

• Gently remove it from the bag and roll it into small balls with oiled hands. Place the balls in jars with olive oil and the herbs of your choice. They will keep for up to 2 weeks in the refrigerator.

Basil tzatziki

Mint is traditional in tzatziki, but try adding shredded basil for a change. This creamy tzatziki is terrific served with grilled meat or as an accompaniment to couscous dishes.

500 ml natural yoghurt, strained
  overnight

I Lebanese cucumber, de-seeded
  and grated (leave the skin on)

I clove garlic crushed with
  I teaspoon salt

I teaspoon dried mint

½ cup fresh basil, leaves only,
  chopped

juice of I lemon

salt and pepper

- Mix all the ingredients together in a large bowl and season. Line a sieve with muslin or a tea-towel and strain for a further 4–6 hours.
- Chill until required.

Other yoghurt recipes

Basboussa, page 6
Baba Ghanoush, page 113
Tahini Whipped with Yoghurt, page 252

Sticky lemon-yoghurt cake

This moist tangy cake is delicious on its own with a cup of coffee, or served with a big blob of King Island cream and some fresh berries.

250 g butter

200 g castor sugar

4 teaspoons lemon zest

4 eggs

50 g plain flour

2 teaspoons baking powder

250 g fine semolina

200 g ground almonds

6 tablespoons lemon juice

120 g plain yoghurt

SYRUP

1 cup lemon juice

175 g castor sugar

½ tablespoon brandy

• Cream together the butter, sugar and lemon zest until the mixture is pale and smooth. Then beat in the eggs, one by one, ensuring each one is completely incorporated before adding the next. Sift the flour and baking powder over the top, and gently fold in with the semolina and ground almonds. Then mix in the lemon juice and yoghurt. Pour the mixture into a well-greased 20 cm spring-form tin, and bake in a preheated 170°C oven for 50–60 minutes, or when the cake is firm to the touch and golden-brown.

• Combine the lemon juice, sugar and brandy in a small pan and bring them to the boil. Reduce the heat and simmer for 5 minutes to make syrup.

• Remove the cake from the oven and pierce it all over with a skewer. Pour the syrup over the hot cake and allow it to soak in. The cake will keep well in an airtight containers for 3–4 days.

Zucchini

One of Greg's favourite home-cooked meals – cooked by his mother, that is – is Koussa Mahshi. This is zucchini (or baby marrows) stuffed with a mixture of rice, minced lamb and pine nuts, flavoured with allspice, and gently braised in a tomato sauce. It is a hugely popular Lebanese dish, and just one way of cooking the infinitely versatile zucchini.

Like its cousins the marrow and squash, the zucchini is a type of edible gourd which grows close to the ground under a riot of lush leaf cover. The best zucchini are small-to-medium in size and firm to the touch. They can be a lovely, shiny dark-green, or paler and speckled-looking, or even a butter-bright yellow. Sadly, they are often allowed to grow too large, which makes their flesh spongy and bitter. Greg's father has a fantastically productive vegetable garden, and we are often the lucky recipients of his bounty. The best zucchini of all are picked fresh and tender from his vines, no bigger than a finger, with their gorgeous golden flower still attached.

SELECTING AND STORING ZUCCHINI

Ideally, zucchini should be firm, shiny and unscarred, but all too often they are droopy, soft, wrinkled and blemished. Avoid these! Zucchini do not keep terribly well and even in the refrigerator they have a tendency to get wet and slimy quickly, so eat them within a day or so of purchase. Choose larger ones for stuffing, medium or small ones for slicing and frying.

USING ZUCCHINI

Wash larger zucchini well and carefully pat them dry. Slice off and discard the ends. The zucchini can then be sliced into discs, on the angle, or lengthways into long strips, or they can be grated. It is best not to boil zucchini, as they quickly become waterlogged and collapse into a soggy, flavourless mass. They are far better steamed, or sautéed in a hot pan with a little olive oil or butter. Add a good squeeze of lemon juice at the end of cooking and throw in a handful of fresh herbs – dill, mint and thyme are all good choices. The tiny babies can be sautéed whole, for the briefest of moments, in a little olive oil, a hint of garlic and a good squeeze of lemon juice.

Zucchini are also excellent chargrilled on a griddle pan or on the barbecue. Slice them lengthways, brush with extra-virgin olive oil, season well and sear on the grill until they are soft and golden. Grilled zucchini are equally delicious eaten hot or allowed to cool, and dressed with lemon juice and garlic-infused olive oil.

In the eastern Mediterranean zucchini are often prepared as a salad for a mezze selection, in a yoghurt dressing with mint or dill; or sliced wafer thin, and tossed in a vinaigrette with thin slices of Spanish onion, currants and pine nuts.

Cheese and eggs are natural allies of zucchini. Grate them and combine with beaten eggs, onion, parsley and a touch of garlic to make a sort of Arabic frittata called an 'eggah'. Zucchini and cheese is a classic Judeo-Spanish combination. Bake lightly steamed slices in the oven with a mixture of creamy ricotta style cheese, a couple of eggs and a pinch of nutmeg. Another equally good version uses salty fetta and mint.

Zucchini flowers are considered very chichi. Some upmarket green grocers sell baby zucchinis with flowers attached and they are very pretty cooked whole. The flowers from larger plant can be removed and stuffed. The preparation method is described on page 295, but always make sure you cook them as quickly as possible after purchase. The petals will start to close up once they have been picked, which can make the whole exercise very fiddly and frustrating.

ZUCCHINI RECIPES

Koussa mahshi

This is probably one of the most popular home-cooked Lebanese family meals. Ideally choose baby marrow, which are squat and bulbous – they are easy to hollow out. Zucchini work well too, but require a little patience and a long thin knife (like a fish filleting knife) to scrape out the insides, while maintaining the whole long shape of the vegetable. Koussa makes a simple supper dish, served with a big blob of thick creamy yoghurt.

8 baby marrows (no smaller than 150 g each)

STUFFING

250 g lamb mince

125 g long-grain rice

¾ teaspoon allspice

¾ teaspoon cinnamon

¾ teaspoon black pepper

½ teaspoon salt

I teaspoon extra-virgin olive oil

⅓ cup cold water

SAUCE

I tablespoon butter

I tablespoon olive oil

I medium onion, finely chopped

2 cloves garlic, finely chopped

½ teaspoon dried mint

I can crushed tomatoes (400 g)

2 tablespoons tomato paste

400 ml water

salt and pepper

¼ teaspoon cinnamon

¼ teaspoon allspice

• Trim off the marrows at the narrow end. With a melon baller or a long, thin knife, carefully hollow out the insides of each marrow. The idea is to have as thin a shell as possible, but without piercing the skin. Reserve the pulp for the sauce.

• To make the stuffing, use wet hands to mix the lamb mince, rice, pepper, salt, extra-virgin olive oil and cold water. Divide the mixture into 8 portions and loosely stuff each marrow about three-quarters full, which leaves space for expansion during cooking.

• Melt the butter with the oil and gently sauté the onion for about 5 minutes, until it is soft and translucent. Then add the garlic and mint. Cook for a few more minutes, then add the roughly chopped marrow pulp, followed by the tomatoes, tomato paste and water.

• Season with salt, pepper and additional spices. Stir well.

• Place marrows in the sauce and bring to the boil. Then cover and simmer over a low heat for 40–45 minutes. About 10 minutes towards the end of the cooking time, remove the lid and raise the heat to reduce the sauce by a quarter.

Battered zucchini flowers stuffed with goat's cheese

One of the most pleasing aspects of the zucchini is its summery-looking yellow flower, which is delicious dipped in a light batter and fried, or carefully stuffed with a light cheese and breadcrumb filling.

120 g goat's cheese

1 teaspoon dried mint

1 teaspoon parsley leaves, chopped

1 tablespoon extra-virgin olive oil

12 baby zucchini with flowers attached

½ litre olive oil and vegetable oil blend for deep-frying

½ cup plain flour for dusting

Chickpea Batter (page 57)

salt

- Mash the cheese with the mint, parsley and extra-virgin olive oil.
- Carefully open each zucchini flower and pinch out the stamen. Roll a lump of the cheese stuffing into a thumb-sized sausage shape between the palms of your hands, and gently stuff it into the flower. Twist the top of the flower to seal.
- Heat the oil olive and vegetable oils to 200°C (when a blob of batter will sizzle to the surface and colour within 30 seconds). Hold the zucchini and carefully dust each flower in the flour and then the Chickpea Batter. Gently place in the oil – cook no more than four at a time – until the batter turns crisp and golden. Remove and drain on kitchen paper. Season with salt and serve immediately.
- Serves four as a starter.

Other zucchini recipes

Risotto with Zucchini, Prawn and Preserved Lemon, page 231

Soused zucchini and eggplant

This is one of our favourite ways of preparing zucchini. Serve them with all meat, poultry and fish.

2 medium eggplants

4 medium zucchini

100 ml olive oil

2 cloves garlic, finely sliced

1 tablespoon parsley, chopped

1 tablespoon oregano leaves

½ teaspoon sumac

MARINADE

8 teaspoons sherry vinegar

4 teaspoons honey

8 teaspoons water

• Trim the ends from the eggplants and cut them lengthways into 1½ cm thick slices. Place them in a colander, lightly salt, and let them sit for half an hour. Rinse well and pat dry.

• Trim the ends from the zucchini, slice them in half lengthways and season with salt.

• Heat the oil in a large heavy pan and fry the zucchini and eggplant slices until they are lightly coloured. Tip them into a large dish.

• Boil marinade ingredients for one minute and pour over the pan-fried vegetables. Sprinkle with the garlic, chopped parsley, oregano leaves and sumac. Leave in the marinade overnight.

• When you are ready to serve, remove the vegetables from the marinade and warm them through gently in a pan or in the oven. Serve with a drizzle of extra-virgin olive oil.

Bibliography

Al Hashimi, Miriam, *Traditional Arabic Cooking*, Garnet, UK, 1993

Alexander, Stephanie, *Stephanie's Australia*, Allen & Unwin, Sydney, 1991

—— *The Cook's Companion*, Viking, Melbourne, 1997

Bareham, Lindsay, *Onions Without Tears*, Michael Joseph, London, 1995

Beer, Maggie, *Maggie's Orchard*, Viking, Melbourne, 1997

Boxer, Arabella, *Mediterranean Cookbook*, Penguin, UK, 1981

David, Elizabeth, *Mediterranean Food*, Penquin, UK, 1950

—— *Harvest of the Cold Months*, Penguin, UK, 1994

Davidson, Alan and Davidson, Jane, *Dumas on Food*, Oxford University Press, Oxford, 1978

Danon, Simy et Denarnaud, Jacques, *La Nouvelle Cuisine Judeo-Marocaine*, ACR, Paris, 1994

Der Haroutunian, Arto, *The Yoghurt Book*, Penguin, UK, 1983

Dosti, Rose, *Mideast and Mediterranean Cuisines*, Fisher Books, USA, 1993

Greenberg, Sheldon and Lambert Ortiz, Elisabeth, *The Spice of Life*, Michael Joseph, UK, 1983

Grigson, Jane, *Vegetable Book*, Michael Joseph, UK, 1978

—— *Fruit Book*, Michael Joseph, UK, 1982

Grigson, Sophie, *Ingredients Book*, Pyramid Books, London, 1991

Guinaudeau, Madame, *Traditional Moroccan Cooking*, Serif, UK, 1994

Humphries, John, *The Essential Saffron Companion*, Grub St, London, 1996

Jaffrey, Madhur, *Eastern Vegetarian Cooking*, Arrow Books, London, 1990

Lassalles, George, *Middle Eastern Food*, Kyle Cathie, London 1991

McGee, Harold, *On Food and Cooking*, Collier Books, New York, 1988

Owen, Sri, *The Rice Book*, Doubleday, London, 1993

Roden, Claudia, *A New Book of Middle Eastern Food*, Penguin, UK, 1986

—— *The Book of Jewish Food*, Viking, UK, 1997

Root, Waverley, *Food*, Simon & Schuster, New York, 1980

Saleh, Nada, *Fragrance of the Earth*, Saqi Books, London, 1996

Shaida, Margaret, *The Legendary Cuisine of Persia*, Penguin, UK, 1994

Simmons, Shirin, *Entertaining the Persian Way*, Lennard Publishing, UK, 1988

Tannahill, Rheay, *Food in History*, Penguin, UK, 1973

Time-Life, *Food of the World* series, Time-Life, New York, 1968-78

Time-Life, *The Good Cook* series, Time-Life, New York, 1978-81

Toussaint-Samat, Maguelonne, *The History of Food*, Blackwell, USA, 1992

Visser, Margaret, *Much Depends on Dinner*, Penguin, Canada 1986

Whittaker, Noel, *Sweet Talk*, Macmillan, UK, 1998

Wolfert, Paula, *Good Food from Morocco*, John Murray, 1973

—— *Mediterranean Cooking*, Harper Collins, New York, 1994

Index